ADOBE® PHOTOSHOP® CS6

ESSENTIALS

CERTIFIED ASSOCIATE
Approved Courseware

Scott Onstott

WILEY

John Wiley & Sons, Inc.

Acquisitions Editor: Mariann Barsolo
Development Editor: Stef Jones
Technical Editor: Jeffrey Greene
Production Editor: Rebecca Anderson
Copy Editor: Judy Flynn
Editorial Manager: Pete Gaughan
Production Manager: Tim Tate
Vice President and Executive Group Publisher: Richard Swadley
Vice President and Publisher: Neil Edde
Book Designer: Happenstance Type-O-Rama
Compositor: Craig Johnson, Happenstance Type-O-Rama
Proofreader: Sheilah Ledwidge, Word One New York
Indexer: Ted Laux
Project Coordinator, Cover: Katherine Crocker
Cover Designer: Ryan Sneed
Cover Image: Scott Onstott

Dear Reader,

Thank you for choosing *Adobe Photoshop CS6 Essentials*. This book is part of a family of premium-quality Sybex books, all of which are written by outstanding authors who combine practical experience with a gift for teaching.

Sybex was founded in 1976. More than 30 years later, we're still committed to producing consistently exceptional books. With each of our titles, we're working hard to set a new standard for the industry. From the paper we print on, to the authors we work with, our goal is to bring you the best books available.

I hope you see all that reflected in these pages. I'd be very interested to hear your comments and get your feedback on how we're doing. Feel free to let me know what you think about this or any other Sybex book by sending me an email at nedde@wiley.com. If you think you've found a technical error in this book, please visit http://sybex.custhelp.com. Customer feedback is critical to our efforts at Sybex.

Best regards,

NEIL EDDE
Vice President and Publisher
Sybex, an Imprint of Wiley

To Merlin and all the future Photoshop wizards

ACKNOWLEDGMENTS

I'd like to thank the professional team at Sybex (an imprint of Wiley), including acquisitions editor Mariann Barsolo, developmental editor Stef Jones, production editor Rebecca Anderson, technical editor Jeffrey Greene, copyeditor Judy Flynn, and Pete Gaughan, Connor O'Brien, and Jenni Housh in the editorial department. Special thanks to Richard Trueman for his photography.

ABOUT THE AUTHOR

 *Scott Onstott is the* author or coauthor of six previous Sybex books, including *AutoCAD 2012 and AutoCAD LT 2012 Essentials* (2011), *Enhancing Architectural Drawings and Models with Photoshop* (2010), *AutoCAD Professional Tips and Techniques* (2006, with Lynn Allen), *Enhancing CAD Drawings with Photoshop* (2005), M*astering Autodesk Architectural Desktop 2006* (2005), and *Mastering Autodesk VIZ 2005* (2004, with George Omura). Since 2002 he has been independently producing and publishing instructional videos, among them *Photoshop for Architects, 3ds Max for Architects,* and *Mastering SketchUp.* Scott is a columnist at *Photoshop User Magazine* and has taught over one thousand students in brick and mortar classrooms. His website is ScottOnstott.com.

Contents at a Glance

CONTENTS

CHAPTER 3   Digital Imaging Fundamentals   55

CHAPTER 4   Painting   83

INTRODUCTION

Welcome to the fascinating world of Photoshop. It will give you great personal satisfaction to learn the essentials of Photoshop and use your skills in ever more creative ways. In this book, you will start by learning the fundamentals of the design process, get acquainted with Photoshop's user interface, and then get a primer on digital imaging. You'll then learn how to paint, draw, and write the Photoshop way and how to accurately select pixels, work with layers and masks, design and apply styles, create comps, shape paths, employ smart objects, apply adjustments, and use filters. You'll learn how to develop photos in Camera Raw, how to retouch images to make them more perfect than they are in reality, how to merge multiple photos into panoramas and high dynamic range images, and finally, how to manage color and create output that looks as close as possible to how it appears onscreen.

Who Should Read This Book

The list of potential Photoshop users is long, and it includes photographers, graphic and web designers, painters, architects, businesspeople, scientists, students, hobbyists, and many more. Essentially anyone who uses images in their work—or wants to—should read this book. No experience is required, and I do not assume you have any skills with software other than being able to surf the Web and send email.

What You Will Learn

You will gain skills by completing projects, making it incredibly easy to learn the essentials of Photoshop simply by following the exercises step-by-step. Therefore, I recommend you start at the beginning and work your way through the book in a linear fashion. Even experienced users might pick up a few tips along the way, and complete novices and those with intermediate skills alike will appreciate my architectural background as I build a firm foundation for you first and then proceed to construct everything you need to become a productive Photoshop user in the course of the journey that this book represents.

What You Need

To complete the projects in this book, you will need Adobe Photoshop CS6 or Photoshop CS6 Extended. See www.adobe.com/products/photoshopfamily.html for more information about the Photoshop family of software.

What Is Covered in This Book

Photoshop CS6 Essentials is organized to provide you with the knowledge needed to master the basics of digital imaging:

Chapter 1: Design Basics   This chapter delves into essential composition principles—ways of seeing rather than just looking—while discussing the design process and such important topics as intellectual property rights. It also includes a photography and scanning primer.

Chapter 2: Getting Acquainted with Photoshop's User Interface   Just as you need to know about an automobile's pedals, shifter, switches, buttons, knobs, and levers do to drive a car, so too must you understand Photoshop's menus, bars, workspaces, tools, panels, tabs, and icons—collectively called the user interface—in order to successfully use the program. This chapter familiarizes you with Photoshop's user interface.

Chapter 3: Digital Imaging Fundamentals   Fundamental concepts such as pixels, colors, channels, modes, aliasing, bit depth, canvas size, image size, resolution, and much more are covered in this chapter, which will help you to understand what's really going on in Photoshop behind the scenes.

Chapter 4: Painting   You'll learn how to create gradients, select paint colors, use brushes, paint with a tablet, paint from history, and use the mixer brush in this chapter. Painting skills are used for more than painting—you'll use what you learn here to select pixels, retouch photos, and work with layer masks in later chapters.

Chapter 5: Drawing   Here you will use vector tools to create crisp clean lines, rectangles, circles, and other geometric shapes. You'll learn how to manipulate shapes and paths to create complex custom shapes typical of most graphic design projects.

Chapter 6: Writing   In this chapter, you will learn not only how to create single-line and paragraph text, but also the basics of typography so that what you write will be readable and look good. You'll learn how to fine-tune type and use text as a mask for special effects.

Chapter 7: Selecting Pixels   Selecting pixels is the key to manipulating portions of images. You will learn how to select pixels with marquees and lassos, draw with vector tools, paint raster selections of varying opacity, select by color, and use Quick Select and Refine Edge to make accurate selections.

Chapter 8: Working with Layers and Masks   Here you will learn how to use layers to split images up into different movable portions that can be blended with each other in a variety of ways. You'll learn the basics of masking, which means hiding content on layers selectively.

Chapter 9: Using Layer Styles and Comps   By learning how to design and apply layer styles, you open new vistas of creativity. In this chapter, you'll apply layer effects, work with layer styles, and use layer comps to record all the layers styles, positions, and visibility settings.

Chapter 10: Transforming Paths, Layers, and Smart Objects   By learning how to position, orient, scale, align, distribute, and deform layers and paths you will gain essential graphic design skills with tools that play roles akin to the roles glue, scissors, and a photocopier with an enlarger play in traditional media.

Chapter 11: Adjusting and Filtering   This chapter teaches you how to assign adjustments and filters directly to images as well as how to use nondestructive methods with adjustment layers and smart filters. In this chapter you'll learn about tools that give you fine control over the final appearance of most all digital images.

Chapter 12: Developing Photos   Adobe Camera Raw (ACR) is the interface you will use to develop your RAW photos. You'll make global development decisions as well as localized adjustments all within the nondestructive and parametric environment of ACR. In addition, you will learn how to use Adobe Bridge as a digital light box to review and tag your shots before developing them.

Chapter 13: Retouching Photos   Not all pictures are perfect as seen through the camera viewfinder. In this chapter you will learn how to retouch photos to remove unwanted elements, remove blemishes, selectively control exposure, redirect attention with blur, and add special effects.

Chapter 14: Merging Photos   By combining multiple exposures of the same subjects, you will be able to expand dynamic range and create panoramic photos. In addition, you will stack images to get rid of all the moving objects, such as removing all the pedestrians or cars from a busy street.

Chapter 15: Working with Color   From the concept of gamut to color spaces and profiles specific to printers and the papers they print on, you'll learn how to manage, correct, adjust, and proof color to maintain all of its vibrance.

Chapter 16: Creating Output   No matter what type of project you are working on, there comes the time when you must supply deliverables. This chapter focuses on creating the print or electronic forms of output that you will ultimately require.

Companion Files   Sample files are provided for each chapter; they can be downloaded from the book's companion web page at www.sybex.com/go/ photoshopessentials.

The Essentials Series

The Essentials series from Sybex provides outstanding instruction for readers who are just beginning to develop their professional skills. Every Essentials book includes these features:

▶ Skill-based instruction with chapters organized around projects rather than abstract concepts or subjects.

▶ Suggestions for additional exercises at the end of each chapter so you can practice and extend your skills.

▶ Digital files (via download) so you can work through the project tutorials yourself. Please check the book's web page at www.sybex.com/ go/photoshopessentials for these companion downloads.

Certification Objective

The certification margin icon will alert you to passages that are especially relevant to Adobe Certified Associate in Visual Communication with Photoshop CS6 certification.

How to Contact the Author

Wiley strives to keep you supplied with the latest tools and information you need for your work. Please check their website at www.wiley.com for additional content and updates that supplement this book. Enter the book's ISBN—978-1-118-09495-2—in the Search box (or type **photoshop cs6 essentials**), and click on the product to get to the book's update page.

If you have any questions or comments about this book, I encourage you to contact me by visiting my website ScottOnstott.com and using the web contact form there.

CHAPTER 1

Design Basics

The best photographers, graphic designers, and creative thinkers use specific technical knowledge to manipulate images without ever losing sight of basic composition principles. So before you dive into the fascinating world of Photoshop, it behooves you to study the fundamentals of design and fully understand the process of capturing digital images with digital cameras and scanners.

▶ **Understanding the design process**

▶ **Learning composition principles**

▶ **Understanding your rights to use images**

▶ **Photography and scanning primer**

Understanding the Design Process

Design isn't some esoteric process that only those who have graduated from the most exclusive schools can understand. Most of the design process is simply good common sense. Everyone working on a project should understand its fundamentals. With every project, from the smallest to the most complex, communication and collaboration skills are mission critical. By its very nature, the design of real-world objects necessitates images (and possibly drawings or models) to communicate visual information. So the ability to effectively create and present visual ideas is a must for those involved in design. Finally, design is a process that can take on a life of its own.

Understanding Project Fundamentals

Certification
Objective

Every project is fundamentally a story. When researching any story, it is helpful to employ the maxim of Five Ws (and one H). Let the answers to these six questions inform your concepts of what the project will fundamentally be about, something I call a project plan.

Why?   Why is the project being undertaken? Discuss the client's mission statement to make certain everyone on the team understands what you are all trying to accomplish. Evaluate how the proposed project meets the client's goals and determine the objective of the project as it pertains to audience demographics, such as age, occupation, gender, education, residence, and ethnicity.

How?   How will you and/or your team create the project deliverables? How will responsibilities be divided among different individuals to take best advantage of each team member's professional strengths?

What?   What are the project deliverables? List which types of documents, images, drawings, models, videos, and/or printed matter that need to eventually be delivered to the client. What tasks will need to be undertaken to produce these deliverables?

Who?   Who will be involved and what are their responsibilities within the project? Gather each person's contact information and store it in a centralized address database that is shared with all project members. Delineate each team member's anticipated responsibilities within the project.

When?   When do project milestones occur in time? Develop a timeline that graphically illustrates anticipated milestones (significant events) in the life of the project. Assign one team member, usually the project manager, with the task of monitoring all team members' progress in achieving milestones on the timeline.

Where?   Where is the project located? If team members work on the project from distributed locations, then work out secure file transfer details to enable electronic collaboration. For example, distribute usernames and passwords to an FTP site or to a third-party file hosting service. If the project deliverables include printed matter, communicate with print professionals to obtain specific technical requirements for high-quality results. If the project is a building, study the larger context of the built and natural environments.

Once you have developed a project plan by answering all of the preceding questions, the next step is to develop a project plan. The plan usually takes the form of a task list, which will identify the actors, their tasks, and the time in which they are slated to perform their roles. The project plan will alleviate common problems relating to methodology, miscommunications, feature creep, and budget overruns.

Figure 1.1 shows an example project plan, which was created using a spreadsheet program.

Task	Client	Due By	Estimated Hours	Actual Hours
Planning				
Budget				
Analysis				
Designing				
Building				
Testing				
Delivery				

F I G U R E 1 . 1 Sample project plan

The project plan can easily be converted into a time sheet used to track the actual hours spent on tasks for each client. Time sheets can be used for client billing.

Collaborating with Others

Certification Objective

Most design is the product of collaboration with other people. Even if you design something entirely by yourself, you must eventually present it to your client, your audience, or to the world at large. This reality implies a relationship between yourself and others.

Effective communication is the key to building healthy relationships. However, conflict often brews because of misunderstandings arising from the lack of effective communication between related parties working on a project.

The keys to effective communication include listening, keeping an open mind, being honest, and getting to the point as efficiently and tactfully as possible. These keys help in business and in life!

The keys to effective communication are all common sense, but it's remarkable how many projects end in litigation because one or more of these keys weren't respected. Consciously studying communication should be a part of every team member's education. Here are a few more tips for professional collaboration:

▶ Reply to correspondence or requests for information promptly.

▶ If you don't understand something, don't be afraid to say so.

▶ Assume responsibility for your own action or lack of action.

▶ Always maintain a courteous professional tone.

Presenting Images

For onscreen presentation within Photoshop, open the files produced from the layer comps, enter full screen mode, and press Ctrl+Tab to advance through the images.

When preparing for a face-to-face client meeting, consider creating high-quality prints for a formal presentation or showing images onscreen for a more informal presentation.

Photoshop has a feature called layer comps (see Chapter 9, "Using Layer Styles and Comps") that simplify the presentation of design variations. There is a script you'll learn about in Chapter 9 that is used to convert layer comps into individual files.

Adobe Bridge is a separate program that comes with Photoshop (see Chapter 12, "Developing Photos"). As an alternative method of presenting images, you can use Bridge to create an onscreen slide show complete with a soundtrack or output a web gallery for online presentation on a website.

Participating in the Design Process

The design process can perhaps best be visualized as a helix because this 3D shape combines the notion of forward progress through time with cycles of design revision (see Figure 1.2). The radius of the helix diminishes with height as you or your design team converges on final design solutions through time.

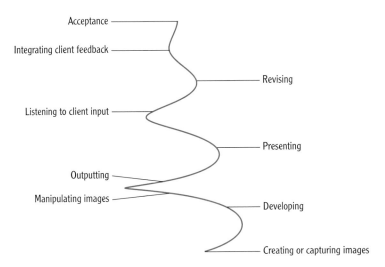

Acceptance

Integrating client feedback

Revising

Listening to client input

Presenting

Outputting

Manipulating images

Developing

Creating or capturing images

FIGURE 1.2 The design process can be visualized as a 3D helix.

Every project is different, and complex projects with many actors can seemingly take on lives of their own. Every project, no matter the scale, is an opportunity to learn something new and refine your technical skills while strengthening your professional relationships.

Learning Composition Principles

Certification Objective

Seasoned creative professionals have developed an eye for composition that informs their work and personal styles. We all know, or more accurately *feel*, beauty when we see and experience it. The key to "learning how to see" is to bring your conscious attention to understanding what gives you aesthetic feelings.

Learning how to see with an artist's, designer's, or photographer's eye is largely an ineffable process that naturally grows and matures over many years.

Learning how to frame compositions and employ composition themes is a means of stimulating this process.

Framing Compositions

Positioning and proportioning a frame around a subject is one of the most powerful tools you have in creating art. Consider filling the frame with the most intriguing part of the picture to generate interest. Sometimes this means zooming in or moving closer to the subject. Rotating the frame also adds a dynamic tension that can be compelling (see Figure 1.3).

Photo courtesy of iStockphoto, © Bayram Tunc, Image #10497430

FIGURE 1.3 Framing compositions is an art.

Part of framing compositions is removing unwanted elements from the picture. The easiest way to do this is in the camera's viewfinder or LCD screen at the time a photo is captured.

When framing compositions, you should also consider the dimension of depth, which can be thought of as foreground, subject, and background. Don't include foreground or background elements at the expense of your subject. In landscapes, show more of the sky or ground according to which element you'd like to accentuate. In portraiture, the rule of thumb is to show more of the foreground than the background or risk losing the viewer's attention in compositional depth. Leonardo da Vinci bends this rule in the most famous painting of all time by painting two different landscapes with slightly different viewpoints behind Mona Lisa, accentuating the mysterious visual tension started in her enigmatic smile (see Figure 1.4).

You can also reframe images postcapture by cropping or retouching in Photoshop to remove unwanted elements.

MONA LISA BY LEONARDO DA VINCI (1503–1505)

FIGURE 1.4 Learn composition by studying the masters.

Don't forget that your artistic license allows you to bend composition rules for dramatic effect. Being aware that you are purposefully bending composition rules is better than being oblivious. Conscious awareness of why something works aesthetically will help you to learn how to see as an artist.

The rule of thirds, a compositional technique dating back to the eighteenth century, is used to locate subject matter within a frame divided into three parts both horizontally and vertically. Photoshop's Crop tool incorporates the rule of thirds in its crop guide overlay (see Chapter 3, "Digital Imaging Fundamentals"). Aligning subject matter with the rule of thirds grid can help you create more aesthetically pleasing compositions as compared with centering the subject (see Figure 1.5). Some other artful usages for the Crop tool and rule of thirds: cropping to emphasize the proximity or groupings of images within a frame, and cropping that takes advantage of white space within an image to place more emphasis on its focal point.

The golden rectangle has been known since the Renaissance as the most aesthetically pleasing proportion. Anyone can construct a golden rectangle with a straightedge and compass (see Figure 1.6). Draw a circle, divide it into four quadrants, and draw a square outside. Draw a diagonal line from point A to B. Draw an arc centered at A from B to C. Extend the lines of the square and draw in the last edge to complete the golden rectangle. If you remove the original square, you are left with another golden rectangle. It seems Leonardo may have used this proportion to lay out the *Mona Lisa*.

FIGURE 1.5 Centering the subject (left) and employing the rule of thirds (right)

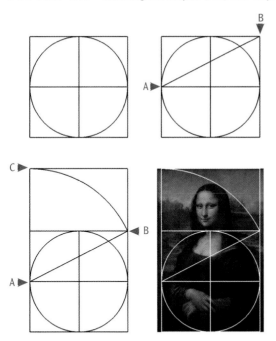

FIGURE 1.6 Drawing a golden rectangle as a proportioning tool

> The golden rectangle has a fixed width-to-height ratio of 1 to 1.618. You can set the Marquee tool options to use this fixed ratio (see Chapter 7, "Selecting Pixels").

Employing Composition Themes

Most images can be classified using one or more composition themes. Images often employ multiple themes but don't necessarily need to. Simplifying images to accentuate one or two themes often produces the most compelling results. The first step is to train yourself to become conscious of themes resident in your images. As your Photoshop skills grow, you will become aware of things you can do to accentuate themes and make your images stand out. The following is not an exhaustive list of composition themes, but it should give you enough to chew on.

Linear form   A line is the shortest distance between two points. Lines connect the dots, implying logic, efficiency, and mechanism. Horizontal lines are restful, vertical lines are strong, and diagonal lines imply motion. Converging lines direct the eye to a goal. Lines are masculine.

PHOTO COURTESY OF ISTOCKPHOTO, © TOMOGRAF, IMAGE #4823532

Curved form   Curves take time to get where they are going. Curves can be sensuous and beautiful and imply relationship. Curves are feminine.

PHOTO COURTESY OF ISTOCKPHOTO, © BEN KLAUS, IMAGE #7751145

Negative space   Closed forms define shapes. Positive space exists inside shapes and negative space is the emptiness surrounding shapes and forms. That is, positive space is that which is occupied by objects and negative space is the field in which the objects exist. Space and form can be thought of as the dance between positive and negative space. Instead of habitually looking at the positive space, shift your perception to the negative space and see if it isn't more compelling.

Photo courtesy of iStockphoto, © Patrick A. Krost, Image #5851563

Texture and pattern   Texture is the surface quality—smooth, bumpy, wispy, scratchy, and so on. Texture is closely related to pattern, which is a recurring design that gives a surface distinctive quality.

Photo courtesy of iStockphoto, © Gijs Bekenkamp, Image #3701501

Tonal gradations   Tone refers to a particular quality in brightness or color value. Images that play with gradations in tone have a soft, sensuous feeling. This effect comes from subtle variations in mid-tones.

PHOTO COURTESY OF ISTOCKPHOTO, © KEVIN DAVIDSON, IMAGE #12076591

Brightness and contrast   Images that contrast light with dark invoke a dramatic quality. Images with extremes in brightness and darkness by definition don't include most of the mid-tones. Thus this theme is the opposite of the theme of tonal gradations.

ST. JEROME BY CARAVAGGIO (1606)

Silhouettes   Silhouettes highlight objects as dark shapes against a bright background illuminated only by a backlight such as the setting or rising sun. Silhouettes are an intriguing way to play with form.

PHOTO COURTESY OF iSTOCKPHOTO, © ANDREA HILL, IMAGE #5474184

Complementary colors Juxtaposing opposites always has an appeal. Complementary colors are opposite each other on the color wheel (see Chapter 15, "Working with Color," for more information). Colors appear more intense when shown against their opposite hue.

PHOTO COURTESY OF RICHARD TRUEMAN

Analogous colors Analogous colors are adjacent to each other on the color wheel. Similar hues, intensities, or color values work well together and create a harmony that ties objects together.

PHOTO COURTESY OF RICHARD TRUEMAN

Color saturation   Contrasting saturated colors and objects drained of their hue creates a tension that highlights the colorful objects. This is a way to draw attention to the colorized objects.

PHOTO COURTESY OF RICHARD TRUEMAN

Rhythm   Setting up or capturing a repeated pattern of objects in space can have a musical appeal. Regular visual rhythms are soothing but can also be boring. Syncopated or varied rhythms give your eyes something to follow and keep your interest too.

PHOTO COURTESY OF ISTOCKPHOTO, © SANDSUN, IMAGE #9339689

Repetition   Closely related to rhythm, repeated shapes can imply movement or set up a dynamic tension that leads the eye somewhere.

PHOTO COURTESY OF iStockPHOTO, © CHARLES SCHUG, IMAGE #7103336

Motion blur   Motion blur is an artifact of the photographic process of capturing an image of reality in a slice of time. The viewer understands that objects moving during the time the shutter was open appear blurry.

Because viewers subconsciously expect fast-moving objects to appear blurry, pros sometimes use neutral density filters to induce blur in daylight time-lapse photography.

PHOTO COURTESY OF RICHARD TRUEMAN

Depth of field   Photographers can either expand or narrow the depth of the spatial field that appears in focus by adjusting the size of the lens aperture. By narrowing the depth of field, you can direct a viewer's attention where you want it—people naturally look where images appear their sharpest.

PHOTO COURTESY OF ISTOCKPHOTO, © ABEL MITJA VARELA, IMAGE #12522936

Vanishing point   The further away objects are, the smaller they appear. In perspective drawings and in real life, parallel lines appear to converge at one or more vanishing points in the distance. One-point perspective images seeming to converge on a single vanishing point imply a visual journey that invites you along.

PHOTO COURTESY OF ISTOCKPHOTO, © JUHA HUISKONEN, IMAGE #1765743

Worm's eye viewpoint   Looking up at objects gives the viewer the point of view of a child, and this causes objects to appear tall, mighty, and even bigger than life.

PHOTO COURTESY OF RICHARD TRUEMAN

God's eye viewpoint   Looking down on objects from a great height gives the viewer a godlike point-of-view. You can accentuate the god-complex in aerial photography or in shots taken from tall buildings by boosting saturation and narrowing the depth of field, which can make objects below appear almost like playthings.

PHOTO COURTESY OF ISTOCKPHOTO, © JOAN VICENT CANTÓ ROIG, IMAGE #14561946V

Contrasting scale　Contrasting objects at different scales can have a surrealistic or humorous effect. Playing with perspective or using oversized or miniature props can help achieve this effect.

PHOTO COURTESY OF ISTOCKPHOTO, © NIKO GUIDO, IMAGE #11557789

Macro Scale　Taking close-ups of small subjects is the subject of macro photography. Macro shots can create an otherworldly effect or can be intended simply to study the texture and forms of small objects in detail.

PHOTO COURTESY OF ISTOCKPHOTO, © ILYA BUSHUEV, IMAGE #4475700

Understanding Your Rights to Use Images

Certification
Objective
While some indigenous peoples hold the belief that cameras steal one's soul, and some psychics tune into a person's energy using a photo, before you start snapping photos of people or scanning printed matter, it pays to educate yourself about the law. I'll compare and contrast using your own images versus using other people's images.

Using Your Own Images

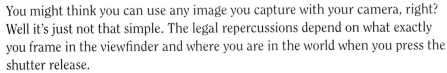

I'm not a lawyer, so take my recommendations with a grain of salt and research the law as it applies where you live.

You might think you can use any image you capture with your camera, right? Well it's just not that simple. The legal repercussions depend on what exactly you frame in the viewfinder and where you are in the world when you press the shutter release.

If a photo contains a recognizable human face, then you must get permission from the model to use their likeness.

Get models to sign release forms. It is a very good idea to get the subjects of your photos to sign model release forms (also known as liability waivers) so that they have less chance of successfully suing you should you ever make money off of their image. Do a Google search for "model release form" for some boilerplate templates.

See http:// en.wikipedia .org/wiki/ Model_release for more information on model releases.

In addition, be aware that some jurisdictions have personality rights applying to living individuals and even those recently deceased. It is your responsibility to ensure that you do not infringe upon someone else's personality rights by publishing their image without their written permission. This is especially critical should you ever decide to use a person's image for parody or social commentary or should the model feel that your image of them is unflattering.

Copyright your work. In some jurisdictions, copyright is implied in anything you create, while in others it is not. No matter where you are it is advisable to register your copyright with the relevant authority because this improves your chances of winning a court battle should someone not respect your copyright. In the United States and Canada, it is very easy to register copyright and costs only a nominal fee. You should also use the copyright symbol © with your name or business name and year of publication (which is required in at least 20 countries).

In the United States: www.copyright.gov

In Canada: www.cipo.ic.gc.ca

Watermark your images.   Traditional watermarks are recognizable symbols that appear within the structure of paper in transmitted or reflected light and are used to identify the paper maker. Digital watermarks serve the same purpose in identifying the maker of an image. However, electronic watermarks can be visible or invisible. Visible watermarks can be as subtle as your business logo or name in the corner of each image, faded out to avoid competing with the images, or as obvious as big red opaque X in the middle of each image, greatly deterring the theft of your intellectual property (but also making the image harder to enjoy viewing). Invisible watermarks encoded within image data can be used to prove that an image is your intellectual property.

Another approach to protecting intellectual property is to post low-resolution thumbnails on your website and offer password-protected high-resolution files suitable for printing for sale.

Using Others' Images

There are many sources of digital images made by other people. However, before you use images made by others, it is your responsibility to determine whether you have the right to do so. For example, many of the images on Wikipedia (`www.wikipedia.org`) and Wikimedia Commons (`http://commons.wikimedia.org`) have Creative Commons licenses, which forge a balance between the "all rights reserved" copyright model and releasing something into the public domain by granting specific abilities to share, remix, and/or reuse digital content. In some cases there are legal exceptions allowing you to fairly use copyrighted material without acquiring permission from the copyright holders. Finally, paying a fee for stock photographic content is another common route to licensing images made by others.

Using creative commons images   Creative Commons (`www.creativecommons.org`) is a nonprofit organization offering a set of licenses supporting cultural innovation on the Internet and elsewhere. All Creative Commons licenses require that you attribute the work in a manner specified by the author or licensor (but not in a way that suggests that they endorse you or your use of the work). Some of the Creative Commons licenses stipulate noncommercial use only and some disallow derivative works; others allow derivative and/or commercial works. You must be careful to find images allowing the particular uses you have in mind.

Under copyright law, works in the public domain may be used by anyone without the need to acquire permission or attribute the author and with no restriction on making derivative and/or commercial works.

Understanding fair use and fair dealing   In many countries, specific exceptions to copyright law allow you to use copyrighted images without permission under certain circumstances. In the United States, *fair use* is the doctrine that enables commentary, criticism, news reporting, teaching, scholarship, and library archiving of copyrighted images. In Canada and other common law jurisdictions, a similar but more restrictive principle called *fair dealing* applies.

There is no way to categorically determine whether a copyrighted image can safely be used without hiring a lawyer because fair use is decided on a case-by-case basis, taking all the circumstances into consideration. However, here are a few general guidelines:

▶ If it is possible to shoot a similar image, then fair use doesn't apply. For example, if you find a beautiful copyrighted picture of a subject you discuss in some cultural context but anyone with a camera could go and photograph that same subject, then fair use might not apply. If on the other hand the copyrighted photo is of something that doesn't exist in the present but did in the past or is planned to exist in the future, then fair use might apply.

▶ You must demonstrate that your use of a copyrighted image either advances knowledge or the progress of the arts through the addition of something new and transformative rather than being merely a derivative work.

▶ Use the entire copyrighted image to avoid tarnishing or misrepresenting it.

▶ Display copyrighted images for online use in a size and resolution sufficient to maintain the quality intended by the company or organization without it being unnecessarily high resolution.

Common misunderstandings about fair use and fair dealing include (but are not limited to) thinking that any use is fair use, noncommercial use is inevitably fair, strict adherence to fair use protects you from being sued, and using copyrighted images in free events or educational institutions is automatically acceptable.

Using stock content   Using stock images is a way to avoid entering into legal gray areas, but this privilege comes at a price. High-quality professional stock photography has been around for many decades but has traditionally been rather expensive. Corbis and Getty Images are the two largest traditional stock photography agencies by revenue. Both offer complex "rights-managed" licenses where price is based on how an image is to be used.

Selling your best images at a microstock agency is a business opportunity worth contemplating.

Microstock photography agencies have sprung up and surged in popularity within the last 10 years. Microstock companies "crowdsource" their images, using the Internet exclusively, and sell royalty-free content usage licenses at very low rates (some for less than $1). Shutterstock uses a subscription model and Fotolia employs a credit-based model, while iStockphoto (owned by Getty Images) uses both. Microstock agencies not only license photographs but also make available illustrations, audio, video, and animations.

Photography and Scanning Primer

So you've picked up this book on Photoshop. But do you understand photography or scanning basics? Not everyone using Photoshop comes to it with a photography or desktop publishing background. If all you've ever used is a point-and-shoot camera, if you don't understand your camera's manual mode, or if you have never scanned anything, then this primer is for you. This primer discusses such fundamental topics as understanding pixels, choosing the right digital camera and lenses, setting light sensitivity, adjusting exposure, focusing, and scanning.

Certification
Objective

Understanding Pixels

Before you choose which digital camera to buy, it's important to understand how images are digitized. Digital cameras have sensor arrays that record myriad light samples during the time the shutter is open. Every point in the sensor array is sampled in red, green, and blue wavelengths. Each triplet of light intensity is recorded numerically. When the numbers are transferred to a computer, each triplet of red, green, and blue intensities combines to form a single solid-color picture element onscreen, called a *pixel*. Digital photos assembled from these pixels are something like a mosaic of tiny ceramic tiles (see Figure 1.7).

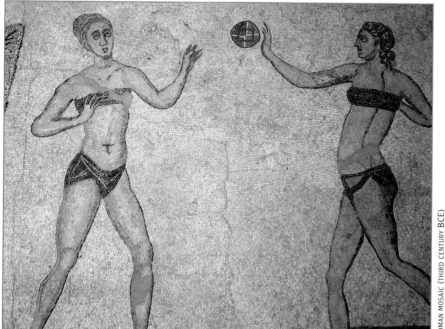

ROMAN MOSAIC (THIRD CENTURY BCE)

F I G U R E 1 . 7 Digital images are analogous to mosaics made of many tiles.

When you stand back from a mosaic, a perceptual shift occurs and you see the picture made up of the tiles. The same thing happens in digital imaging with pixels. Figure 1.8 shows the pixels within the red rectangle centered on the ball in Figure 1.7.

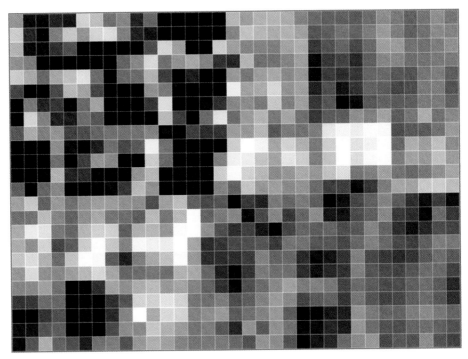

FIGURE 1.8 Any digital image shown at full magnification (3200%) will appear as a grid of pixels.

Selecting a Digital Camera

Camera manufacturers commonly advertise how many megapixels (millions of pixels) their camera sensors sample. While more pixels means more detailed images, more pixels also means more information to be stored. Processing large amounts of data can slow down your computer and require additional investment in storage for your photos. Unless you plan to make large-sized prints, you probably don't need to maximize the number of megapixels.

An often-overlooked and more important factor in the quality of photos a camera can produce is the sensor size, a rectangular area measured in millimeters. The full frame size of traditional 35mm cameras actually measures

3624 mm. All but the highest-end digital cameras have sensor sizes smaller than full frame (see Figure 1.9). Larger sensors capture more pixels with a greater dynamic range and can operate in lower light conditions and with less noise.

PHOTO COURTESY OF SPHL UNDER THE CREATIVE COMMONS ATTRIBUTION-SHARE ALIKE 3.0 UNPORTED LICENSE

FIGURE 1.9 Charge coupled device image sensor

Professional and advanced amateur cameras have the ability to store unprocessed sensor data called RAW files, which can be thought of as digital negatives. Lower-end cameras lack this ability and process sensor data into JPEG digital positives within the camera circuitry, losing a great deal of information and image quality in the process but also minimizing file storage requirements.

Modern digital cameras are now better than film cameras in every respect. Disposable film cameras remain popular however, and film photography will probably always exist as a creative anachronism.

Consumer point-and-shoot cameras and many smartphones are convenient for shooting photos and video, but the downside is low picture quality due to their very small lenses. Digital single-lens reflex (DSLR) cameras on the other hand are designed to accommodate interchangeable lenses of varying use, cost, and quality. The two most fundamental lens parameters are focal length and maximum aperture.

◄

Kodak stopped making traditional 35mm film cameras in 2004, and the once ubiquitous Kodachrome film was discontinued in 2009.

Lens Focal Length

Focal length determines the magnification of the image converging on the camera sensor. A lens with a long focal length magnifies the image as compared to a lens with a short focal length. Focal length is measured from the center of the outer lens to the light sensor and is typically measured in millimeters (see Figure 1.10).

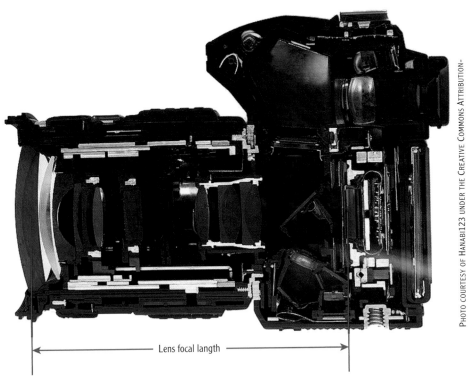

Lens focal length

FIGURE 1.10 Focal length is measured from the outer lens to the light sensor.

The interaction of a lens's focal length with the camera's sensor size determines the angle of view. The angle of view approximating human vision is 50. On a full-frame DSLR, this angle of view corresponds to a "normal" lens with a 43 mm focal length.

Lenses with angles of view wider than 60 are called wide-angle lenses. They have correspondingly smaller focal lengths. Wide-angle lenses are useful in enclosed spaces such as building interiors because the wide angle of view captures more of the space. However, extreme wide-angle lenses such as fisheyes introduce a large amount of geometric distortion.

Telephoto lenses have longer focal lengths that magnify the image received by the light sensor. These are used to make the subject appear closer to the photographer than it really is. Long focus lenses are often used in nature and sports photography.

Zoom lenses have adjustable focal lengths, while prime lenses have fixed focal lengths.

Lens Aperture

Interchangeable lenses have the ability to modulate the intensity of light striking the sensor by adjusting the size of the aperture, similar to how the pupils of our eyes work. The f-stop ring was used in days gone by to manually adjust the diameter of the iris diaphragm, but this is automatically driven by a motor on modern lenses (see Figure 1.11).

◄

All lenses have aberrations (imperfections) that Photoshop can help correct (see Chapter 10, "Transforming Paths, Layers, and Smart Objects").

Iris diaphragm

Lens aperture

F-stop ring

FIGURE 1.11 Selecting an f-stop controls the size of the lens aperture.

F-stops follow the geometric sequence f/(1, 1.4, 2, 2.8, 4, 5.6, 8, 11, 16, 22), where each successive stop has half the light intensity of the previous stop.

The f-stop measurement is the ratio of focal length to aperture diameter. The smaller the f-stop ratio is, the larger the aperture.

Lenses are rated by their maximum aperture, which is also known as lens speed. Lenses with larger maximum aperture open up more to deliver more light to the sensor and therefore allow faster shutter speeds, which reduce blurring in low-light conditions. Faster lenses cost more than slower lenses. Prime lenses are generally faster than zoom lenses. A fast prime lens can easily cost more than several point-and-shoot cameras put together.

Adjusting Exposure

Exposure refers to the amount of light received by the sensor. An underexposed image didn't receive enough light and an overexposed image received too much light (see Figure 1.12).

PHOTOS COURTESY OF RICHARD TRUEMAN

FIGURE 1.12 Underexposed foreground (left) and overexposed background (right)

Exposure is primarily modulated by aperture and shutter speed. All digital cameras automatically choose a combination of f-stop and shutter speed in Program mode. All but the least expensive digital cameras allow you to manually select aperture, shutter speed, or both.

In low-light situations, natural light can be reflected onto a model (see Figure 1.13) or supplemented by electronic flashes, which can be diffused by studio umbrellas or portable soft boxes.

Bracketing is the practice of taking multiple shots of the same subject at different shutter speeds or apertures in the hope that one combination will produce the proper exposure. Most DSLR cameras have auto-bracketing features, which allow you to rapidly expose multiple photos with varying shutter speeds or apertures.

FIGURE 1.13 Bouncing natural light onto a model with a reflector

However, it is not always possible to properly expose all parts of images that exhibit great variations in brightness (called *dynamic range*). Figure 1.12 shows how the image can be bracketed to properly expose either the house or the brighter background, but not both at the same time. High dynamic range (HDR) images combine multiple bracketed shots into a single image. You'll learn how to create images like Figure 1.14 in Chapter 14, "Merging Photos."

> ◄
>
> It is preferable to bracket in aperture priority mode to maintain the same f-stop and vary the shutter speed across multiple exposures.

PHOTO COURTESY OF RICHARD TRUEMAN

FIGURE 1.14 HDR image maps tones from the bracketed shots in Figure 1.12 into a single image.

Focusing

All modern cameras have an autofocus feature that works well in most situations. However, there are times when you'll want to focus on something in the foreground but the camera will focus on the background. To solve this problem, try centering the frame on an object in the foreground, pressing the shutter release button halfway down to engage autofocus, and then reframing the composition the way you like it before depressing the shutter release all the way to take the shot.

In panorama photography, it is necessary to control focus manually to maintain the same focal depth across multiple exposures. In Chapter 14 you'll merge multiple such photos into a seamless panorama.

Every lens focuses precisely at only one distance at a time. The width of the spatial region in sharp focus is called *depth of field*. You control depth of field by adjusting the lens aperture. Small apertures tend to keep everything from the foreground to the background in focus. Large apertures tend to narrow the depth of field. The rule of thumb is *depth of field increases with f-stop* (see Figure 1.15).

PHOTO COURTESY OF ISTOCKPHOTO, © LAJOSREPASI, IMAGE #9109571

FIGURE 1.15 Narrow the depth of field by using a small f-stop ratio.

Selecting Light Sensitivity

Photographic film stocks had different sensitivities affecting how much light was required to drive the chemical reaction. Fast-reacting film that was used for shooting in low-light situations or to capture fast action was grainy, whereas slow film was fine grained. Film speeds were measured using various standards in the past, including DIN, ASA, and ISO.

In digital photography, we still use the ISO system to calibrate the light sensitivity of the sensor (see Figure 1.16). Digital light sensors are far more sensitive to light than film with ISO equivalents up to 102,400.

> Just to put modern ISO capabilities in perspective, the original Kodachrome film had an ISO of 6.

PHOTO COURTESY OF ISTOCKPHOTO, © LEONSBOX, IMAGE #9022259

FIGURE 1.16 Exposure is a combination of shutter speed, f-stop, and ISO value.

Increasing the ISO value in your camera's menu will enable you to use faster shutter speeds and smaller apertures. However, at extremely high ISO values (above 2,000), digital cameras start to experience problems with *noise*, or random fluctuations of light intensity. You should therefore set your camera to use the lowest ISO value that yields the shutter speeds and apertures you need.

Scanning Tips

Two-dimensional matter is best captured on a scanner (see Figure 1.17) rather than with a camera. Like cameras, scanners use light sensors to digitize images. However, scanners supply their own light in a moving bar that scans stationary subjects. By moving the bar very slowly, the scanner can record an image at incredibly high resolutions.

PHOTO COURTESY OF ISTOCKPHOTO, © LISE GAGNE, IMAGE #90395

The key to using scanners successfully is never to scan more area or resolution than is needed for the specific use you have in mind for the image.

FIGURE 1.17 Flatbed scanner

Scanners come with their own software supplied by their manufacturers. This software will allow you to specify which region of the scanning bed you wish to sample and at what resolution (see Chapter 3 for a discussion of resolution).

Scanned images often suffer because they do not use the full dynamic range available in the image file. Figure 1.18 shows a histogram (which you'll learn more about in Chapter 3) representing the full dynamic range. The white portion of the graph (on the left side) means the pixels are not distributed properly to take advantage of the darkest tones available in the image file. You'll learn how to adjust the histogram with the Levels command in Chapter 11, "Adjusting and Filtering."

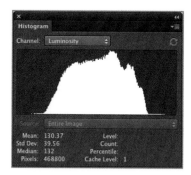

FIGURE 1.18 The histogram shows that this scanned image does not take advantage of the full dynamic range.

Professional printing presses create rows and columns of cyan, magenta, yellow, and black colored dots. In much the same way as with mosaics and pixels, we perceive continuous tone when printed dots appear small enough in printed matter. A problem called *moiré* (see Figure 1.19) sometimes arises with scans because of the interference between the grid of printed dots and the grid of pixels in the scan.

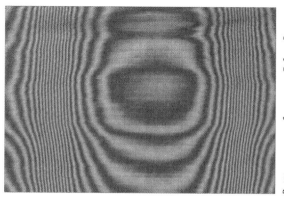

PHOTO COURTESY OF iSTOCKPHOTO, © CHRIS PRICE, IMAGE #8786558

FIGURE 1.19 Moiré interference pattern

Good scanning software comes with a de-screen filter that you can use to remove moiré patterns. If your scanning software does not come with such a filter, you can try scanning at twice the desired resolution and then halving the image size in Photoshop to reduce the unpleasant interference (see Chapter 3, "Digital Imaging Fundamentals" under "Setting document size and resolution").

THE ESSENTIALS AND BEYOND

In this chapter you have considered the big picture in the design process, learned specific techniques for framing compositions, studied a variety of composition themes, pondered the ramifications of using your own images versus using the work of others, and digested the fundamentals of photography and scanning.

ADDITIONAL EXERCISE

Take your digital camera outside and go for a walk. Identify a subject, which might be a person, building, small object, or anything that you find interesting. Take at least 20 pictures of this subject from a variety of different focal lengths, apertures, shutter speeds, distances between camera and subject, height of camera, tilt of camera, orientations, depths of field, and so on. Fully explore the subject and how you can capture it photographically.

CHAPTER 2

Getting Acquainted with Photoshop's User Interface

Just as you need to know what an automobile's pedals, shifter, switches, buttons, knobs, and levers do to drive a car, so too must you understand what Photoshop's menus, bars, workspaces, tools, panels, tabs, and icons do—collectively called the user interface—in order to successfully use the program. Let's launch Photoshop and take it for a spin.

▶ **User interface overview**

▶ **Accessing commands**

▶ **Working with documents**

▶ **Using tools**

▶ **Arranging panels**

▶ **Recalling workspaces**

Certification
Objective

User Interface Overview

Giving a document a name in the New dialog box is optional. You will have another opportunity to name the document when you save the file.

▶

A lot of thought has gone into the design of Photoshop's user interface (UI) over its more than 20-year existence. Along the way palettes became dockable panels, and the preferred display of tools went from two columns to one. Let's create a new document and take a look at Photoshop's UI.

1. Launch Photoshop from the operating system's Dock or Applications folder on the Mac or the Start menu on Windows.

2. Open the File menu and choose New.

3. In the New dialog box, select Web from the Preset drop-down menu. Select 800 × 600 from the Size drop-down menu and leave all the other parameters at their default values. Notice that the image size is estimated at 1.37M (megabytes) in the lower-right corner of the New dialog box (see Figure 2.1). Click OK.

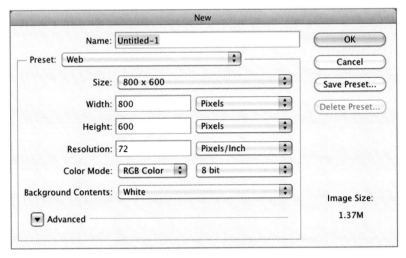

FIGURE 2.1 Creating a new blank document

EPHEMERAL VERSUS LONG TERM STORAGE

Images take up space according to how many pixels they are made of. Remember that pixels are combinations of red, green, and blue numerical values that must all be stored, even if all the pixels are white. Right now a new "blank" document is stored only in your computer's random access memory (RAM). If Photoshop were to crash or if your computer suddenly lost electrical power, you would lose this document. Although this would be no big loss at this point, it's important to understand the difference between ephemeral RAM and the long-term storage of images as files on your hard drive or solid-state drive.

Figure 2.2 shows Photoshop's Mac UI and Figure 2.3 shows its Windows UI. Note how similar the two user interfaces appear. The only visual difference has to do with how each operating system manages windows. The Mac has Close, Minimize, and Maximize buttons (red, yellow, and green respectively) in the top left corner and

The Windows version of Photoshop CS6 does not have an Application frame.

Windows has its equivalent buttons in the upper right corner. This book will use the Mac UI in general but as you can see this is no problem for Windows users.

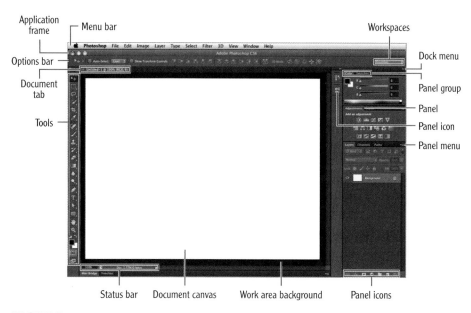

FIGURE 2.2 Photoshop's Mac OS UI

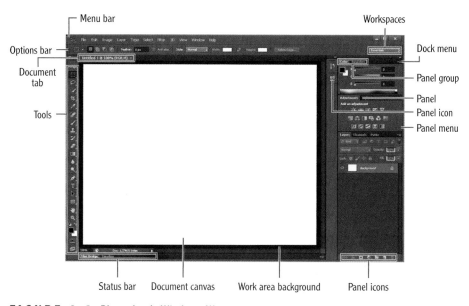

FIGURE 2.3 Photoshop's Windows UI

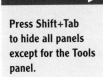

Press Shift+Tab to hide all panels except for the Tools panel.

4. Press the Tab key. The tools and panels are reduced to thin vertical strips along the left and right edges of the screen. The options bar disappears completely.

5. Hover the cursor over the strip along the right edge of the screen. The panels are revealed. Move the cursor away from the panels and they will auto-hide again.

6. Press Tab again to show the tools, options bar, and panels and keep them displayed continuously.

Setting Application Preferences

Certification Objective

Photoshop has a number of configurable settings, or preferences, dealing with many aspects of the program. At this point you won't know what many of the preferences do, but at least you will know where to look if and when you want to change how Photoshop works. Most applications have preferences, and Mac OS and Windows differ in how you access them. Let's open the Preferences dialog box.

1. On Mac OS, application preferences are located in the application menu. On Windows, preferences are located in the Edit menu. Preferences are further categorized in cascading submenus (see Figure 2.4). On Mac OS, choose Photoshop ➢ Preferences ➢ General. On Windows, choose Edit ➢ Preferences ➢ General.

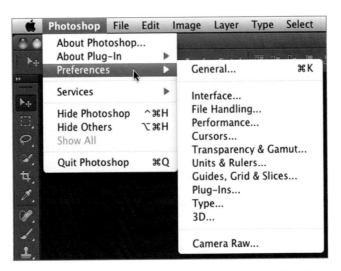

FIGURE 2.4 Accessing Photoshop preferences on Mac OS

2. Select the Zoom Resizes Windows check box (see Figure 2.5) if it is not already selected. You will use this feature in Chapter 3, "Digital Imaging Fundamentals."

FIGURE 2.5 Changing an application preference

3. The Preferences dialog box has a page interface. Click the Next button repeatedly and take a look at what's under the hood. Click OK when you're done poking around.

You can change the color theme of the UI to one of four choices on the Interface page in Preferences.

RESETTING DEFAULT PREFERENCE

If you are worried after changing some preferences that you have messed something up, don't. That's not really possible. However, you can reset the preferences to the way they were when you first installed Photoshop. To do so, press and hold Option+Command (⌘) +Shift (Mac OS) or Alt+Ctrl+Shift (Windows) when you launch Photoshop. Release the keys when you see a message asking whether you want to delete the current preferences and choose Yes.

Accessing Commands

You can access commands equally well from menus or from the keyboard. Beginners tend to use the menus a lot while they are learning the commands, and that is perfectly natural. Intermediate-level Photoshop users tend to increasingly use default keyboard shortcuts as they memorize more of them, while pros tend to make their own keyboard shortcuts to work more efficiently. Photoshop's default preferences are loaded with a set of keyboard shortcuts, and there is generally no reason to change them because they are well thought out as a cohesive system. However, in the following steps you will make two new keyboard shortcuts.

1. Open the Image menu and examine some of the commands listed there. In particular notice that the commonly used commands Crop and Trim (see Chapter 3) do not have keyboard shortcuts assigned to them by default.

Menu items often have cascading submenus indicated by black disclosure triangles.

2. Choose Edit ➤ Keyboard Shortcuts. Scroll down and expand the Image menu item by clicking its disclosure triangle. Keep scrolling down until you locate Crop and Trim.

3. Select the shortcut field next to the Crop command. Press Opt+Shift+Cmd+X and click Accept.

MODIFIER KEYS, ABBREVIATIONS, AND SYMBOLS

Typewriters have one modifier key, Shift, which computers obviously inherited. Windows has three additional modifier keys: Control (Ctrl), Alternate (Alt), and the Windows key. However, the Windows key can't be used within Photoshop.

Mac OS has three modifier keys in addition to Shift, which are Command (⌘), Option (Opt), and Control. Mac Command (⌘) is equivalent to Windows Ctrl. One way to remember this is to think of commanders controlling their troops. Modern Mac keyboards have the words Option and Alt printed on the same key, illustrating their equivalence.

What makes this confusing is that Windows and Mac OS both have Control keys but they are not equivalent because Windows Ctrl = Mac OS Command (⌘). Mac OS's Control key is not used in Photoshop's default set of keyboard shortcuts but it can be assigned to custom shortcuts.

(continues)

MODIFIER KEYS, ABBREVIATIONS, AND SYMBOLS *(Continued)*

Mac OS uses the following symbols to identify modifier keys in menus.

⇧ Shift
⌘ Command
⌥ Option
^ Control

In this book I will consistently use the following abbreviations:

▶ Cmd refers to the Mac Command (⌘) / Windows Ctrl key

▶ Opt refers to the Mac Option / Windows Alt key

▶ Enter refers to the (carriage) return key

Whenever I use the Mac Control key, I will explicitly say so to avoid potential confusion.

4. Select the shortcut field next to the Trim command. Press Opt+Shift+ Cmd+T. In this case you are overriding the default shortcut, which triggers the message "Create a duplicate while transforming again" (see Figure 2.6). Click Accept and OK.

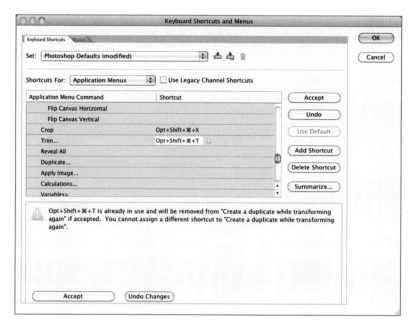

FIGURE 2.6 Setting Keyboard Shortcuts

5. Open the Image menu and observe the two new shortcuts you just made appear in the menu as symbols on the Mac or abbreviations on Windows (see Figure 2.7).

6. Press Cmd+W to close the open document. (Click Don't Save if prompted.)

FIGURE 2.7 New Crop and Trim keyboard shortcuts appear in the Image menu

Working with Documents

Certification
Objective
Whatever you open in Photoshop appears within a document tab or window. Each document is stored in RAM, so the more memory your computer has, the larger and more documents you can open at the same time. In the following steps you will open several documents and learn to arrange them in several ways.

1. Go to the book's Downloads page at www.sybex.com/go /photoshopessentials. Browse to Chapter 2 and download the sample files.

2. In Photoshop, press Cmd+K to open the Preferences dialog box. Select the Interface page in the Preferences dialog box and select Open Documents As Tabs if it is not already selected. Click OK.

3. Press Cmd+O (Open), select all four JPG files, and press Enter. Four documents appear as tabs across the top of the work area background (known as tabbed documents). Click each tab to view one photo at a time.

4. Select Window ➢ Arrange ➢ 4-up (known as n-up viewing).

5. Press Z to select the Zoom tool. Select Zoom All Windows on the options bar and click twice inside one of the images until the magnification is 50%. Figure 2.8 shows the result.

The zoom level that allows you to see all four images in their entirety depends on your monitor's display resolution.

PHOTOS COURTESY RICHARD TRUEMAN

FIGURE 2.8 Arranging tabs in a grid and adjusting the zoom level in all of the images

6. Select Window ➢ Arrange ➢ Float All In Windows. Drag one image's title bar into the document window of another image and two tabs will be automatically generated within the single document window (see Figure 2.9).

7. Open the Screen Mode drop-down menu in the Tools panel and select Full Screen Mode With Menu Bar. Hold the Cmd key and press the = (equals) key twice to zoom to 100% magnification.

8. Right-click in the work area background and choose Select Medium Gray from the shortcut menu.

9. Press F to cycle to the next screen mode, which is Full Screen Mode. If this is the first time you've entered this mode you will be warned that you must press Esc (or F) to exit the mode. Hold the Cmd key and press the = (equal) key twice to zoom into each image. To create a manually-advanced slideshow, press Cmd+` (next to the 1 key) repeatedly to view each successive image. When you are done, press Esc to return to Standard Screen Mode.

Full Screen Mode maintains its own background color, black by default. You can change it by right-clicking in the work area if desired.

FIGURE 2.9 Arranging documents with windows and tabs

Using Tools

Certification Objective

Photoshop's many tools are arranged in a streamlined interface called the toolbox. To work successfully with Photoshop, you need to know where to look to find the right tool for the job among tool groups and flyout menus, how to access tool options, and how to enter numerical values efficiently. I'll round out this discussion by showing you how to create tool presets that will save you loads of time in the long run.

Understanding Tool Groups and Flyout Menus

Photoshop has had a single column toolbox since CS3, when all Adobe applications got a UI facelift, but the former two-column toolbox is still available (toggle between them by clicking the arrows in the upper right corner). No matter how many columns you prefer in your toolbox, the tools are organized into the same groups (see Figure 2.10).

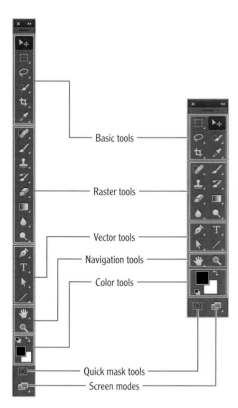

Basic tools

Raster tools

Vector tools

Navigation tools

Color tools

Quick mask tools

Screen modes

FIGURE 2.10 Single- and double-column toolboxes show the same tool groups

The tool groups are as follows:

Basic tools These tools include Move, selection tools (Marquees, Lassos, and Wands), Crop and Slice, and a variety of tools for measurement and annotation. You'll learn about these tools in Chapter 3, "Digital Imaging Fundamentals," and Chapter 7, "Selecting Pixels."

Raster tools Raster tools directly create, manipulate, or retouch pixels. Many of these tools use the technology behind the Brush tool, which you'll learn about in Chapter 4, "Painting."

Vector tools Vector tools are based on mathematical objects that create pixels very precisely. Vector tools include drawing and text tools that you'll learn about in Chapter 5, "Drawing," and Chapter 6, "Writing."

Navigation tools Navigation tools are used for getting around 2D and 3D space (these tools are available in the Extended version of Photoshop only).

Color tools   The color tools feature the foreground and background colors themselves plus an icon to set the default colors (black/white) and the toggle for switching foreground and background color.

Quick mask toggle   Quick mask mode allows you select pixels by painting. You'll learn how to do this in Chapter 7.

All but two of the tools in the toolbox (Move and Zoom) have additional tools under them. The small black triangle in the lower-right corner indicates the presence of additional tools. Let's explore the toolbox.

1. Hover the cursor over any tool for a few seconds to display a tooltip that reveals its name.

2. Click and hold a tool for a couple of seconds to open its flyout menu (or right-click it to immediately open it). Figure 2.11 shows a typical flyout menu.

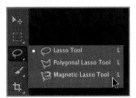

FIGURE 2.11 Flyout menu contains additional tools.

3. Observe that the keyboard shortcut (L in this case) is listed on the flyout. All the tools on the same flyout share the same keyboard shortcut. Hold Shift and press the shortcut key to cycle through all the tools on the flyout, one at a time. For example, press L to select the Lasso tool. Hold Shift and press L and the Polygonal Lasso tool appears on top (ready for use).

4. Press Shift+L and the Magnetic Lasso tool is on top. Press Shift+L and you cycle back to the Lasso tool.

5. Spend a few minutes familiarizing yourself with the various tools and their icons. Figure 2.12 shows an overview of the tools and their locations within the toolbox.

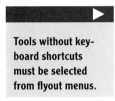

Tools without keyboard shortcuts must be selected from flyout menus.

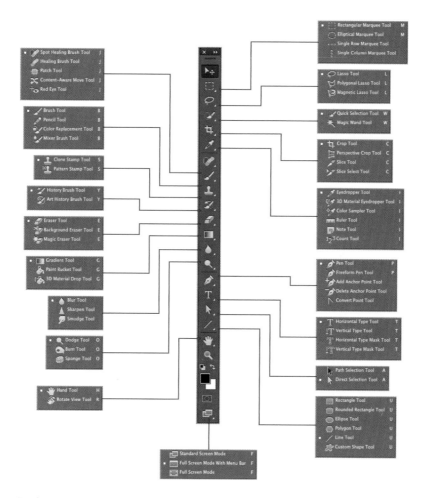

FIGURE 2.12 Tools overview

Selecting Tool Options and Entering Numerical Values

Each tool has a variety of settings configurable on the options bar. Let's take a look at tool options and I'll give you a few tips on entering numerical values to save time.

 1. Select the Rectangle tool. The options bar contains many important controls, including tool presets, drawing modes, fill and stroke types, path controls, geometry options and more that you'll learn about in Chapter 5.

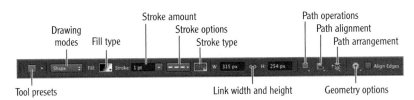

FIGURE 2.13 Identifying the parts of the options bar

2. Select Pixels drawing mode and how the tool-specific options change (see Figure 2.14).

FIGURE 2.14 Selecting a different drawing mode presents different options

3. The least efficient means of entering values is to type them. Double-click the Opacity text box on the options bar to highlight the numerical value and type **50%**.

4. A faster way to changes values is to scrub the label. Position the cursor over the word *Opacity* on the options bar. Drag to the left or right to rapidly change values. Hold Opt while dragging to go slower or hold Shift to change values much more quickly.

5. A more precise approach is to use the arrow keys to change values. Press the up arrow or down arrow key to increment or decrement the value by 1 unit per press. Hold Shift and press the arrow keys to change values by 10 units per press.

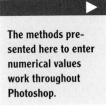

The methods presented here to enter numerical values work throughout Photoshop.

Creating Tool Presets

Tool presets provide a way to save time on configuring options. You can save tool presets for any tool and recall them using the tool preset drop-down menu. Let's create a new tool preset.

1. Select the Polygon tool and set Sides to 5. Open Geometry options and select Star. Open the Fill type drop-down and select Gradient mode. Select the Orange, Yellow, Orange preset gradient, and select Radial type. Set stroke amount to 8 pt. Open the Stroke type menu and select solid color and click the black swatch (see Figure 2.15).

Orange, Yellow, Orange gradient

Shape mode | Gradient fill | Black stroke

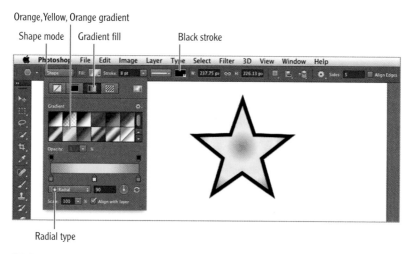

Radial type

FIGURE 2.15 Selecting the Star option and Shape Layers mode

2. Drag out a star. Let us suppose for whatever reason you would like to create a tool preset from all the options you have configured for this particular tool. That way you can avoid having to reconfigure the options every time you want to make a star like this one.

3. Open the tool preset drop-down menu on the options bar and click the Create New Tool Preset button. Type **5 Point Gradient-Fill Black-StrokeStar** in the New Tool Preset dialog box and select Include Color (see Figure 2.16). Click OK.

FIGURE 2.16 Creating a new tool preset

4. Reopen the tool preset drop-down menu and uncheck Current Tool Only. Scroll down and see that your new preset is among many other

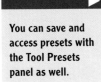

You can save and access presets with the Tool Presets panel as well.

If you need to delete a preset, go to the Preset Manager, select the preset, and click Delete.

presets that come with Photoshop (see Figure 2.17). As you gain more experience with Photoshop, you'll probably find that you are reaching for the same tools and configuring their options the same way time after time, so consider saving tool presets to save time configuring. It's like reaching for a hammer and a bag of nails compared to a pressing the trigger on pneumatic nail gun.

FIGURE 2.17 The new tool preset is available in the drop-down menu on the options bar.

Arranging Panels

Certification Objective

Photoshop has over two dozen panels and extensions that would completely fill the screen if they were to be displayed all at once. Photoshop's panel and dock architecture lets you configure the user interface to suit the kinds of tasks you are performing while leaving plenty of room onscreen to work. In the following steps you will arrange panels and see how easy it is to change the UI.

1. Click the arrows in the upper-right corner of dock 2 to expand the panels (see Figure 2.18). The History and Properties panels appear in their entirety.

Expand panels   Minimize to icons

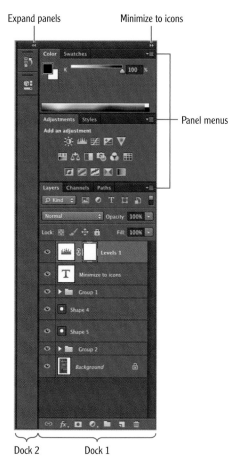

Panel menus

Dock 2   Dock 1

FIGURE 2.18 Panel and dock controls

2. Choose Window ➢ Brush. The Brush and Brush Presets panels appear in a panel group at the bottom of dock 2 (see Figure 2.19). Depending on your screen resolution, some of the panels might minimize in order to accommodate the new panels. If a panel is part of a panel group, all the panels in that group will appear when any one of the panels is chosen. Select the Brush tool to activate the Brush panel.

3. Move the Brush panel out into the document work area by dragging its tab. Brush becomes a floating panel by itself.

FIGURE 2.19 Brush panel group displayed in dock 2

4. Click the arrows in the upper-right corner of dock 2 to minimize the panels to icons. Drag the left edge of dock 2 to the left to reveal the icons and their titles.

5. Drag the Brush panel in between the Color/Swatches panel group and the Adjustments/Styles panel group in dock 1. A horizontal blue bar will appear as you are dragging, indicating a potential panel drop zone. Double click the Brush panel to maximize it. Figure 2.20 shows the result.

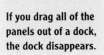

If you drag all of the panels out of a dock, the dock disappears.

FIGURE 2.20 Altering the UI by dragging panels

6. Every panel has a unique panel menu. Expand the Layers panel, open its panel menu, and choose Panel Options. Select the medium thumbnail size in the Layers Panel Options dialog box (see Figure 2.21). Click OK.

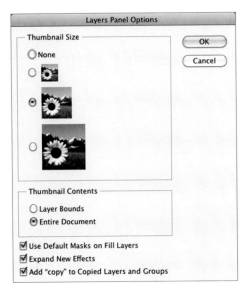

FIGURE 2.21 Changing Layers panel options

7. Choose Window ➢ Timeline. Three panels have landscape orientation: Mini Bridge, Timeline, and Measurement Log. The first two appear by default along the lower edge of the UI.

Recalling Workspaces

Certification
Objective

Use the Workspace Switcher to quickly navigate and select workspace configurations. The Live Workspace feature auto-saves any changes made to a task-specific user workspace. If switched to a different configuration, and then back, the panels will return to their original position.

Workspaces allow you to save and quickly restore panel locations, states, and sizes plus keyboard shortcuts and/or alterations made to the menus. Photoshop comes with several default workspaces that are preconfigured for a variety of tasks. Let's compare a few default workspaces.

1. Click the word Essentials on the options bar to see all the workspaces listed in the drop-down menu. Choose Reset Essentials.

2. Select the Typography workspace on the options bar. The Character and Paragraph panels are important in web or graphic design because they fine-tune how text appears (you'll learn more about these in Chapter 6).

3. Select the Painting workspace on the application bar. Brush presets are located in the center of dock 1 and the Brush panel icon appears in dock 2. Both of these are obviously important when painting.

4. Select the Photography workspace. The Histogram panel shows at a glance how the pixels in a photo are balanced in terms of highlights, mid-tones, and shadows. Adjustments are often needed when retouching (see Chapter 13, "Retouching Photos"). Figure 2.22 shows the Typography, Painting, and Photography workspaces side by side for comparison.

The Extended version of Photoshop has 3D and Motion workspaces.

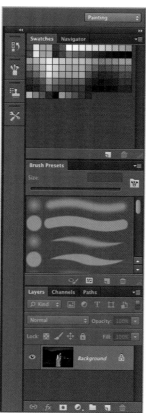

FIGURE 2.22 Comparing the Typography (left), Painting (center), and Photography (right) workspaces

THE ESSENTIALS AND BEYOND

In this chapter you have assimilated the essentials of Photoshop's user interface. You should feel more comfortable with Photoshop now that you have learned how to access commands, work with documents, use tools, arrange panels, and recall workspaces.

ADDITIONAL EXERCISE

Create your own workspace by arranging panels and by opening new panels from the Window menu and dragging and dropping them into position. To get rid of a docked panel, drag it into the work area background to make it a floating panel and then click its close box. Once your panels match the following screen shot, choose Window ➢ Workspace ➢ New Workspace. Type your own name in the New Workspace dialog box and click OK. Observe that your name now appears as a workspace button on the application bar, making it easy to restore the panels in this configuration with a single click.

CHAPTER 3

Digital Imaging Fundamentals

My experience with teaching people who already have a good working knowledge of Photoshop has been that they are often confused by fundamental digital imaging concepts. How is color represented in channels? What is aliasing? What does bit depth really mean? What is the relationship between canvas size, image size, and resolution? Should I use RGB, CMYK, or Lab color? No matter whether you are an absolute beginner or already have some Photoshop experience, this chapter will answer all of these pressing questions and many more.

▶ **Working with pixels**

▶ **Understanding color**

▶ **Storing data**

▶ **Setting document size and resolution**

Working with Pixels

Certification Objective

After many years of working with digital images, I still marvel at the fact that cameras somehow magically convert light into numbers. This digital alchemy boils down to recording myriad blocks of color, better known as pixels. In the following sections, you will learn the benefits of maximizing megapixels, how to choose the correct pixel aspect ratio for the kind of work you are doing, how to deal with aliasing, and finally, how to navigate through millions of pixels with ease.

Maximizing Megapixels

Every year manufacturers seem to produce cameras that can capture more pixels. Modern sensors capture so many pixels in every photo that the pixels number in the millions (megapixels). Figure 3.1 shows a photo captured with a Panasonic Lumix 5-megapixel point-and-shoot camera. Figure 3.2 shows the same scene photographed with a Canon EOS 5D Mark II 21.1-megapixel digital single-lens reflex (DSLR) camera.

PHOTO COURTESY RICHARD TRUEMAN

FIGURE 3.1 Photo shot with 5-megapixel camera

PHOTO COURTESY RICHARD TRUEMAN

FIGURE 3.2 Photo shot with 21-megapixel camera

The insets in Figure 3.1 and Figure 3.2 show that more megapixels means you can digitally zoom in much further and still have good quality. The cat on the mat in Figure 3.1 is far more blurry and noisy compared with Figure 3.2.

On the downside, greater numbers of pixels consume more RAM and take up more file storage space. If you are shooting photos for the Web but not for print, you can get away with using fewer megapixels. However, resampling large images down to the desired size will always result in higher-quality photos compared to shooting fewer megapixels to start with. The adage that *you get what you pay for* rings true for digital cameras.

More pixels generally mean more detail can be captured and with less noise.

Selecting the Pixel Aspect Ratio

If you are creating output for the Web or for print, then you will always use square pixels (see Figure 3.3).

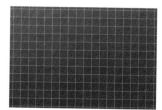

FIGURE 3.3 Square pixels shown at maximum magnification

The Extended version of Photoshop can do video editing and people can easily get confused when dealing with video files having non-square-pixel aspect ratios. It's really very simple, however. Choose the pixel aspect ratio on the View menu according to the video format you are using.

Figure 3.4 shows pixels that are 1.5 times as wide as they are tall according to the DVCPRO HD 1080 standard. At 100% magnification, an image shown with the wrong pixel aspect ratio would appear either too narrow or too wide. The amount of stretching in standards D1/DV NTSC or D1/DV PAL is very subtle because these standards have aspect ratios closer to square.

In Photoshop CS6 Extended you can paint, clone, and even add text over multiple frames of a video sequence using the Movie Paint feature. Select Layer ➢ Video Layer ➢ New Video Layer From File... and your video clip will be imported as a single video layer that you can paint on non-destructively.

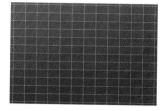

FIGURE 3.4 Pixels with an aspect ratio of 1.5 shown at maximum magnification

VIEWING THE PIXEL ASPECT RATIO

The pixel aspect ratio becomes evident if you zoom in so far that you can perceive the actual pixels. Choose View ➤ Show ➤ Pixel Grid if you don't see grid lines revealing the pixel aspect ratio.

Dealing with Aliasing

Aliasing is a problem that arises out of the practice of representing continuous tones in a grid of pixels. When linear elements don't align with the grid, a stair-stepping type of distortion occurs. Figure 3.5 shows two lines: the red line exhibits aliasing, and the blue line has been *anti-aliased*. Anti-aliasing blurs the edge by *dithering* pixels adjacent to the edge with gradually decreasing values that blend into the surrounding pixels.

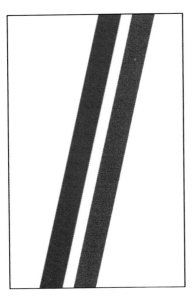

My book *Enhancing Architectural Drawings and Models with Photoshop* (Sybex, 2010) includes in-depth coverage on working with aliased line drawings in Photoshop.

▶

FIGURE 3.5 The blue line is anti-aliased and the red line is aliased. The image on the left is shown at 100% magnification and the image on the right is at 500%.

Most of the time you'll want to anti-alias the shapes that you draw (see Chapter 5, "Drawing"). However, there are occasions when you might want to intentionally alias lines, especially when they are horizontal, vertical, or at 45 degree angles because these orientations produce crisp lines without any fringe pixels.

Navigating Pixels

When you're viewing millions of pixels on screen, you'll need to learn how to navigate to get around any digital photo. The Zoom and Hand tools are all that you need to navigate in 2D. Let's gain some experience navigating a 21-mega-pixel photo.

1. Go to the book's Downloads page at `www.sybex.com/go` `/photoshopessentials`, browse to Chapter 3, get the file `Cabin` `.jpg`, and open it in Photoshop.

2. Press Cmd+K to open the Preferences dialog box on the General page. Select the following check boxes: Animated Zoom, Zoom Resizes Windows, Zoom With Scroll Wheel, Zoom Clicked Point To Center, and Enable Flick Panning. Click OK.

   ◀

   Animated Zoom and Flick Panning are available in Preferences only if your computer's graphic subsystem supports OpenGL.

3. Choose Window ➤ Arrange ➤ Float In Window. Select the Zoom tool. Click several times on the cat on the mat in front of the cabin door. The window enlarges because of the Zoom Resizes Windows option. The cat stays centered in the view because of the Zoom Clicked Point To Center option.

4. Hold the Cmd key and press the - (minus) key to zoom out one step. Hold Cmd and press the = key to zoom in one step. This is an alternative to using the Zoom tool.

5. Press Z to reselect the Zoom tool. Select Scrubby Zoom on the options bar. Position the cursor over the silver chimney cap and drag from left to right to zoom in there. Keep dragging until you reach the maximum magnification level of 3200%, which is listed on the document title bar. Drag from the right to the left to zoom back out.

6. Deselect Resize Windows To Fit on the options bar (the same as the Zoom Resizes Windows preference) and repeatedly click on the pair of green chairs on the right to zoom in there. The pixels will fluidly animate between magnification stops due to the Animated Zoom preference.

7. Hold down the spacebar and drag to pan the picture. Drag and release while the cursor is moving and the picture will keep panning (this is the Flick Panning preference at work). Release the spacebar to return to the Zoom tool.

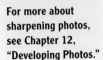

Fit Screen respects
the document's
aspect ratio, whereas
Fill Screen respects
your monitor's
aspect ratio.

For more about
sharpening photos,
see Chapter 12,
"Developing Photos."

8. Hold down Opt and click to zoom out. Notice how holding down Opt temporarily toggles the Zoom Out button on the options bar.

9. Click the Fit Screen button on the options bar (or double-click the Hand tool). You can see the whole image with its aspect ratio preserved. Click Fill Screen and it might zoom in or out depending on your monitor's aspect ratio so that pixels fill the entire screen. Double-clicking the Zoom tool displays the actual pixels at 100% magnification.

10. Click the Print Size button. The picture zooms to approximate the document's resolution (see "Setting Document Size and Resolution" later in this chapter). Double-click the Zoom tool. The document zooms to 100% magnification. This is equivalent to clicking the Actual Pixels button on the options bar. You will want to view photos at 100% when sharpening them.

Understanding Color

Certification
Objective

Color is a very powerful visual element, and numerous books have been written on the subject. In the following sections I'll discuss the fundamentals: how color is represented by primary colors, why primaries are stored in channels, the differences between color modes, and how to pick color in Photoshop.

See Chapter 15,
"Working with
Color" for more
information about
managing, correct-
ing, adjusting, and
proofing color.

Using Primary Colors

Although the human eye can distinguish between about 10 million different colors, we can agree on names for less than a dozen. Figure 3.6 lists additive primaries in white, subtractive primaries in black, and tertiary colors in gray.

Just as any point can be represented in 3D space as a set of coordinates taken along the X, Y, and Z primary directions, any color can be represented as a combination of three primary colors. However, color is complicated because the nature of light changes depending on whether it shines directly in your eyes or reflects off a surface before entering your eyes.

Light emitted from a computer monitor, or light captured by a digital camera or scanner sensor, is additive. Red, green, and blue (RGB) are the primary colors of additive light. Cyan, magenta, and yellow are secondary colors in the RGB system. Figure 3.7 shows that if you add equal intensities of red, green, and blue light together, you get pure white. All the colors of the rainbow are in white light.

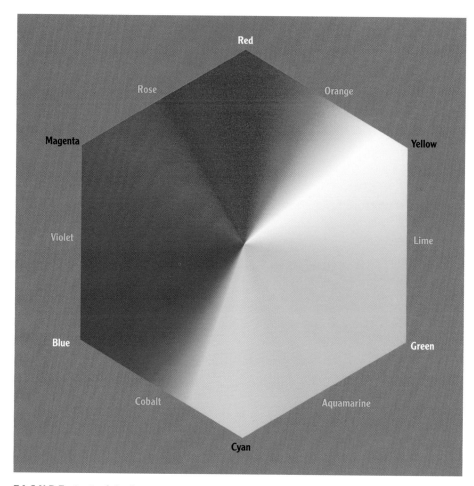

FIGURE 3.6 Color hexagon

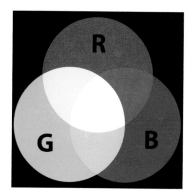

FIGURE 3.7 RGB are additive primaries.

Reflected light, on the other hand, behaves differently. If you start with a white source and reflect it off of a printed surface, the surface will absorb some of the light. The reflected light will have some of its wavelengths subtracted compared with the source. Cyan, magenta, and yellow (CMY) were chosen as the primary colors of subtractive light in order to differentiate them from the RGB system. In the CMY system, red, green, and blue are secondary colors. In theory, if you mix cyan, magenta, and yellow paints, pigments, or inks, you should get pure black (see Figure 3.8).

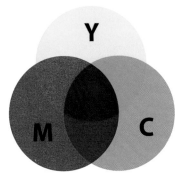

FIGURE 3.8 CMY are subtractive primaries.

However, no real-world paints, pigments, or inks are perfect. Every painter knows that if you mix multiple paints together, the result is a muddy brown, not black as would match color theory. For this reason black (represented by the letter *K*) was added to the subtractive primaries so that cyan, magenta, yellow, and black form a four-color system called CMYK.

WHAT ABOUT RED, YELLOW, AND BLUE AS PRIMARY COLORS?

If, like me, you learned in school that red, yellow, and blue (RYB) were the primary colors used in painting, then you're probably confused by the CMYK color system. The source of this confusion dates to Goethe's *Theory of Colors* (1810) wherein the German poet described color in terms of its psychological effects. The RYB system is still taught in many art schools. However, modern scientific color theory shows that the colors in the CMYK color system are truly the subtractive primary colors. CMYK is used universally today in professional offset printing presses.

Storing Color in Channels

You might be surprised to learn that camera sensors do not directly record unique colors. For example, there is no orange sensor. Orange is recorded as a combination of red, green, and blue light intensities represented as (255,168,0) in 8-bit color. The human eye has three types of cones mapping roughly to red, green, and blue wavelengths, so there is a strong correlation between how we record additive color and how we see.

In Photoshop, color is stored in channels. Channels are nothing other than grayscale images. In RGB color there are three channels, one for each primary. So an RGB file has three grayscale pictures in one file. Ponder the paradox—there is literally no color in the digital representation of color. Figure 3.9 shows an RGB image created entirely from its three constituent grayscale channels.

FIGURE 3.9 Red (left), Green (middle), and Blue (right) channels

Each channel in the Photoshop file is sent to corresponding red, green, and blue subpixels for display on your monitor. When this light enters your eyes, three types of cone structures pick up varying intensities of red, green, and blue light and turn this information into a color picture in your mind (see Figure 3.10).

FIGURE 3.10 Color photo created from RGB channels

In the following steps you will explore the channels in a sample file.

1. Go to the book's Downloads page at www.sybex.com/go /photoshopessentials, browse to Chapter 3, get the file Businesswoman.tif, and open it in Photoshop.

2. Select the Channels tab to bring it to the front of the Layers/Channels/ Paths panel group. Select the Red channel (see Figure 3.11).

FIGURE 3.11 Channels panel

3. Press Cmd+4 to select the green channel. Press Cmd+5 to select the blue channel. Observe how each channel's grayscale information is slightly different (shown in Figure 3.9, earlier in this chapter).

4. Select the Alpha 1 channel. Alpha channels are additional optional channels beyond the color channels. In this case the Alpha 1 channel is a mask that hides the background (with black) and reveals the businesswoman in white. Shades of gray appear in her hair where the foreground and background blend slightly.

5. Select the RGB composite channel. The RGB, Red, Green, and Blue channels highlight in the Channels panel because the RGB channel isn't really a channel in its own right. RGB is merely a convenient switch that sends each color channel to its corresponding subpixels in the monitor so you perceive the color image on screen.

6. Toggle on the visibility of the Alpha 1 channel by selecting its eye icon in the Channels panel. A transparent red mask indicates where the alpha channel masks the color image (see Figure 3.12).

Photo courtesy of iStockphoto, ©Neustockimages, Image #7007990

FIGURE 3.12 Red tinted mask shown when Alpha 1 channel is toggled on

Selecting Image Modes

Photoshop's image modes correspond to different systems for handling color and/or light intensity. The following are Photoshop's color modes:

Bitmap   Bitmap mode stores black and white pixels only, without any intermediate shades of gray. Bitmap files are extremely small because binary information (1 for black and 0 for white) is all that is required to describe them. Bitmap mode may be entered only from grayscale mode.

Grayscale   Black, white, and intermediate shades of gray are represented in grayscale mode. No hues are recorded, only light intensity values.

Duotone   Duotone, tritone, and quadtone images using two to four inks can be created in this mode that employs but a single channel. Duotone is a specialized printing technique in which shadows are typically printed with black ink and the mid-tones and/or highlights are printed with one or more separate ink colors, producing an old-fashioned cyanotype or sepiatone look. Duotone mode may be entered only from grayscale mode.

Indexed color   A color index is a list of up to 256 colors that reference a single channel. Indexed color mode produces small image files that are suitable for deployment on the Web in file formats such as GIF or PNG. This mode does not support layers or filters. In addition, many adjustments are unavailable in indexed color mode, greatly limiting its image manipulation capabilities.

RGB   Red, green, and blue color is used to capture photographic and scanned images and to display additive color on computer monitors. Everything on the Internet is shown in RGB color. In addition, the RGB color space is widely used in desktop printers, including ink-jets and color laser printers.

The majority of the world's professionally printed material is produced in CMYK.

CMYK   The subtractive cyan, magenta, yellow, and black color space is used primarily in professional printing where ink is offset from a metal plate to a rubber blanket and then transferred to the printing surface in four separate runs. CMYK files are larger than RGB files because of the addition of the fourth channel.

Lab   Lab color isn't processed in a laboratory as its name might suggest. Lab stands for Lightness, a, and b color channels. In this unique system, detail is carried in the Lightness channel and color is carried using a combination of a and b channels. Lab is most useful when you want to isolate the image detail for sharpening or for grayscale conversion.

Multichannel   Multichannel is an advanced mode that doesn't support layers. Use multichannel only if your professional printer requires it.

In the following steps you will convert an image into several modes and investigate the results in the Channels panel.

1. Go to the book's Downloads page at `www.sybex.com/go /photoshopessentials`, browse to Chapter 3, get the file `Taj.jpg`, and open it in Photoshop (see Figure 3.13).

PHOTO COURTESY OF ISTOCKPHOTO, ©TERRY J ALCORN, IMAGE #14990625

FIGURE 3.13 RGB image of the Taj Mahal

2. Open the Channels panel and observe the Red, Green, and Blue channels. Choose Image ➢ Mode ➢ CMYK Color. Select each of the channels one at a time (see Figure 3.14). The blue sky is carried mostly on the Cyan channel and a little on the Magenta channel where the pixels appear darker. There is very little yellow in the sky and that is why the sky appears white on the Yellow channel. The pavement is carried mostly in the Magenta and Yellow channels. Press Cmd+2 to select the CMYK composite channel.

PHOTO COURTESY OF ISTOCKPHOTO, ©TERRY J ALCORN, IMAGE #14990625

FIGURE 3.14 Cyan, Magenta, Yellow, and Black channels shown from left to right

3. Choose Image ➢ Mode ➢ Lab Color. Select the channels one at a time (see Figure 3.15). The image detail is carried in the Lightness channel while color information is stored using a combination of the a and b channels.

FIGURE 3.15 Lightness, a, and b channels of Lab color shown left to right

Use the Black & White adjustment (see Chapter 11, "Adjusting and Filtering") for finer control in the conversion to grayscale.

4. Press Cmd+3 to select the Lightness channel. This channel looks most like a black-and-white photograph because it carries most of the image detail. Choose Image ➤ Mode Grayscale. When prompted to choose whether you want to discard the other channels, click OK. You are left with a single Gray channel (see Figure 3.16).

FIGURE 3.16 Grayscale mode reduces the file to a single channel

5. Choose Image ➤ Mode Bitmap. Select Halftone Screen in the Bitmap dialog box (see Figure 3.17). Click OK.

Halftone is a technique that simulates continuous tone by varying dots in size, shape, or spacing. Many comic books and newspapers print with halftone screens.

FIGURE 3.17 Lightness, a, and b channels of Lab color shown left to right

6. In the Halftone Screen dialog box that appears, enter **65** as the frequency in lines per inch and 0 for degrees, and select Round as the shape. Click OK. The single Bitmap channel carries black or white pixels only. Figure 3.18 shows the resulting image.

Picking Color

The default colors are exchanged in layers masks and alpha channels.

Photoshop uses foreground and background colors for a variety of tasks. The default colors are black in the foreground and white in the background. Pressing D restores the default colors and X exchanges the foreground and background colors.

FIGURE 3.18 Bitmap image shown with halftone screen

There are many ways of picking colors. In the following steps you will explore some of the methods of selecting foreground and background colors.

1. Choose File ➤ New, select the Web preset and a size of 800 × 600 pixels. Click OK to accept the default options.

2. Press B to select the Brush tool (which you'll learn more about in Chapter 4, "Painting"). On the Mac, hold down Cmd+Opt+Control and drag using the left mouse button in the document window. On Windows, hold down Shift+Alt and drag using the right mouse button in the document window. On either operating system, you can release the modifier keys after the heads up display (HUD) color picker appears but keep dragging the mouse button (see Figure 3.19). Drag the hue slider up or down and then drag the target around the square color ramp to select saturation (left to right) and brightness (top to bottom) levels before finally releasing the mouse button. Make a brush stroke in the document window by dragging, select another color in the HUD picker, and make another brush stroke.

FIGURE 3.19 HUD hue strip color picker

3. Press Cmd+K to open the Preferences dialog box. Select Hue Wheel (Small) from the HUD Color Picker drop-down menu on the General page and click OK. Open the HUD color picker with the same modifier keys you used in the previous step and select a hue using the color wheel. Select saturation and brightness using the square color ramp in the center of the wheel (see Figure 3.20).

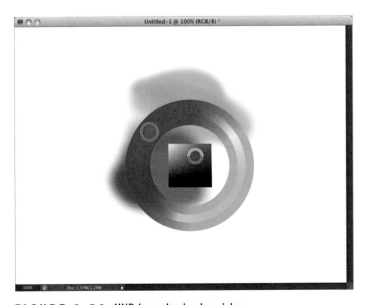

FIGURE 3.20 HUD hue wheel color picker

4. Click the background color well on the Tools panel. The Color Picker (Background Color) dialog box appears. With the H (hue) radio button selected, the controls are much like the HUD hue strip. Drag the hue arrows up or down to select a hue and use the color ramp to select saturation and brightness levels. The new color you are picking appears as the top swatch while the former background color appears underneath in an adjacent swatch (for the purpose of comparison). Notice that all the numbers in the various color modes change as you pick a color. You can enter values using the radio buttons for all of the following color systems: HSB, RGB, Lab, CMYK, and the # text box is for hexadecimal color (see Figure 3.21).

When the color picker is open, you can sample color from any open document within Photoshop. Use the Eyedropper tool to accomplish this without the color picker.

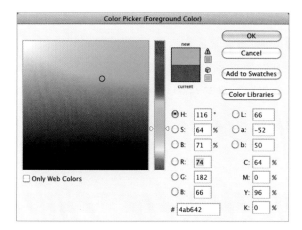

FIGURE 3.21 Using the color picker

5. Click the Color Libraries button. The Color Picker dialog box is swapped for the Color Libraries dialog box (see Figure 3.22). Scroll through the Pantone Sold Matte library and select Pantone 203M.

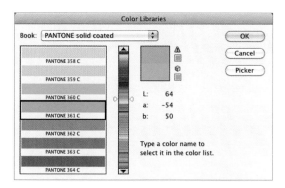

FIGURE 3.22 Selecting a color from a library

USING A COLOR MATCHING SYSTEM

Pantone is an example of a standardized system used to color-match painted, printed, and manufactured goods. You can take a Pantone formula guide book into the field and match a specific color, make a note of its color number, and match the color using one of Photoshop's color libraries.

The Color panel provides another way to pick color.

6. Click the Picker button to swap the Color Libraries dialog box for the Color Picker dialog box. Click the Add To Swatches button, type the Pantone number (Pantone 203M in this case), and click OK. Select the Swatches panel to bring it to the front of the Color/Swatches/Styles panel group. The color you just saved appears as the last swatch for easy recall at some future time (see Figure 3.23).

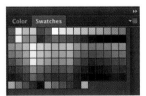

FIGURE 3.23 Adding a color swatch

Storing Data

Once you understand that digital pictures are made up of 1s and 0s, it makes sense to learn a bit about data, its relationship with detail, and how data can be compressed when stored.

Certification Objective

Bits and Bit Depth

A *bit* is the most fundamental unit of computer storage, a transistor that is either on or off, which is represented numerically by 1 or 0. A bitmap is the most primitive type of image because each pixel is mapped to 1 bit (black or white).

To create black-and-white or color photos, more bits per pixel are clearly required. With 8 bits per pixel, or 2 raised to the eighth power, there are 256 tonal gradations possible. 256 gradations is enough data to represent smooth tonal transitions in black-and-white photos in a single Grayscale channel.

As you learned in the previous section, color photos usually have three channels. RGB images have 8 bits/channel or 24 bits/pixel. Two raised to the 24th power offers more than 16 million possibilities for every pixel, which is enough data to represent color photos. Figure 3.24 shows photos of increasing bit depth.

◄

CMYK images having four 8-bit channels yield a bit depth of 32 (8x4).

PHOTO COURTESY OF ISTOCKPHOTO, ©KAREN MOLLER, IMAGE #3228224

FIGURE 3.24 1-bit (left), 8-bit (middle), and 24-bit (right) images

Professional DSLR cameras have the ability to shoot at higher bit depths up to 16 bits/channel. An RGB image shot at 16 bits/channel would be a 48-bit image, requiring much more storage space and RAM than a similar image having 8 bits/channel.

It is advantageous to shoot at 16 bits/channel if you can afford to support the increased memory and storage requirements because manipulations made to images can be "destructive," which is something you'll learn about in the next section. High dynamic range (HDR) images have even higher bit depths at 32 bits/channel (see Chapter 14, "Merging Photos").

Data versus Detail

Just because you shoot a 24-bit photo doesn't mean you have taken advantage of the full tonal range stored in the image. In other words, you might be "paying" for the data even if you are not filling all of it with detail. Histograms provide a way to take a look at how data is distributed across the tonal range.

Figure 3.25 shows a typical histogram. Thin vertical bars are arranged in a statistical representation of where pixels fall across the tonal range, from shadows on the left through mid-tones to highlights (bright areas) on the right. The histogram is color coded to show the contribution from each channel and its complements. The gray graph represents the sum total of all the channels.

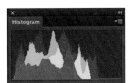

Shadows Mid-tones Highlights

FIGURE 3.25 Using the Histogram panel to see how pixels are distributed

This particular histogram tells us that the brightest highlights aren't as bright as they should be. The peaks in the shadows show that this image is also dark. After the image is manipulated by increasing brightness and adjusting the highlight input level (which you'll learn more about in Chapter 11, "Adjusting and Filtering"), the histogram shows a better distribution across the tonal range (see Figure 3.26).

After the image is manipulated, the number of pixels hasn't changed so the amount of data hasn't changed either. However, tiny gaps in the histogram show that some of the initial detail has been irretrievably lost. This emphasizes the fact that there is a difference between data and detail.

FIGURE 3.26 Histogram showing redistribution across tonal range and consequent detail loss

In Chapter 12, "Developing Photos," you will learn nondestructive workflows in which you will apply color corrections, make multiple tonal adjustments, reduce noise, and sharpen all at once through the Adobe Camera Raw interface.

Compressing Data

Although a set number of pixels consume a given amount of RAM, it is possible to compress the data so the file takes up less storage space. For example, the Cabin.jpg sample file you opened earlier in this chapter is a 21-megapixel image, which consumes 60.2 MB of RAM. However, as a JPG file, the size on the hard drive is only 6.1 MB (showing almost tenfold compression).

Compression works in principle by efficiently representing patterns in the data. For example, if there were a million 1s in a row, it would be more efficient to state that fact rather than literally listing one million 1s in the file. Compression schemes are obviously more technical than this, but you get the general idea.

There are two types of compression: lossless and lossy. Lossless compression represents data concisely and without error but doesn't compress the data as much as lossy methods do. Tagged image file format (TIFF) files support lossless compression schemes and are good for printing because they don't sacrifice any detail.

Lossy compression sacrifices some of the detail for the sake of smaller file sizes. The Joint Photographic Experts Group (JPEG) format is widely used on the Web because of the small file sizes made possible with lossy compression. Figure 3.27 compares lossless versus lossy compression in terms of quality. You can plainly see JPEG *artifacts* in the lower image due to the extreme level of lossy compression used.

PHOTOS COURTESY RICHARD TRUEMAN

FIGURE 3.27 Lossless compression (top) versus lossy compression (bottom)

Setting Document Size and Resolution

Certification Objective

Document size and resolution are inversely proportional. That means if you increase document size, the resolution decreases and vice versa. In the following sections, you will learn guidelines on setting resolution for print and for display on the Web. You will also learn how to resample images, change the canvas size, and trim and crop images.

Setting Resolution

The term *resolution* refers to pixel density measured in pixels/inch or pixels/cm (centimeter). Contrary to popular belief, resolution is only important for print work. Every computer monitor has a different resolution, so there is no way to ensure that an image with a specific document size will appear at any specific actual size on the Web.

WHAT IS SCREEN RESOLUTION?

Photoshop's default is to create new documents having the resolution of 72 pixels/inch using the Web, Mobile & Devices, and Film & Video presets in the New dialog box. This "screen" resolution was chosen because traditional typography has 72.27 points per inch. Windows uses 96 pixels/inch as its screen resolution. But neither screen resolution is truly of any consequence because all monitors are different. Pixel dimensions are all that matter on the Web because it is pixel dimension that is coded in HTML tags and never resolution.

Resolution is very important in printed matter. Each device has different limits on how many dots or lines per inch (or cm) it can print. In general, the minimum resolution for an acceptable-quality print is 200 pixels/inch (80 pixels/ cm). Photoshop's default is to create new print documents having a resolution of 300 pixels/inch (120 pixels/cm) because most output devices support at least this equivalent print density. In the following steps, you will change the resolution of an image without changing its pixel dimensions.

You can set the default print and screen resolutions on the Units & Rulers page of the Preferences dialog box.

1. From the book's Downloads page at www.sybex.com/go/ photoshopessentials, open the sample file Taj.jpg.

2. Choose Image ➤ Image Size. Deselect the Resample Image check box if it is currently checked. Right now the document size measures 7.264 inches by 11.111 inches with a resolution of 72 pixels/inch.

3. Change the resolution to 300 pixels/inch (see Figure 3.28). The document size is automatically reduced to 1.743 inches by 2.667 inches to compensate for the increased resolution.

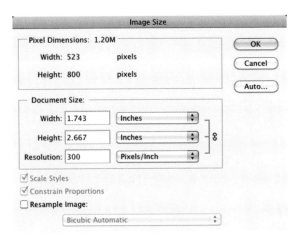

FIGURE 3.28 Trading document size for resolution

You can't print this particular image out at a larger size at a reasonable level of quality because it doesn't have enough pixels. At 523 × 800 pixels, this document would function well as a large sized web graphic but can't print much larger than a postage stamp.

Resampling Images

Image *resampling* is changing the overall pixel dimensions of the image. Image *scaling* is changing the size of the print without changing the number of pixels in the image.

The Resample Image check box in the Image Size dialog box allows you to change the number of pixels. At first blush you might think your postage stamp printing problems are solved if you can change the number of pixels at will, right? Unfortunately it's not that simple: Increasing the number of pixels in a photo increases the amount of data without increasing detail. That's why Photoshop enlargements generally don't improve print quality.

USE THE BLOW UP 2 PLUG-IN FOR QUALITY ENLARGEMENTS

If you need to print a web graphic larger than a postage stamp, the Blow Up 2 Photoshop plug-in can help. It uses a sophisticated algorithm that converts raster images into vector representations. Vector objects can be resized without losing quality, so the vector representation is blown up and then rasterized, leaving you with smooth, crisp edges and natural-looking textures. See www.alienskin.com/blowup/.

On the other hand, Photoshop does an excellent job of reducing images. In the following steps you will reduce the pixel dimensions of a large image by resampling it.

1. Open the sample file Cabin.jpg.

2. Choose Image ➢ Image Size. Right now the image measures 18.72 × 12.48 inches with a resolution of 300 pixels/inch. Select Resample Image and observe that the pixel dimension text boxes become enabled. Select the Bicubic Sharper (Best For Reduction) algorithm from the drop-down menu if it is not already selected.

3. Although you could directly change the pixel dimensions, in this case you will adjust the document width in order to fit the photo on letter-sized paper. Change the document width value to 10 inches. Observe that both the document height and pixel dimensions change at the same time while the resolution remains constant (see Figure 3.29).

Additional resampling algorithms include Nearest Neighbor (for hard edges), Bilinear, Bicubic (for smooth gradients), Bicubic Smoother (for enlargements), Bicubic Sharper, and Bicubic Automatic.

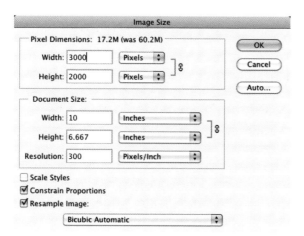

FIGURE 3.29 Resampling an image to fit on smaller paper

Check the Scale Styles box to ensure that any Layer Styles in the file are scaled in proportion.

This image can now print in high quality at 106.66 inches with a resolution of 300 pixels/inch. By resampling the image, you reduced the file that would be sent to printer from 60 MB down to 17 MB so it will print that much faster and take up less than a third of the storage space.

Changing the Canvas Size and Trimming

Using the analogy of fine art painting, the document window is sometimes referred to as the *canvas*. A painter would never change their canvas size after they started painting, but such a thing is possible in Photoshop. Changing canvas area is fundamentally different from changing the image size because pixels are never resampled when the canvas is altered—just added or removed. Trimming is like cropping except the trimming algorithm can automatically cut away all the pixels up to the edges of an object. In the following steps you will alter the canvas size and trim it to get a feel for these important tools.

1. From the book's Downloads page at www.sybex.com/go /photoshopessentials, open the sample file Star.png. The edges of the digital art's circular composition are tangent to the square canvas on all four sides.

2. Choose Image ➢ Canvas Size, or press Cmd+Opt+C if you added this keyboard shortcut in Chapter 2, "Getting Acquainted with Photoshop's User Interface." Select Relative and change the Width drop-down menu to percent. Type **25** in the Width text box (see Figure 3.30).

Use the anchor buttons to control where pixels are added or clipped.

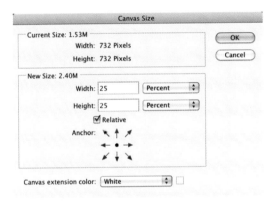

FIGURE 3.30 Changing the canvas size

3. Open the Canvas Extension Color drop-down menu and select Other. The color picker appears. Instead of picking a color within the Select Canvas Extension Color dialog box, move the mouse over the canvas and see the cursor appear as an eyedropper, meaning you can select a color from the canvas itself. Click the area outside the circle to select medium gray and click OK twice. A gray border is added around the artwork.

4. Choose Image ➢ Canvas Size again. Deselect Relative and change the Width drop-down menu to Pixels. Type **800** in the Height text box and click OK. A warning dialog box appears that says, "The new

canvas size is smaller than the current canvas size; some clipping will occur." Click Proceed. Figure 3.31 shows the result.

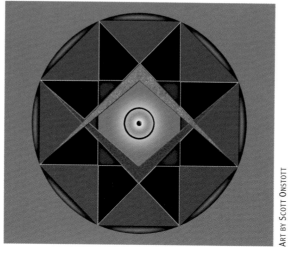

ART BY SCOTT ONSTOTT

FIGURE 3.31 Artwork's canvas size added to in both directions and then clipped in height

5. Choose Image ➤ Trim. In the Trim dialog box, you can choose to base the trim operation on the top left or bottom right pixel color. Both corners will work the same way in this case because medium gray surrounds the image. Click OK. All the pixels added with Canvas Size have been removed with Trim.

Cropping

Many photographers tend to crop in the viewfinder or in Live Preview mode on their cameras, but there are times you'll want to crop photos in Photoshop no matter how you shoot pictures. In the following steps you will crop a photo using the rule of thirds (see Chapter 1, "Design Basics").

1. From the book's Downloads page at `www.sybex.com/go/photoshopessentials`, open the sample file `Ferry.jpg`.

2. Choose the Crop tool and drag out a window within the canvas. Select Rule Of Thirds from the View drop-down menu on the options bar if it is not already selected.

3. Drag the corner and/or side handles until the guides appear as shown in Figure 3.32. Press Enter to commit to the cropping operation.

FIGURE 3.32 Cropping an image using the rule of thirds grid

THE ESSENTIALS AND BEYOND

In this chapter you have learned the fundamentals of digital imaging, and this knowledge should hold you in good stead as you continue to learn more about Photoshop's tools and techniques. In particular, you should now understand pixels, bits, compression, anti-aliasing, the basis of additive and subtractive color, the relationship between resolution and document size, resampling, changing the canvas size, trimming, cropping, and much more.

ADDITIONAL EXERCISE

Open the Logo.jpg sample file on the book's Downloads page at www.sybex.com /go/photoshopessentials and trim away the medium gray border. Reduce the image down to a size of 400×400 pixels. When you're finished, the image should look the way it does here.

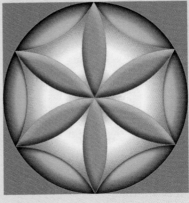

Painting

By providing you with digital painting tools, Photoshop can keep you from suffering the fate of many a traditional painter: turpentine, mercury, and heavy metal poisoning linked to the use of chemical solvents and pigments. In addition, Photoshop is infinitely more flexible and efficient compared to traditional media. Digital painting skills aren't just for creating fine art; you'll use what you learn in this chapter later in the book to select pixels, retouch photos, and work with layer masks.

▶ **Creating gradients**

▶ **Selecting paint colors**

▶ **Using painting tools**

▶ **Exploring brushes**

▶ **Painting with a tablet**

▶ **Painting from history**

▶ **Using the mixer brush**

Creating Gradients

Gradients are used to create smooth tonal variations between different colors or pixel luminance values. Creating perfect gradients is very difficult in traditional painting, but they can be created quite simply in Photoshop by dragging from one point to another. In the following steps you will create an artist's color palette using the Gradient tool that you will then use in the next section to select paint colors.

1. Press Cmd+N to create a new document. Change the Width dropdown to Pixels and type 800 in both the Width and Height text boxes. Type **Color Gradient** in the Name text box (see Figure 4.1) and click OK.

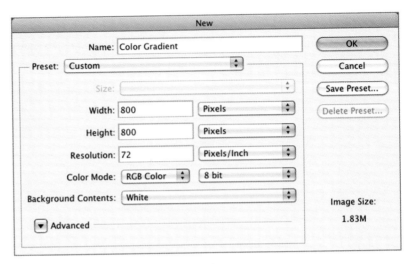

FIGURE 4.1 Creating a new square image

2. Press Cmd+R to display the rulers. Right-click either one of the rulers and select Percent from the shortcut menu if these units are not already shown.

3. Select the Gradient tool in the Tools panel. Open the gradient picker drop-down menu on the options bar and select the Spectrum gradient (see Figure 4.2).

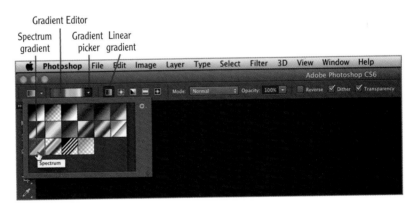

FIGURE 4.2 Gradient options

4. Click the gradient swatch itself to open the Gradient Editor (see Figure 4.3). You can add color and/or opacity stops by clicking above

or below the gradient bar. Stops are colors represented by the repositionable markers. There is nothing you need to do to the Spectrum gradient, so click Cancel.

Gradients are blends that are interpolated between stops. Existing stops can be shifted by dragging left to right or removed by dragging up or down.

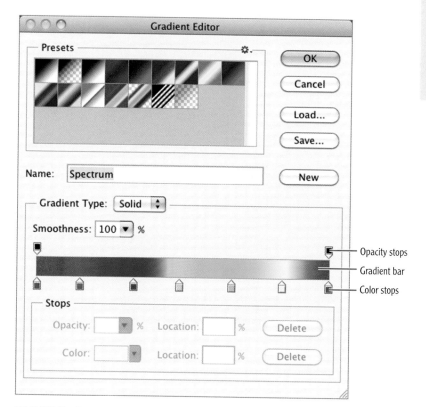

FIGURE 4.3 Gradient Editor

5. Select the Linear Gradient mode on the options bar if it is not already selected. Position the cursor on the canvas at 50% vertically. Start dragging to the right, hold down Shift to constrain the gradient horizontally, and continue moving the cursor all the way to the right edge at 100% on the horizontal ruler. When you release, a color gradient fills the document window.

6. Press D to set the default colors. Open the gradient picker and select Foreground To Transparent. Select Transparency on the options bar. Position the cursor at 100% vertically (at the bottom). Start dragging upward, hold down Shift to constrain the gradient, and continue moving the cursor up until it is level with 60% on the vertical ruler.

Hold the cursor still for a few seconds to read the tooltip identifying a gradient by name. Once a tooltip appears you can move the cursor over other gradient swatches to read their names without delay.

The bottom of the document window now fades to black. Press X to exchange the foreground and background colors.

7. Position the cursor at 0% vertically. Start dragging downward, hold Shift, and continue until you reach 40% vertically. Release the mouse or trackpad button and the top of the document fades to white. Repeat this entire step to brighten the gradient at the top. Press Cmd+R to toggle off the rulers. Figure 4.4 shows the result.

FIGURE 4.4 Color ramp with tints at the top and shades on the bottom

TINTS AND SHADES

Traditional painters start by squeezing colored paint onto their palettes and then mix either white or black into each hue to produce corresponding tints and shades of the respective hues. Gradients allow you to mix color with great subtlety in Photoshop.

8. Choose Filter ➤ Distort ➤ Polar Coordinates. Select the Rectangular To Polar option in the Polar Coordinates dialog box and click OK. Figure 4.5 shows the resulting color gradient wheel.

9. Save your work as Color Gradient.psd.

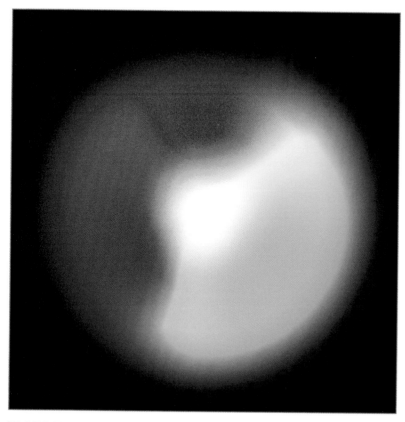

FIGURE 4.5 Color gradient wheel

Selecting Paint Colors

You learned in Chapter 3, "Digital Imaging Fundamentals," how to select color
using the Color Picker dialog box, the HUD hue strip, and color libraries. Those
methods are most suitable when you are interested in selecting a singular color,
but the color wheel you developed in the previous section is something a painter
would prefer because it shows the analogous and complementary relationships
between hues, plus their shades and tints. In the following steps you'll use color
wheels and the Color panel to learn more about color in conjunction with the
Eyedropper tool to sample multiple colors from existing images.

**Certification
Objective**

1. If the color gradient wheel isn't still open, go to the book's Downloads
   page at www.sybex.com/go/photoshopessentials, browse to
   Chapter 4, get the file Color Gradient.psd, and open it in Photoshop.

2. Select the Color panel in the Color/Swatches/Styles panel group in the Essentials workspace. Open the Color panel menu and select HSB Sliders (the sliders are shown in Figure 4.6).

FIGURE 4.6 Using the Color panel in HSB mode

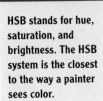

HSB stands for hue, saturation, and brightness. The HSB system is the closest to the way a painter sees color.

3. Select the Eyedropper tool and choose Point Sample from the Sample Size drop-down menu on the options bar. Drag the eyedropper slowly outward from the center of the color wheel and observe how the sliders in the Color panel change. Color saturation ramps up until you reach the ring of full saturation and brightness. Brightness ramps down to black as you continue sampling color out to the edge of the color wheel. Hues change around the wheel, while analogous colors surround every point and complementary colors are on the opposite side of the wheel (see Figure 4.7).

Point samples measure the color of individual pixels. Larger sample sizes take the average color of grids of pixels, which can be useful when sampling photos.

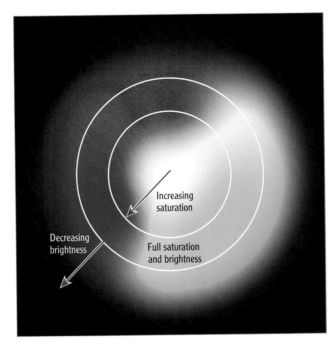

FIGURE 4.7 Understanding saturation and brightness

4. In the Color panel, drag the cursor from the top to the bottom of the gradient at the bottom of the panel. Saturation ramps up until the halfway mark and then brightness ramps down. Changing hues (and analogous colors) are available to the left and right, but there is no way to choose complementary colors on a strip.

5. Press Cmd+N and create a new blank document measuring 800×800 pixels.

6. Press Cmd+K to open the Preferences dialog box. Select Hue Wheel in the HUD Color Picker drop-down menu and click OK. You can use the HUD picker to select color in any image.

7. Press B to select the Brush tool. On the Mac, hold down Cmd (⌘)+Opt+Control and drag the left mouse button in the document window. On Windows, hold down Shift+Alt and drag the right mouse button in the document window. On either operating system you can release the modifier keys after the heads up display (HUD) color picker appears, but keep dragging the mouse button (see Figure 4.8). Drag the hue ring around the wheel and then move the cursor into the square color ramp inside the wheel. Drag the target around to select a combination of saturation (left to right) and brightness (top to bottom) levels before finally releasing the mouse button.

> If you are painting an image that will ultimately be output on an offset printer, select CMYK Spectrum from the Color panel menu.

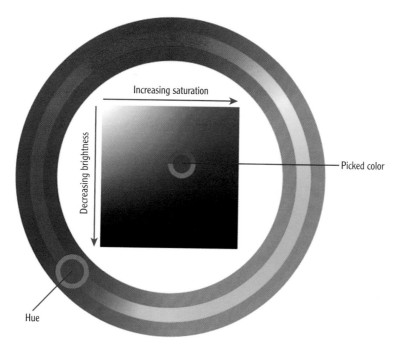

FIGURE 4.8 HUD hue wheel

Unlike the color wheel you developed using gradients and the gradient strip in the Color panel, the HUD hue wheel allows you to select varying levels of both saturation and brightness while simultaneously being able to select analogous and complementary colors. Therefore, I recommend using the HUD hue wheel to select colors whenever you are painting.

Using Painting Tools

Now that you have a handle on color, it's time to familiarize yourself with the various instruments used for applying and removing pixels from the canvas. You'll try your hand at sketching with a pencil, painting with a brush, pouring paint from a bucket, and using a variety of erasers.

Sketching with a Pencil

The Pencil tool creates aliased lines that are suitable for sketching rough ideas, as one might do on a cocktail napkin (a favorite pastime of architects). In the following steps you will practice sketching the ancient Egyptian temple of Luxor by tracing an image made from a 3D model.

1. Go to the book's Downloads page at www.sybex.com/go /photoshopessentials and browse to Chapter 4, get the file Luxor.jpg, and open it in Photoshop (see Figure 4.9).

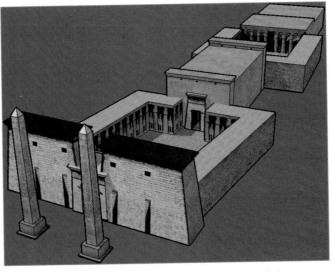

FIGURE 4.9 3D rendered image of Temple of Luxor

2. Create a new layer by clicking the Create A New Layer button at the bottom of the Layers panel. Rename this layer **Sketch**.

3. Select the Pencil tool, which is on the flyout menu under the Brush tool. You can either open the flyout menu or press Shift+B to cycle through its tools until the Pencil tool icon appears.

4. Press the left or right bracket keys until the brush size reads 4 (pixels) on the options bar.

5. Start tracing the edges of the building.

6. Press R to select the Rotate View tool. Drag the canvas to rotate it clockwise or counterclockwise so you can align the lines you wish to draw with your hand's natural arc of motion, much as you might rotate a cocktail napkin when sketching with a real pencil. Press B to return to the Pencil tool and continue sketching (see Figure 4.10).

7. After you have sketched in the major lines, decrease the brush size to 1 pixel by pressing the left bracket key three times. Sketch in any finer details you wish to capture with the Pencil tool.

> You can click, hold Shift, and click again to draw a straight line. Sketching is easier with a stylus and tablet (Wacom's tablets are excellent) than with a mouse.

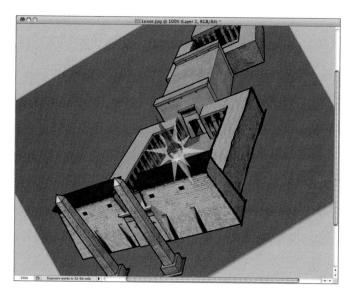

FIGURE 4.10 Rotating the view in order to sketch lines more comfortably

8. Select the Background layer in the Layers panel. Choose Layer ➤ New Fill Layer ➤ Solid Color. Click OK to accept the default name

of Color Fill 1 in the New Layer dialog box. Select white in the color picker that appears and click OK. Your sketch now appears against a white background (see Figure 4.11).

9. Save your work as Sketch.tif.

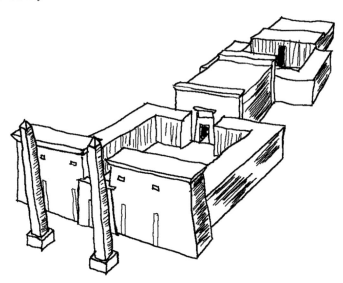

FIGURE 4.11 Completed pencil sketch against white background

Painting with a Brush

The Brush tool has far more nuance than the Pencil tool. Before we delve into the complexities of the Brush tool (which we will do in the section "Exploring Brushes" later in this chapter), let us get acquainted with the most basic brush first: the default soft round brush. In the following steps you will paint the sketch you developed in the previous section.

1. Open your version of Sketch.tif if it is not already open.

2. Select the Color Fill 1 layer and then click the Add A New Layer button. Rename this layer **Painting**.

3. Toggle off layer Color Fill 1. Press I to select the Eyedropper tool. Select 31 By 31 Average from the Sample Size drop-down on the options bar. Sample a color from a surface of the original 3D rendering; it becomes the new foreground color. Toggle on Color Fill 1.

4. Select the Brush tool. Right-click the canvas and the Brush Preset picker appears. Select the first brush (Soft Round) and then drag the Size slider to 15 px and the Hardness slider to 50% (see Figure 4.12).

FIGURE 4.12 Choosing a brush and configuring its size and hardness

5. Paint over all the surfaces having the color you sampled in step 3. Repeat step 3 and sample another color from a different surface.

6. You should enlarge the brush size to cover larger areas quickly and shrink the brush size to paint in between narrowly spaced lines. You can interactively change the brush size by holding Opt+Control and dragging the left mouse button on the Mac or by pressing Alt and dragging the right mouse button on Windows. Continue painting the rest of the surfaces while getting used to the brush. Figure 4.13 shows the result.

7. Save your work as `Painted Sketch.tif`.

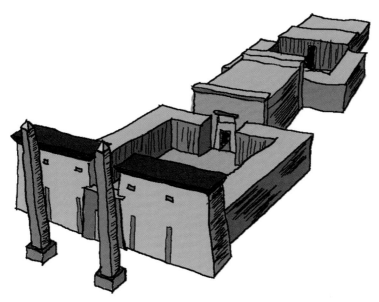

FIGURE 4.13 Painted sketch

Pouring Paint from a Bucket

Although the Paint Bucket tool doesn't artistically stream paint out of a bucket like Jackson Pollock did in the mid-twentieth century, it evenly floods bounded areas with paint. In the following steps you will experiment with different methods of pouring in background color to surround the painted sketch you have been developing.

1. Open your version of `Painted Sketch.tif` if it is not already open.

2. Press Shift+Cmd+N to create a new layer, type **Paint Bucket** in the New Layer dialog box, and click OK.

This file is also available on the book's Downloads page.

3. Press Cmd+[to move the Paint Bucket layer down until it is below the Painting layer in the Layers panel.

4. Click the foreground color swatch on the Tools panel and select a dark-brown color such as #3e3220 in the Color Picker dialog box that appears. Click OK.

5. Press Shift+G to select the Paint Bucket tool under the Gradient tool. On the options bar, set Tolerance to 0 and deselect Anti-Alias, Contiguous, and All Layers. Click inside the document window and brown paint will flood the Paint Bucket layer, creating a dark background in the painted sketch. This method works well when the elements of a composition are on layers separate from the background.

6. Press the Delete key to get rid of the Paint Bucket layer. This time you will pour paint onto a flattened composition. Choose Layer ➢ Flatten Image.

7. Click in the white area surrounding the sketch to flood it with paint. Observe any white fringes that may appear around the edges of the building (see Figure 4.14). Fringes appear along the edges of these brushstrokes because they were made with a brush having 50% hardness. The Paint Bucket tool floods only pure-white pixels when Tolerance is set to 0%.

8. Press Cmd+Z to undo. On the options bar, set Tolerance to 30 and select Anti-Alias. Click the white background to flood it with brown paint. This time no fringe appears because the increased tolerance floods more whites and anti-aliasing blends the transition between background and the painted sketch.

9. Save your work as `Flattened Flooded Painted Sketch.tif`.

FIGURE 4.14 White fringes appear around the painted sketch because of the Paint Bucket's zero tolerance setting.

Using Eraser Tools

Photoshop has three specialized erasing tools: the Eraser, Background Eraser, and Magic Eraser. The Eraser paints with the background color; the Background Eraser allows you erase pixels themselves, leaving only transparency; and the Magic Eraser works like the Paint Bucket tool in reverse, removing pixels within a bounded area.

The Eraser tool doesn't really erase: It simply paints using the background color and this can look like erasure. The Eraser tool has three different modes— you can erase using the pencil, brush, or fixed-size block. In the following steps you'll erase any areas where paint went outside the lines.

1. Open your version of Flattened Flooded Painted Sketch.tif if it is not already open.

2. Zoom into any areas where paint went outside the lines of the sketch. Press I to select the Eyedropper tool. Hold down Opt and click on the brown background to sample it as the background color.

This file is also available on the book's Downloads page.

3. Press E to select the Eraser tool. Select Brush from the Mode drop-down menu on the options bar.

4. Paint over any paint that bleeds into the background and the pixels will be replaced with the background color (see Figure 4.15).

5. Save your work as Luxor Final.tif.

Block mode is best used in conjunction with the Shift key to precisely erase rows and/or columns of pixels.

Erase areas like this where the paint went outside the lines.

FIGURE 4.15 Erasing to the background color

The Background Eraser actually removes pixels (in contrast to the Eraser tool, which paints pixels in the background color). Using the Background Eraser on the Background layer automatically converts it into a regular layer that accommodates transparency. The Background Eraser has three different modes that you'll use in the following steps.

1. Open your version of Luxor Final.tif if it is not already open.

2. Press Shift+E to select the Background Eraser tool. Open the Limits drop-down menu on the options bar and select Contiguous. Set Tolerance at its minimum value of 1% and deselect Protect Foreground Color if it is currently selected.

This file is also available on the book's Downloads page.

3. Select the Sampling: Continuous button on the options bar. Starting over the background color on one side of the sketch, make a swipe across the building until you reach the background on the other side. Pixels are removed continuously.

 4. Select the Sampling: Once button on the options bar. Make a second swipe across the building. This time only the background pixels are removed because the Background Eraser is set to sample only once (where you start dragging).

5. Select the Sampling: Background Swatch button on the options bar. Before using the Background Eraser, hold the Opt key and observe that the cursor changes to the Eyedropper icon. Click the top of the building to sample its color. Press X to exchange foreground and background colors so that the color you just sampled is now in the background. Make a third swipe across the building. Only the roof pixels are removed because they match the background color. Figure 4.16 shows the results of your three experiments.

6. Save your work as `Background Eraser Experiments.tif`.

— Continuous

— Once
— Background Swatch

FIGURE 4.16 Testing the Background Eraser

The Magic Eraser works something like the Paint Bucket in reverse: The Magic Eraser removes pixels in a bounded area. In the following steps you will remove the dark-brown background color you added earlier with the Paint Bucket.

1. Open your version of `Luxor Final.tif` if it is not already open.

2. Press Shift+E to select the Magic Eraser tool. On the options bar, set Tolerance at 30% and select Anti-Alias. Click once on the dark-brown background. It disappears—but so too do some of the darker pylon roofs because they were a similar dark-brown color (see Figure 4.17).

◄

This file is also available on the book's Downloads page.

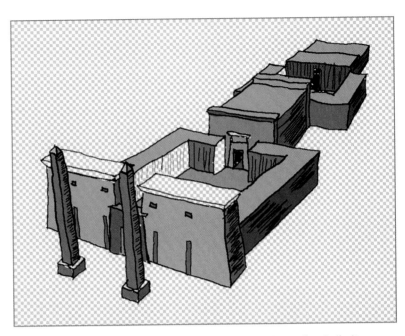

FIGURE 4.17 Magic Eraser removes pixels based on color similarity.

3. Press Cmd+Z to undo.

4. Set Tolerance at 10% and click on the dark-brown background. Most of the pylon roof remains this time, but if you look closely, you'll see some missing pixels inside the structure where the pixels were similar in color to the background.

5. Press Cmd+Z again to undo.

6. Select Contiguous on the options bar and click again on the dark-brown background. This time, only background pixels were removed. Dark brown pixels inside the building were left alone because they are not contiguous with the background.

7. Close the document without saving by pressing Cmd+W and then press N for No when asked to confirm your action.

Exploring Brushes

Certification
Objective

Brushes have numerous parameters beyond size and hardness to control how paint is applied to the canvas. Photoshop ships with a plethora of preset brushes that should suit many of your needs. You will also learn to adjust brush parameters to have them work exactly the way you want them to.

Opacity and Flow

Opacity and Flow are parameters on the options bar that control how paint comes off the brush. You will experiment with them in the following steps.

1. Press Cmd+N to create a new document. In the New dialog box, select Web from the Preset drop-down menu and 800×600 from the Size drop-down. Click OK.

2. Open the Color panel and choose a dark-red color by dragging along the color strip.

3. Press B for brush and open the Brush Preset picker on the options bar. Select the 59-pixel Spatter brush.

4. Reduce Flow on the options bar to 10%. Painting with reduced flow allows you to build up paint in successive strokes.

5. Make a few brushstrokes on the canvas that overlap in one area. You can perceive what appear to be individual hairs in the brush because of the brush's scattered shape. Paint is more saturated where the brushstrokes overlap because of the reduced flow.

6. Set Opacity to 10% and Flow to 100% on the options bar. Make a few more brushstrokes and observe how reducing the opacity makes the paint appear like a wash (paint mixed with water). Opacity builds where brushstrokes overlap. Figure 4.18 shows the result.

Hold the cursor still over a preset brush for a few seconds to display its name in a tooltip.

FIGURE 4.18 Painting at 100% opacity and 10% flow (above) and 10% opacity and 100% flow (below)

Brush Panel

The Brush panel is the one-stop shop for all parameters relating to brushes. You will customize a preset brush with the Brush panel and get a feel for the complexity of brush parameters and what you can do with them.

1. Press Cmd (⌘)+Delete on the Mac or Ctrl+Backspace on Windows to fill the canvas with the white background color.

2. Click the Brush panel button on the options bar to toggle it on. Click Brush Tip Shape on the left side of the panel to open a list of preset brush icons. Scroll down the list and select the 112-pixel Dune Grass brush (see Figure 4.19).

FIGURE 4.19 Selecting a preset brush in the Brush panel

3. Select a dark-green color in the Color panel.

4. Notice that Spacing is selected and set to 25% in this preset. Brushstrokes are really a series of copies of the brush shape in the direction of the stroke. Increasing Spacing above a few percent allows you to perceive the individual copies. Make a horizontal brushstroke across the top of the canvas and you'll see the individual blades of grass.

5. Click Scattering to toggle on this feature and open its page as the parameters on the right side of the Brush panel change. Drag the Scatter slider to 66% and make another horizontal brushstroke in the middle of the canvas. The grass is scattered vertically in a random fashion.

6. Click Color Dynamics to toggle on this feature and open its page in the Brush panel. Drag Hue Jitter to 15%. Jitter refers to randomization, so hue jitter will make the color vary along the brushstroke. Make another horizontal brushstroke along the bottom of the canvas. Figure 4.20 shows the results of these experiments.

7. Close the document without saving.

Photoshop CS6 has two new brush features: Erodible Tip and Airbrush Tip. Erodible brush settings allows rough edges for more realistic strokes. Airbrush tips are best used with a pen tablet where applied pressure and angle affects the brush stroke.

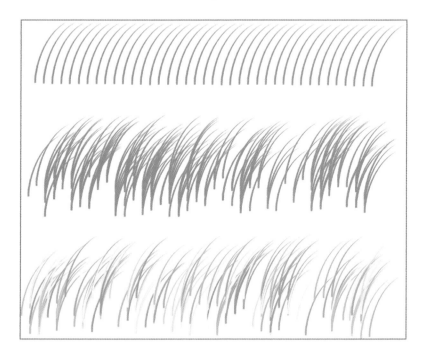

FIGURE 4.20 Spacing (top), Scattering (middle), and Hue Jitter (bottom)

Spend a few minutes experimenting with parameters in the Brush panel. This should give you a feel for the complexity you can build into brushstrokes. Consider the artistic possibilities!

Painting With a Tablet

Certification Objective

The mouse is a terrible instrument for painting. It's like painting with a bar of soap. If you want to get serious about painting in Photoshop, you need a pressure- and tilt-sensitive tablet (see Figure 4.21). Much of the nuance and subtlety of painting can be captured only with pressure and tilt sensitivity—these two dimensions are not captured with a mouse. Using the stylus input device on a tablet is very much like holding a paintbrush or pen in your hands.

PHOTO COURTESY OF ISTOCKPHOTO, ©DORI O'CONNELL, IMAGE #2818905

There is less abstraction with a tablet and this makes painting and drawing much more intuitive.

FIGURE 4.21 Using a stylus on a pressure- and tilt-sensitive tablet

In addition, tablets use absolute positioning, which means, for example, that when you hold the stylus in the lower-right corner of the tablet, the cursor will always be in the lower-right corner of the screen. Mice use relative positioning, so the mouse could be in the upper-left corner of the mouse pad while the cursor could be in the lower-right corner of the screen.

Taking Advantage of Pressure Sensitivity

Pressure sensitivity gives you another dimension of input. Pressure is most often set to modulate the brush size, but you can configure pressure to modulate hue, scattering, opacity, flow, rotation, and many other parameters if you wish. If you have a pressure-sensitive tablet, try the following steps.

1. Press Cmd+N to create a new document. In the New dialog box, select Web from the Preset drop-down menu and 800×600 from the Size drop-down. Click OK.

2. Open the Color panel and choose a light-blue color by dragging along the color strip.

3. Click the Brush panel button on the options bar to toggle it on. At the top of the Brush panel, click the Brush Presets button to open the Brush Presets panel. Select the third preset, whose tooltip reads Soft Round Pressure Size. Drag the Size slider to 100 px (see Figure 4.22).

Brushes whose size is controlled by pressure have tapered brushstroke thumbnails in the Preset Brushes panel.

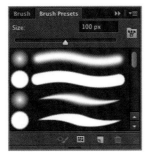

FIGURE 4.22 Selecting a pressure-modulated brush in the Brush Presets panel

4. Make a horizontal brushstroke starting with light pressure on the right and increasing in pressure as you drag to the left (see Figure 4.23). You can use pressure to control how much paint is applied, more or less like a real paintbrush.

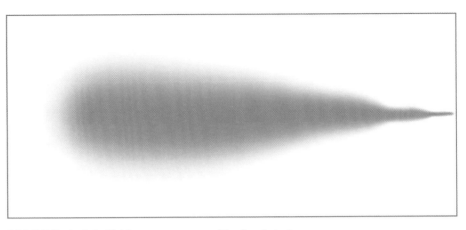

FIGURE 4.23 Making a pressure-sensitive brushstroke

Controlling Bristle Tip Brushes with Tilt Sensitivity

Bristle tip brushes are the most sophisticated brushes because they change shape depending upon how you hold the stylus. If you have a pressure- and tilt-sensitive tablet, try the following steps.

1. Press Cmd (⌘)+Delete on the Mac or Ctrl+Backspace on Windows to fill the canvas with the white background color.

2. Open the Color panel and choose a red color by dragging along the color strip.

3. Scroll down in the Brush Presets panel and locate the icons that look like real brushes: These are the bristle tip brushes. Select the second bristle tip brush (its tooltip reads Round Blunt Medium Stiff). Drag the Size slider to 25 px. Set Flow to 10% on the options bar.

4. Notice that a preview window appears in the upper-left corner of the canvas. As you tilt the stylus, the preview updates in real time (this will not happen with a mouse). Make a few horizontal and vertical brushstrokes, taking care to tilt the stylus differently on each stroke (see Figure 4.24). You can get a wide variety of marks by modulating the pressure and tilt of the stylus, just as you would with a real paintbrush.

Adjustable Bristle Qualities is on the Brush Tip Shape page in the Brushes panel.

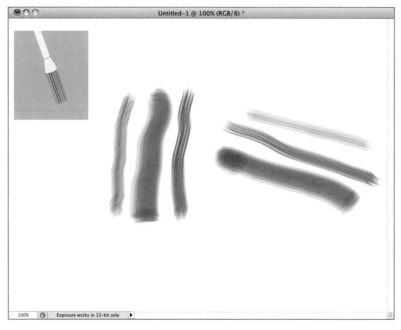

FIGURE 4.24 Making a few strokes with a bristle tipped brush

5. When you are satisfied that you understand how bristle tips apply paint, close the document without saving.

Painting from History

You can use history not only to correct your mistakes but also to selectively paint areas back to the way they were before. In addition, you can use history to create an artistic treatment loosely based on a document's past state.

Certification Objective

Understanding the History Panel

Wouldn't it be great if when you realized you made a mistake you could turn back the clock a few minutes to the moment before it happened? This fantasy is possible (at least in Photoshop) with the History panel. In the following steps you will experiment with the History panel.

1. Press Cmd+N to create a new document. In the New dialog box, select Web from the Preset drop-down menu and 800×600 from the Size drop-down. Click OK.

2. Press B to select the Brush tool. Paint a few brushstrokes.

3. Press E to select the Eraser tool. Erase potions of the brushstrokes.

4. Press B again and paint a couple more brushstrokes. Let's say that at this moment you regret getting rid of what you erased in the previous step.

5. Drag the blue handle upward in the history list until before the Eraser action. What you erased reappears as you effectively "go back in time" (see Figure 4.25).

You can press Cmd+Opt+Z to move backwards through history one step at a time.

Source for History Brush

Turning the clock to this action
Mistaken action

FIGURE 4.25 Using the History panel

6. Press G to select the Gradient tool and drag out a gradient. The Eraser action and the actions following it (brushstrokes in this example) are gone as if they never happened.

Using the History Brush

The History brush allows you to turn back time (or more precisely, your Photoshop actions) but only in the areas you paint. In the following example you'll experiment with the History brush.

As Winston Churchill said, "History is written by the victor," and thankfully that's always you in Photoshop!

The default source for the History brush is the initial state corresponding to how the image appeared when you opened it (in color in this case).

1. Go to the book's Downloads page at www.sybex.com/go /photoshopessentials, browse to Chapter 4, get the file Mountain Freedom.jpg, and open it in Photoshop.

2. Choose Image ≻ Adjustments ≻ Desaturate. The color image turns into a black-and-white photo.

3. Open the History panel if it's not already open. There are only two actions so far: Open and Desaturate.

4. Press Y to select the History brush. Select the Soft Round brush and set its size at 100 px in the Brush Preset picker on the options bar. Paint over the man and observe his red cap and yellow jacket reappear (see Figure 4.26).

PHOTO COURTESY OF iSTOCKPHOTO, ©ANDREW PENNER, IMAGE #6376617

FIGURE 4.26 Painting color back in with the History brush

5. Press the left bracket key repeatedly to reduce the size of the brush down to 20 px. Click the blank box next to Desaturate in the History panel to set a new source for the History brush.

6. Paint over the reflection of the mountain in the lake to desaturate any areas you resaturated in step 4. Now you can appreciate how

useful it is to be able to manipulate history with a brush to create the illusions you wish to convey.

An example file using this technique is available on the book's Downloads page.

7. Save your work as Mountain Freedom History.jpg.

Painting with the Art History Brush

The Art History brush isn't about the history of art (that's what I thought initially), but it does have something to do with making artistic renditions of photos or 3D models. The Art History brush employs gestural algorithms to apply paint sourced from a history state. So you can think of it like the History brush with a twist. Let's experiment with the Art History brush in the following steps.

1. Reopen the photo Mountain Freedom.jpg.

2. Choose Edit ➤ Fill. Open the Use drop-down menu in the Fill dialog box and choose 50% gray (see Figure 4.27). Click OK. This will act like the canvas of a new painting. You could fill with any color or shade of gray if you prefer.

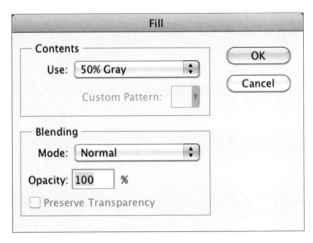

FIGURE 4.27 Filling the canvas with medium gray

3. Press Shift+Y to select the Art History brush. On the options bar, select the Soft Round brush from the Brush Preset picker drop-down, select Tight Medium from the Style drop-down, set Area to 50 px, and set Tolerance to 0. Click the Tablet Pressure Controls Size button if you are using a pressure-sensitive tablet.

4. Press the right bracket key to increase the brush size to 50 px if you are not using a tablet, or press firmly if you are and paint a few brush-strokes on the canvas.

5. Reduce the brush size by either pressing the left bracket key repeat-edly or pressing lightly with the stylus. Paint over areas where you want more detail to appear, such as the silhouette of the mountain chain and the man with outstretched arms. Figure 4.28 shows the resulting artistic painting.

6. Save your work as `Mountain Freedom Art History.jpg`.

The Art History brush sources its paint from the ini-tial history state, which contains the original photograph. The Tight Medium algorithm swirls the paint around in con-trolled strokes.

An example file using this tech-nique is available on the book's Downloads page.

ORIGINAL PHOTO COURTESY OF ISTOCKPHOTO, ©ANDREW PENNER, IMAGE #6376617

F I G U R E 4 . 2 8 Art History Brush painting based on photograph

Using the Mixer Brush

The Mixer brush is the closest a Photoshop tool gets to a real paintbrush. As the name suggests, you can mix paint that's already on the canvas with any percentage of fresh pigment, and blend colors to add to your canvas. In the following steps you will use the Mixer brush to transform the photograph you were working on in the previous section into a fine art painting.

1. Reopen the photo `Mountain Freedom.jpg`.

2. Create a new layer by pressing Shift+Cmd+N. Type **Moist Unloaded** in the Name dialog box and click OK.

3. Select the Mixer brush from the flyout under the Brush tool. On the options bar, select the Spatter 46 px brush from the Brush Preset drop-down. Deselect Load The Brush After Each Stroke and select the Clean The Brush After Each Stroke button. Choose Moist, Light Mix from the drop-down menu and select Sample All Layers. Select the Tablet Pressure Controls Size button if you are using a tablet.

4. Paint over the silhouette of the mountain range. Paint over the rocks in the mountains such that your brushstrokes follow the striations in the rock. Paint vertical strokes over the trees near the lake and horizontal strokes at the edge of the water. Continue painting, being sensitive to the natural directions of the surfaces you are tracing. The pixels of the photo are treated as moist paint that you are pushing around like oil on a canvas.

5. Create a new layer by pressing Shift+Cmd+N. Type **Loaded Heavy Mix** in the Name dialog box and click OK.

6. Click the Current Brush Load drop-down on the options bar to open the color picker. Type the hex color **b878fe** in the # text box and click OK to select a deep-purple hue.

7. Select the Load The Brush After Each Stroke button and deselect the Clean The Brush After Each Stroke button. Increase Load to 100% and Mix to 90%. Now the brush will always be full of purple paint and you will mix 90% of the existing pigment with 10% purple as you paint.

8. Paint horizontal strokes over the sky and swirly strokes over the reflection of the sky in the lake. Paint a few horizontal strokes over the mountains. Paint a few horizontal strokes over the reflections of the mountains in the lake. Purple paint loaded on the brush is mixed with the moist paint on the canvas, resulting in a painting with hues not seen in the original photograph (see Figure 4.29).

9. Save your work as `Mountain Freedom Mixer Brush.jpg`.

An example file using this technique is available on the book's Downloads page.

ORIGINAL PHOTO COURTESY OF iSTOCKPHOTO, ©ANDREW PENNER, IMAGE #6376617

FIGURE 4.29 Mixing in color not present in the original photo

THE ESSENTIALS AND BEYOND

In this chapter you have learned how to paint and manipulate pixels in Photoshop. You have expanded the number of tools you know how to use, from gradients to the Pencil, Brush, and Eraser tools. In addition, you have explored the complexities of customizing brushes, painting with a stylus on a tablet, and using the History brush, the Art History brush, and finally, the Mixer brush. You should now be prepared to push pixels around a canvas in a multiplicity of ways.

ADDITIONAL EXERCISE

Create a fine art digital painting from your own photo using the Art History Brush and/or Mixer Brush tools.

CHAPTER 5

Drawing

You probably haven't thought of Photoshop as a drawing program. Although Adobe Illustrator is more specialized in that department, you might be surprised at how easy it is to create precise drawings in Photoshop. In this chapter you will learn the difference between raster and vector data, how to use the vector tools to draw, and how to manipulate shapes and paths. You will work in all three drawing modes. In short, you'll learn everything you need to know to draw accurately in Photoshop.

▶ **Comparing vector with raster data**

▶ **Drawing with vector tools**

▶ **Manipulating shapes and paths**

▶ **Working with drawing tool modes**

Comparing Vector with Raster Data

Certification Objective

Vector and raster data are the two main types of graphical information stored on computers. They are loosely correlated as drawing and painting, respectively, although some of the drawing tools can be used in a raster mode. The term *vector* refers to mathematical objects defined in a coordinate space. Don't worry, though, because no math knowledge is required to create graphics using vector tools.

You might recall that the term *raster* refers to pixels arranged in a grid. You ultimately rasterize vector objects by filling closed shapes or stroking paths, but as long as they retain their vector representations, you can manipulate them as objects rather than as pixels. In the following steps you will create both types of data to compare their similarities and differences.

> You'll learn more about each of the tool modes: shape, path, and pixels in "Working with Drawing Modes" later in this chapter.

1. Press Cmd+N to create a new document. Select Web from the Preset drop-down and 800×600 from the Size drop-down. Click OK.

 2. Select the Custom Shape tool on the options bar.

3. Select Shape from the tool mode drop-down on the options bar.

4. Open the Custom Shape Picker by clicking its down arrow on the options bar. Select the light bulb shape from the list of icons (Figure 5.1). If you don't see the light bulb in the list, open the Custom Shape Picker menu (right-facing arrow), select Reset Shapes, and click OK when asked to confirm.

FIGURE 5.1 Selecting a shape from the Custom Shape Picker

5. Open the Fill type drop-down, select Solid Color from the Fill type menu, and click the red swatch. Open the Stroke Type drop-down and select None (see Figure 5.2).

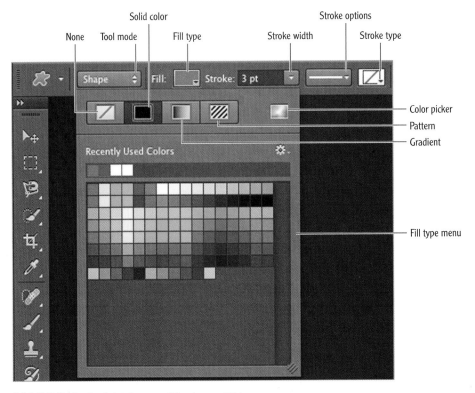

FIGURE 5.2 Selecting a solid color as fill type

6. Press Cmd+R to toggle on the rulers. Right-click one of the rulers and choose Percent from the context menu if Percent is not already selected. Position the cursor at 40% horizontally and 40% vertically, drag down to the right, and hold Shift to constrain the proportions of the custom shape until you reach approximately 50% vertically (see Figure 5.3). This is a vector shape, and you can see that the form of the light bulb shape is quite crisp and sharp. Rename the Shape 1 layer **Vector**.

FIGURE 5.3 Creating a vector custom shape

7. Press Cmd+J to copy the current layer. Rename the Vector Copy layer **Raster**. Open the Fill type menu and select the blue color swatch. Right-click the Raster layer and choose Rasterize Layer from the context menu. Notice that this layer has now lost its vector quality.

8. Press V to select the Move tool. Uncheck Auto-Select on the options bar if it is selected. Drag the blue light bulb to the right until it is a short distance away from the red light bulb. Both bulbs look equally crisp and sharp. The red bulb is vector and the blue bulb is raster. They look the same because vector shapes are ultimately rasterized.

You'll learn more about Free Transform mode in Chapter 10, "Transforming Paths, Layers, and Smart Objects."

The Vector Raster.psd file is provided on the book's website at www.sybex.com /go/photoshop essentials.

9. Hold Shift and select the Vector layer so that both layers are selected. Press Cmd+T to invoke Free Transform mode. Hold Shift+Opt and drag any one of the corner transformation handles outward to scale the layers from their common center while maintaining their proportions until they fill the canvas. Position the cursor inside the transformation bounding box and drag to center both objects on the canvas (see Figure 5.4). Click the Commit Transform button on the right end of the options bar.

10. Save your work as `Vector Raster.psd`.

FIGURE 5.4 Scaling vector (red) and raster (blue) light bulbs illustrates the differences between these types of data

The vector object (red light bulb) can be scaled up or down to any size without loss of quality because its shape is based on a mathematical representation created with the drawing tools you will learn about in the next section. The blue light bulb, on the other hand, was rasterized at a small size so it looks pixelated when enlarged almost 10 times.

Drawing with Vector Tools

Certification Objective

You can draw lines, arrows, curves, circles, squares, ellipses, rectangles, polygons, stars, and much more using Photoshop's vector toolset. These tools can be

used to create anything from simple web graphics to corporate logos, sophisticated technical illustrations, and more. In the following example you will learn
how to use the vector tools on the job by creating a hypothetical corporate logo.

1. Press Cmd+N to create a new document. Type **Logo** in the Name text
   box and select Web from the Preset drop-down and 800×600 from the
   Size drop-down. Click OK.

2. Press Cmd+R to toggle on the rulers if they aren't already on. Drag
   out horizontal and vertical guides from their respective rulers and
   snap them to 50%.

3. Select the Polygon tool and set Sides to 3 on the options bar. Select
   Shape tool mode, open the fill type drop-down and select a blue solid
   color. Position the cursor at the intersection of guides, drag vertically,
   and hold Shift until the cursor is at 10% along on the vertical ruler
   (see Figure 5.5).

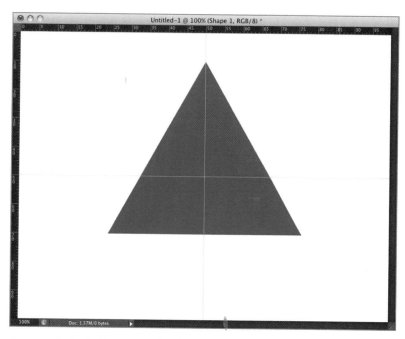

FIGURE 5.5 Drawing a triangle with the Polygon tool

4. Select the Ellipse tool on the options bar and select the Exclude
   Overlapping Shape Areas from the Path operations drop-down on the
   options bar. Open the Geometry Options drop-down and select the

Circle (Draw Diameter or Radius) radio button. Select From Center and then close the Geometry Options menu.

5. Position the cursor at the apex of the blue triangle on the canvas and drag until the diameter of the circle corresponds with the mark on the horizontal ruler at approximately 53.5%. A new blue circle appears. Because the area where it intersects the triangle is excluded, this region appears in white (see Figure 5.6).

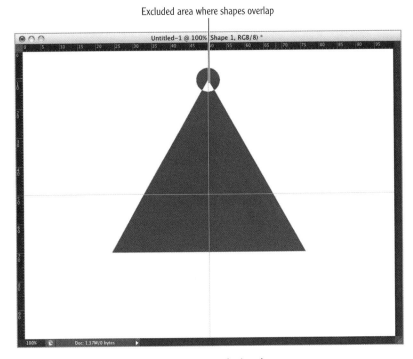

FIGURE 5.6 Drawing a circle on top of triangle

Other Shape Tool options are Rounded Rectangle, Line, and Custom Shape.

6. Select the Rectangle tool Subtract From Shape from the Path operations drop-down on the options bar. Position the cursor at the intersection of the guides at the center of the triangle. Instead of using the Geometry Options menu, this time hold Shift+Opt and drag out a square from the center point until the corners of the square reach the edge of the triangle, as shown in Figure 5.7. Holding Opt creates the rectangle from the center and holding Shift constrains the rectangle's proportions so it will be a square.

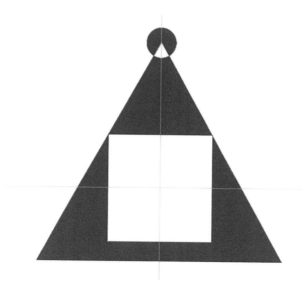

FIGURE 5.7 Subtracting a square from the triangle

7. Save your work as Logo1.psd. You can leave this file open because you will work with it in the next section.

Manipulating Shapes

You are by no means limited to drawing only circles, ellipses, rectangles, squares, or other basic shapes. Once you learn how to manipulate the basic shapes, you will be able to draw a much wider variety of custom forms. In the following steps you will continue the logo you started in the previous section by manipulating its shapes and paths.

Certification Objective

1. If the logo design isn't still open, go to the book's Downloads page at www.sybex.com/go/photoshopessentials, browse to Chapter 5, get the file Logo1.psd, and open it in Photoshop.

2. Press A to select the Path Selection tool (black arrow icon). Click the white square at the center of the blue triangle to select it. Press Cmd+T to enter Free Transform mode. Position the cursor outside the square and observe the rotate icon that appears at the cursor location. Hold Shift and drag the square 45 degrees in either direction until you have a diamond shape (see Figure 5.8).

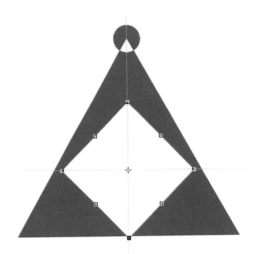

FIGURE 5.8 Rotating a square shape with the Path Selection tool

3. Click the Maintain Aspect Ratio button on the options bar. Click the Width text box used to set the horizontal scale. Repeatedly press the up arrow key until the left and right corners of the diamond touch the edge of the triangle (111% in this case) and the tips of the compasses come to sharp points (see Figure 5.9). Click the Commit Transform button (check mark icon) on the options bar.

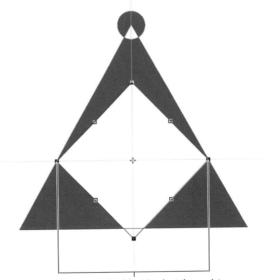

White square touches blue triangle at these points

FIGURE 5.9 Scaling a shape using free transform mode

4. With the Path Selection tool still active, select the circle at the top of the logo. Press Cmd+C and Cmd+V to copy and paste the shape in place. Drag the copied circle down to the lower-left corner of the blue triangle. Use the arrow keys to nudge the copied shape into position so that it is centered on the tip of the blue triangle as shown in Figure 5.10.

The blue portion of the circle disappears because both coincident circles are in Exclude Overlapping Shape Areas mode.

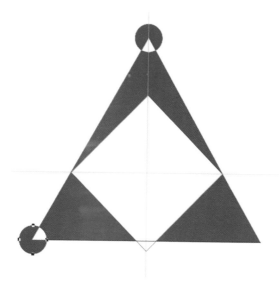

FIGURE 5.10 Copying an existing shape and repositioning it at the lower-left point of the triangle

5. Press Cmd+C and Cmd+V again to make a coincident copy of the second circle. Drag the third circle over the lower-right point of the triangle. Use the left and right arrow keys to nudge the circle so that its center is on the tip of the blue triangle.

6. Hold Shift and select the circle in the lower-left corner of the triangle so that you have both lower circles selected. Open the Path alignment drop-down and select Vertical Centers. Figure 5.11 shows the result.

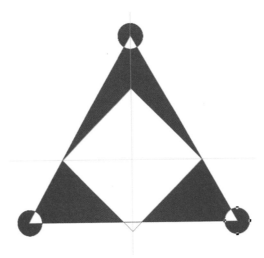

FIGURE 5.11 Copying and aligning the third circle

By merging shape components, you lose independent control over the original shapes but you gain additional anchor points, allowing different types of manipulation.

7. With the Path Selection tool still active, drag out a window around all five shapes the logo comprises. Open the Path operations drop-down and choose Merge Shape Components.

8. Press Shift+A to select the Direct Selection tool (white arrow icon). This tool allows you to manipulate individual anchor points. Click off to the side to deselect all anchor points and then click anchor point A shown in Figure 5.12. Hold Shift and drag to point B. Use the left and right arrow keys to nudge the anchor until it is directly under point C.

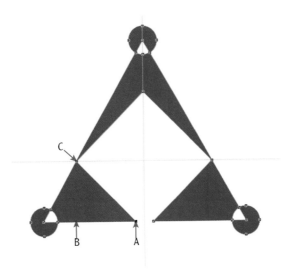

FIGURE 5.12 Moving an anchor point from A to B

9. Make the right half of the logo symmetric to the left by moving the appropriate anchor point. Press Cmd+; to hide the guides and Cmd+R to toggle off the rulers. Figure 5.13 shows the intended result.

FIGURE 5.13 Completed path manipulation

10. Save your work as Logo2.psd. You can leave this file open because you will work with it in the next section.

Working With Drawing Tool Modes

Photoshop's vector tools have three drawing tool modes that allow you to work in several distinct ways. You'll explore shape, path, and pixels drawing tool modes in the following sections.

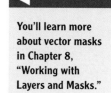

Certification
Objective

Shape Tool Mode

When you draw in Shape tool mode, you are actually drawing a vector mask that can be filled and/or stroked. There are many advantages to this approach: You can easily change the color, gradient, or pattern fill of the shapes by changing the fill type, you can stroke the shapes with a variety of stroke types

◄

You'll learn more about vector masks in Chapter 8, "Working with Layers and Masks."

and options including dashed lines, and the shapes you draw remain editable as vector objects. Let's create a couple of shapes and see how this works.

1. If the evolving logo design isn't still open, go to the book's Downloads page at www.sybex.com/go/photoshopessentials, browse to Chapter 5, get the file Logo2.psd, and open it in Photoshop.

2. Select the Background layer in the Layers panel.

3. Select the Rounded Rectangle tool and type **25 px** in the Radius text box on the options bar. Drag out a rounded rectangle that frames the logo. Open the Fill type drop-down, select the color picker, type hex color **c1c1c1** (light gray) in the # box, and click OK.

4. Select the Direct Selection tool in the toolbox. Drag a window around four anchor points and move them up or down, left or right until one half of the rounded rectangle frames the logo symmetrically. Repeat this by selecting the other four anchor points and move the other half of the rounded rectangle into the approximate positions shown in Figure 5.14.

FIGURE 5.14 Manipulating a rounded rectangle's anchor points to frame the logo

5. Choose Image ➢ Trim and click OK. The white border is trimmed away. Choose Image ➢ Canvas Size. Select Relative in the Canvas Size dialog box and change the drop-downs to Percent. Type **10** in the

Width box and **10** in the Height box. Select White from the Canvas Extension Color drop-down if it is not already selected. Click OK and an even white border surrounds the logo.

6. Choose the Custom Shape tool on the options bar. Open the Custom Shape Picker drop-down and click the right facing arrow to access the custom shape library menu. Select Symbols in the menu that appears and then click OK when prompted whether you want to replace the current shapes with the shapes from Symbols. Select the World shape shown in Figure 5.15.

FIGURE 5.15 Selecting a custom shape from the Symbols library

7. Deselect the Shape 2 layer so that you won't create the custom shape on this layer.

8. Hold Shift+Opt and drag out the world custom shape as shown in Figure 5.16.

FIGURE 5.16 Creating a custom shape layer (shown in red)

Fill and stroke properties remain editable in Shape tool mode.

9. Open the Fill type drop-down and select red as the solid color for the custom shape you already created.

10. Save your work as Logo3.psd. You can leave this file open because you will work with it in the next section.

Path Tool Mode

In Chapter 7, "Selecting Pixels," you'll learn how paths can be used to create accurate selections of hard-edge objects.

You can draw vector objects independently of layers in Path tool mode. Paths are vector objects that can be either open or closed. Open paths can be stroked (thickened) with any brush tool and closed paths can be filled with color. Although paths are vector objects, any stroke or fill that you apply to them appears as raster data (pixels). In the following steps you will use the Pen tool to draw paths, and then after manipulating the form with vector tools, you will stroke the path and create pixels.

1. If the evolving logo design isn't still open, go to the book's Downloads page at www.sybex.com/go/photoshopessentials, browse to Chapter 5, get the file Logo3.psd, and open it in Photoshop.

 2. Select the Freeform Pen tool. Select Paths mode on the options bar and drag out a wavy path under the world shape. Select the Direct Selection tool and see that the sketch you did is vector in nature (it has anchor points). Move some of the anchor points around and see how you can change the shape of the freeform sketch (see Figure 5.17).

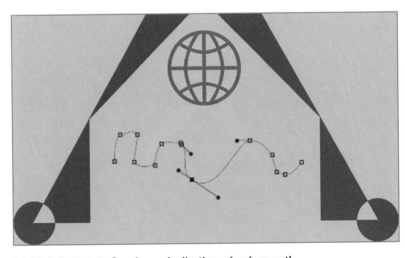

FIGURE 5.17 Drawing and adjusting a freeform path

3. Open the Paths panel and observe that two paths are listed: the Work path and the Shape 3 Shape Path. Any path you draw in Path mode will appear on the work path. If the current layer has a vector mask, its path appears on the Paths panel as well. Right-click the Work path and choose Delete Path from the context menu.

4. Press Shift+P to select the Pen tool (P is used for both the Pen and Freeform Pen tools). Click each one of the five points in the approximate locations shown in Figure 5.18.

◄

Click and drag a point with the Pen tool to shape the curvature of the path passing through that anchor point.

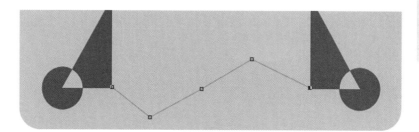

FIGURE 5.18 Sketching a rough path with the Pen tool

5. Open the Pen tool flyout in the Tools panel and select the Convert Point tool (not accessible via the keyboard by default). Drag the central three anchor points to shape the path passing through the anchors into a smooth wave.

6. Press A to select the Direct Selection tool and adjust any of the points and/or their handles as needed to match Figure 5.19.

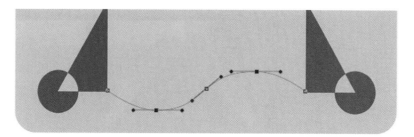

FIGURE 5.19 Shaping the working path into a smooth wave

7. Create a new layer by pressing Shift+Cmd+N, type **Wave** in the New Layer dialog box, and click OK.

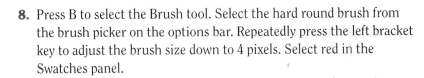

8. Press B to select the Brush tool. Select the hard round brush from the brush picker on the options bar. Repeatedly press the left bracket key to adjust the brush size down to 4 pixels. Select red in the Swatches panel.

9. Open the Paths panel and click the Stroke Path With Brush button (see Figure 5.20).

Make work path from selection
Load path as selection
Stroke path with brush
Fill path with foreground color

FIGURE 5.20 Path tools

Right click the work path and choose Stroke Path if you want to choose which tool to stroke the path with from a list.

10. Delete the Work Path by right clicking it in the Paths panel. Figure 5.21 shows the result. Save your work as Logo4.psd. You can leave this file open because you will work with it in the next section.

FIGURE 5.21 Stroking the wavy working path with a red brush

Pixels Tool Mode

In Pixels tool mode, you use drawing tools to directly generate pixels without creating a work path. This has immediate results but limited editability. In the following steps you will draw a line in Pixels tool mode and complete the logo design with the Paint Bucket tool.

The pen tools do not have a Fill Pixels mode.

1. If the evolving logo design isn't still open, go to the book's Downloads page at www.sybex.com/go/photoshopessentials, browse to Chapter 5, get the file Logo4.psd, and open it in Photoshop.

2. Click the red swatch in the Swatches panel to set the foreground color. Select the Wave layer if it is not already selected.

3. Select the Line tool. Select Pixels tool mode, also on the options bar. Type 3 px in the Weight text box on the options bar.

4. Hold Shift and drag a line between the points where the triangles and compasses intersect. Figure 5.22 shows the intended result. Don't worry if your line passes beyond the blue triangles as it does in the example.

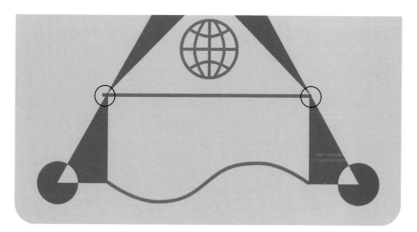

FIGURE 5.22 Drawing a line in Pixels tool mode might overshoot the blue triangles, as shown in the black circles.

5. The "line" you just drew doesn't have the qualities of a vector object. The only way you can alter it is to use raster techniques. Press E to select the Eraser tool. Select Block from the Mode drop-down on the options bar. Roll your mouse wheel forward to zoom in and carefully erase any portions of the red line that extend outside the vertical edges of the blue triangles. Double-click the Zoom tool to show the actual pixels at 100% magnification.

6. Select the Paint Bucket tool. On the options bar set Tolerance to 30% and select Anti-Alias, Contiguous, and All Layers. Click once in between the line you drew in the previous step and the wavy path you stroked in the previous section. Red color floods the bounded area and the logo design is complete. Figure 5.23 shows the result.

FIGURE 5.23 Completed logo project

7. Save your work as Logo5.psd. This file is provided on the book's website for your convenience.

THE ESSENTIALS AND BEYOND

In this chapter you have learned everything you need to know to begin drawing accurately and successfully with Photoshop. By drawing a fictitious corporate logo, you have learned how to use each one of the drawing tools and each of the drawing modes. You have gained experience manipulating shapes and paths and should now have a firm grasp of the differences between vector and raster data.

ADDITIONAL EXERCISE

Draw your own hypothetical corporate logo using the skills you have learned in this chapter.

CHAPTER 6

Writing

Much of the work you'll do will likely mix graphic and photographic elements with text, so it's essential that you learn how to write in Photoshop. In this chapter, you will learn about typography and creating attractive text. You will also learn how to use fonts and font sizes, as well as devices such as line spacing and indentation, to create visual hierarchy in your design.

- ▶ **Typography primer**

- ▶ **Creating point text**

- ▶ **Creating mask text**

- ▶ **Fine-tuning type**

- ▶ **Creating paragraph text**

Typography Primer

**Certification
Objective**

Typography, the art of arranging type, began with the Gutenberg press and continues to this day with your copy of Photoshop. Much of the terminology surrounding type originates from the time when letters were metal objects arranged in rows on a printing press. Although the technology has changed, the conventions developed over the centuries to improve the readability of the written word remain the same.

Figure 6.1 shows the basic anatomy of type. The height of the lowercase letter x is called the x-height, which refers to the height of lowercase letters in general. Lowercase letters *b, d, f, k, l,* and *t* have ascenders that are higher than the x-height. Lower case letters *g, j, p, q,* and *y* have descenders that are lower than the baseline the letter x rests on. The cap height is the x-height plus the ascender; while the font height equals the ascender plus the x-height plus the descender.

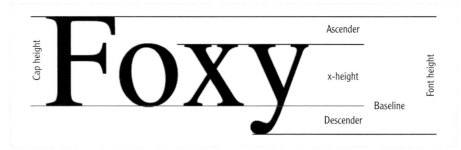

FIGURE 6.1 Anatomy of type

Type is measured points or picas. The following relationships apply:

$$1 \text{ pica} = 12 \text{ points}$$

$$6 \text{ picas} = 72 \text{ points} = 1 \text{ inch}$$

You can think of one pica as the ideal font height for body text. Table 6.1 lists a range of font heights associated with different uses of typography.

TABLE 6.1 Recommended font heights

Text Use in Document	Font Height in Points
Title	25–72
Header	14–24
Body	9–13
Caption	6–8

There are approximately 28 points per centimeter. Metric users are unfortunately not accommodated in the world of typography, whose standards were codified long before the metric system was invented.

You can enter picas or points in Photoshop, and both units are available on the rulers. However, points are the preferred unit of measurement; the font size drop-down lists points only. Photoshop accepts the abbreviation *pt* for point, but no abbreviation is accepted for pica.

A *font* is the vector source for all the glyphs (letters, numbers, and symbols) of a particular typeface. When you installed Photoshop, your operating system integrated a collection of useful font files into its inner workings. You can purchase additional font files from Adobe (see www.adobe.com/type/) or other vendors.

Fonts can be broken down into several categories (see Figure 6.2). The pangram "The quick brown fox jumps over the lazy dog" displays every letter of the alphabet at least once. Alternative pangrams are available in multiple languages for examining letters in typography.

Serif:
The quick brown fox jumps over the lazy dog. Caslon Pro
The quick brown fox jumps over the lazy dog. Garamond Pro
The quick brown fox jumps over the lazy dog. Chaparral Pro
The quick brown fox jumps over the lazy dog. Minion Pro
The quick brown fox jumps over the lazy dog. Times New Roman
The quick brown fox jumps over the lazy dog. Nueva Std
The quick brown fox jumps over the lazy dog. Palatino

Sans Serif:
The quick brown fox jumps over the lazy dog. Arial
The quick brown fox jumps over the lazy dog. Helvetica
The quick brown fox jumps over the lazy dog. Hobo Std
The quick brown fox jumps over the lazy dog. Myriad Pro
The quick brown fox jumps over the lazy dog. Tekton Pro
The quick brown fox jumps over the lazy dog. Poplar Std
The quick brown fox jumps over the lazy dog. Giddyup Std
The quick brown fox jumps over the lazy dog. Futura
The quick brown fox jumps over the lazy dog. Optima

The quick brown fox jumps over the lazy dog. Zapfino

All Caps:
THE QUICK BROWN FOX JUMPS OVER THE LAZY DOG. CHARLEMAGNE
THE QUICK BROWN FOX JUMPS OVER THE LAZY DOG. LITHOS PRO
THE QUICK BROWN FOX JUMPS OVER THE LAZY DOG. TRAJAN PRO
THE QUICK BROWN FOX JUMPS OVER THE LAZY DOG. STENCIL STD
THE QUICK BROWN FOX JUMPS OVER THE LAZY DOG. MESQUITE STD

Monospaced:
THE QUICK BROWN FOX JUMPS OVER THE LAZY DOG. ORATOR STD
The quick brown fox jumps over the lazy dog. Letter Gothic Std
The quick brown fox jumps over the lazy dog. Prestige Elite Std

FIGURE 6.2 Comparison of font types. Every line has the same font height of 24 points.

Both serif and sans-serif fonts are often selected for their emotional impact (see Nueva and Zapfino, for example).

Serif fonts have small horizontal lines, or wedges, at the end of some letter strokes that originate from a time when letters were painted with a brush. Serif fonts are generally easier to read than *sans-serif* fonts (*sans* is French for *without*) because the serifs provide visual cues that help the eye track horizontally and aid the visual cortex in distinguishing individual letters. But the simpler appearance of some sans-serif fonts can be preferable for readability on the Web and/or in larger font sizes.

Fonts with larger x-heights appear larger compared to others at the same font height (for example, compare Myriad Pro to Helvetica). Fonts with larger x-heights are generally easier to read.

The font designer sets the font width within the design of each glyph. You can adjust the spacing between letter pairs with *kerning* or artificially stretch or condense a whole line with *tracking* (see "Fine-Tuning Type" later in this chapter).

Most fonts are *proportional,* which means a different width is allocated to narrow letters like *i* as compared to wider letters like *m*. A small subset of the fonts supplied by Photoshop is *monospaced*—each letter has exactly the same width, as with letters on a typewriter. Notice how the monospaced letters of Orator, Letter Gothic, and Prestige Elite all line up vertically. Monospaced fonts are good for displaying programming code but are harder to read than proportional fonts.

Line length and line spacing both affect readability. The optimal line length for the most efficient reading experience is approximately 10 words or 60 characters long. Spacing between lines is called *leading*, which is pronounced "ledding" because the term originated by inserting strips of lead between rows of movable metal type. Lines spaced too closely or too far apart make for inefficient reading; there is a happy medium balancing x-height, line length, and spacing that is unique for every font.

Paragraphs that are left-justified appear less formal than paragraphs fully justified on both sides. You should select a justification based upon the tone of your document.

Creating Point Text

Certification Objective

The most common form of text in Photoshop is *point text*, which is used to write a line or two. The Text tool creates vector text layers, also called type layers, that can be edited as text later on (very much like Shape tool mode that you learned about in Chapter 5, "Drawing"). In the following steps you will create some text and learn many of the text options in the process.

1. Press Cmd+N to create a new document. Type **Point Text** in the Name text box. Change the Width drop-down to Pixels and type **800** in the Width and Height text boxes. Set the resolution at 72 pixels/inch if it is not already. Click OK.

Sidebar notes:

If you plan on using all capital letters, then it is best to select an all-caps font optimized for that purpose.

Fully justified text looks best when line-ending words are hyphenated because this practice produces more consistent word spacing.

You'll learn about better tools for managing multiple sentences in "Creating Paragraph Text" later in this chapter.

2. Press Cmd+R to toggle on the rulers. Right-click either one of the rulers and select Percent from the context menu that appears.

3. Press V to select the Move tool. Drag out a guide from the vertical ruler to 50% along the horizontal ruler. Drag out another guide from the horizontal ruler to 50% on the vertical ruler. The guides will snap into place at 50% automatically when you get close.

4. Press T to select the Text tool. Click a point near the intersection of the guides and type **Zygote**. The insertion point cursor is blinking at the end of the word, indicating that you can keep on typing.

5. Click the Commit Any Current Edits button at the right end of the options bar (see Figure 6.3). This completes the writing activity.

FIGURE 6.3 Options for completing the writing activity

Pressing Enter while writing advances to the next line. All words and/or lines you type are created as a single text layer.

6. Open the Layers panel and observe the text layer that was created. The layer is named after the word you typed: Zygote. Double-click layer Zygote's thumbnail to select all of the text on that layer for editing.

7. Click the center justification button (see Figure 6.4) and position the cursor a short distance outside of the actual text until the cursor changes to the move icon. Drag the text to the intersection of the guides and snap it into place. (You could alternatively use the Move tool to reposition text, but it is more efficient to use the move function in Text Editing Mode.)

You can select individual letters or words by dragging the Text tool over existing text for editing.

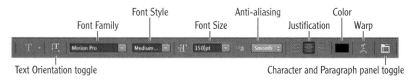

FIGURE 6.4 Text tool options

Each font definition is different; some have no font style options while others may have many family members. Minion Pro has a large family of styles.

8. Rather than opening the Font Family drop-down and selecting a font from the list, click in the Font Name text box and press the up or down arrows to preview how the text looks in each font. Select

Minion Pro when you're ready. Open the Font Style drop-down and select Medium Italic from the list.

9. Open the Font Size drop-down on the options bar and select 72 pt from the list. Although this is the maximum size listed, it isn't the largest font size you can use. Click in the Font Size text box and press Shift+up arrow repeatedly to increase the size rapidly. Let go of Shift when you get close to 150 pt and press the up or down arrow keys to zero in on this value. You can alternatively type a specific font size in the text box.

10. The differences among the anti-aliasing algorithms listed on the options bar are very subtle. Anti-aliasing (or pixel blending) is performed at the edge of each letter, as the vector representations are rasterized. Try out each algorithm in turn. Finally, select Smooth and click the Commit Any Current Edits button. Figure 6.5 shows the result.

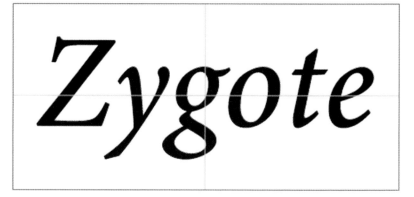

FIGURE 6.5 Editing text by adjusting its options

11. Save your work as Point Text.psd.

Creating Mask Text

Mask text doesn't create visible text by itself; instead, it creates a raster selection in the shape of text. What you do with that selection is up to you. You can use this mask text to reveal a background image within the text body ensuring that the text and image are aligned in a manner that avoid distracting interruptions. In the following steps you will create some mask text and use it to reveal a portion of a gradient fill layer.

1. Open your file from the previous section, or go to the book's Downloads page at www.sybex.com/go/photoshopessentials, browse to Chapter 6, get the file Point Text.psd, and open it in Photoshop.

2. Open the Text tool flyout and select the Horizontal Type Mask tool. Click an arbitrary point on the canvas and type **Egg** (see Figure 6.6). The canvas switches to Quick Mask mode (tinted red) to indicate that you are creating a mask. The text you type retains its vector quality (and editability) before you commit any of the current edits.

You'll learn more about this Quick Mask mode in Chapter 7, "Selecting Pixels."

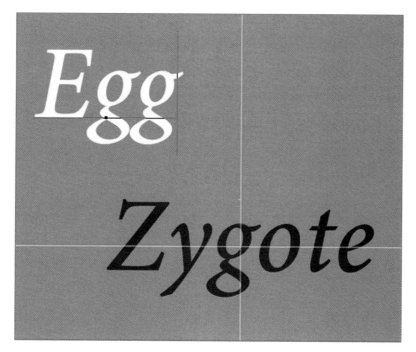

FIGURE 6.6 Creating mask text

3. Click the Toggle Text Orientation button on the options bar. The letters reorient themselves vertically in a column.

You can create
vertical mask
text directly with
the Vertical Type
Mask tool.

4. Move the cursor off the letters until it changes to the move icon. Drag the word down so that the middle letter *g* in the word *Egg* lines up with the letter *g* in the word *Zygote*. Click the Commit Any Current Edits button on the options bar. You are left with a selection (also known as a mask) rather than a text layer (see Figure 6.7).

FIGURE 6.7 Mask text produces a selection rather than a text layer

5. Right now the letters themselves are what is selected. Choose Select ➢ Inverse. Now everything but the letters is selected.

6. Press D to ensure that the default colors are selected (black in the foreground and white in the background).

7. Click the Create New Fill Or Adjustment Layer icon at the bottom of the Layers panel and select Gradient from the menu that appears. In the Gradient Fill dialog box, open the Gradient drop-down and select the Foreground To Transparent gradient (second from top left). Open the Style drop-down and select Radial. Select Reverse so you have a white gradient in the center that fades to black on the outside (see Figure 6.8). Click OK. The letters of the word *Egg* are white because they mask the Gradient Fill 1 layer and thus reveal the white Background layer. The gradient mask is just one example of what you can do with mask text.

◄

The current selection becomes a layer mask when you create new fill or an adjustment layer.

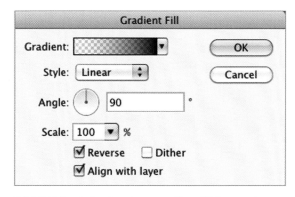

FIGURE 6.8 Creating a gradient fill layer using the letter selection as a mask

8. Press Shift+T twice to cycle through the writing tools until the Horizontal Type tool is selected. Drag over the middle letter *g* of the word *Zygote* to select it alone. Click the color swatch on the options bar, select bright red in the color picker that appears, and click OK. Click the Commit Any Current Edits button.

9. Press Cmd+; to hide the guides and press Cmd+R to toggle off the rulers. Figure 6.9 shows the result.

10. Save your work as Mask Text.psd and close the file. This file is provided on the book's web page for your convenience.

FIGURE 6.9 Finished type experiment

Fine-Tuning Type

  If you ever do any graphic or web design, you will probably need to fine-tune type to fit any number of geometric situations. Fortunately Photoshop has plenty of options for manipulating, transforming, and warping characters to suit almost any conceivable situation. In the following steps you will put together a composition designed to give you an understanding of the many options for fine-tuning type.

1. Press Cmd+N to create a new document. Type **Fine Tuning** Text in the Name text box. Change the Width drop-down to Pixels, type 800 for Width and **600** for Height, and click OK.

T. **2.** Select the Horizontal Type tool and click the canvas to locate the type. Select the Minion Pro font, Regular font style. Type **215 pt** in the Font Height text box, and select the center justify icon. Type **Gnosis** and drag the word to the approximate center of the canvas. Highlight the whole word by dragging across it and click the Toggle The Character And Paragraph Panels button on the options bar. In the Character panel, set the tracking of the selected characters to -25 (see Figure 6.10). The letters get closer together. Press the left arrow key and then the right arrow key to position the cursor in between the *G* and the *n*. Set Kerning to 50. There is now more space between these letters.

FIGURE 6.10 Using the Character panel to fine-tune type

3. Click the Create Warped Text icon on the options bar. Open the Style drop-down and select Wave from the long list of deformations you can apply to text. Drag the Bend slider to +33 and click OK.

4. Click the Commit Any Current Edits button on the options bar. Open the Layers panel and right-click the Gnosis text layer. Choose Convert To Shape from the context menu that appears. The result is a shape layer (see Figure 6.11).

Once you convert text to a shape, there is no going back; the object will no longer be editable as text.

FIGURE 6.11 You can convert type into a shape layer for geometric editing.

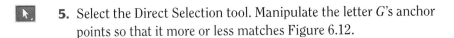

5. Select the Direct Selection tool. Manipulate the letter *G*'s anchor points so that it more or less matches Figure 6.12.

FIGURE 6.12 Changing the shape of an individual letter by manipulating its anchor points

6. Press Shift+U twice to select the Ellipse tool and choose Path from the first drop-down on the options bar. Hold down the Opt key and drag out an ellipse from the center of the word *Gnosis* as shown in Figure 6.13.

FIGURE 6.13 Drawing an elliptical path to surround the word

7. Press T to select the Text tool. Position the cursor over the elliptical path. When the cursor displays the curving path icon, click the path. Set the Font Height to 60 pt. Type the following words with four spaces between each word: **Wisdom Knowledge Understanding Mysteries Arcana Sophia.** The words appear on the elliptical path. Click the Commit Any Current Edits button.

You can also get text to follow an open path drawn with the Pen tool.

8. Press A to select either the Path Selection or Direct Selection tool. Position the cursor over the text wrapping along the elliptical path. Drag when the cursor changes to an icon with two arrows and you'll be able to drag the text around that path. Arrange the words so that *Wisdom* is the word on the upper left.

If you drag text aligned to a path across the path direction, it will flip over vertically.

9. Press T and click the point between the letters *W* and *i* in *Wisdom* where there is too much space. Set Kerning to -100 in the Character panel and the letters are pulled closer together. Click the Commit Any Current Edits button. Figure 6.14 shows the result.

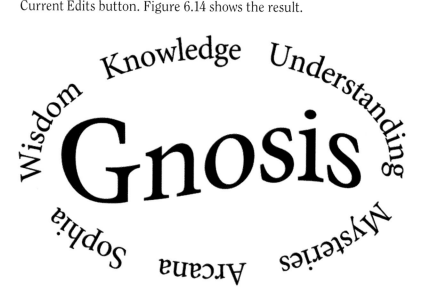

FIGURE 6.14 Completed text manipulation project

10. Save your work as Fine Tuning Text.psd and close the file. This file is provided on the book's web page for your convenience.

Creating Paragraph Text

It is very tedious to write multiple lines of text with point text because this mode does not support word wrap as a word processor does. If you change some text, you may have to manually rewrap every line of text. Fortunately, Photoshop does support word wrap, but not with a specialized tool. In the following steps you will learn how to create paragraph text and fine-tune it.

1. Go to the book's Downloads page at `www.sybex.com/go /photoshopessentials`, browse to Chapter 6, get the file `Paragraph Text.psd`, and open it in Photoshop. This file contains a curved frame that you will fill with text.

 2. Press T to select the Text tool. Instead of clicking an insertion point for point text, drag out a window inside the black border to contain the paragraph text you will write. On the options bar, select the Minion Pro font, Regular font style, 60 pt font height, crisp anti-aliasing, left justification, and black as the color. Type the following text: **Now is the time for all good women to come to the aid of their country.** Figure 6.15 shows the result.

![Writing paragraph text showing the text "Now is the time for all good women to come to the aid of their country." inside a rounded rectangle frame]

FIGURE 6.15 Writing paragraph text

3. Drag the lower-right corner of the paragraph text frame and observe the text wrap from line to line as the frame changes size. Drag the frame large enough so you can see the entire sentence.

You can convert point to paragraph text (and vice versa) by right-clicking any text layer.

4. Click the Toggle The Character And Paragraph Panels icon on the options bar if these panels aren't already visible. Select the Paragraph panel and select the Justify Last Left button. This justifies the paragraph on both sides (by varying the spacing in between the words) but justifies the last line of the paragraph only on the left. (In Figure 6.16, note that the justification icons in the Paragraph panel let you visualize how the text will be justified.)

Justify last left

Indent first line

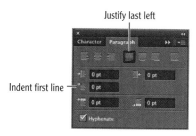

FIGURE 6.16 Using the Paragraph panel to fine-tune paragraph text

5. Type **50 pt** in the Indent First Line text box and click the Commit Any Current Edits button. Press Cmd+W to close the window and press D for Don't Save.

6. Press Cmd+N to create a new document. Type **360** for width and **800** for height in the New dialog box and click OK.

7. When you are working with lengthy layouts, it is helpful to use the filler text that's been traditional since the 1500s. Go to www.1ipsum.com, type 3, choose Paragraphs, and click Generate Lorem Ipsum. Select all three resulting paragraphs and press Cmd+C to copy them to the clipboard.

Filler text is not meant to be read and is used simply for layout purposes. After the layout is complete, you would typically replace the filler with meaningful copy.

8. Switch back to Photoshop and press T to select the Text tool. Drag out a large window and press Cmd+V to paste the filler text inside the frame.

9. Press Cmd+A to select all the text. Set the font height to 12 pt on the options bar. In the Character panel, set Leading to 18 pt to increase the space between the lines. In the Paragraph panel, set the Indent

▶

Notice that some of the words are hyphenated. It is best to hyphenate in full justification to avoid unequal spacing between words.

First Line amount to 30 px to decrease the indent as compared to the first example. Figure 6.17 shows the result.

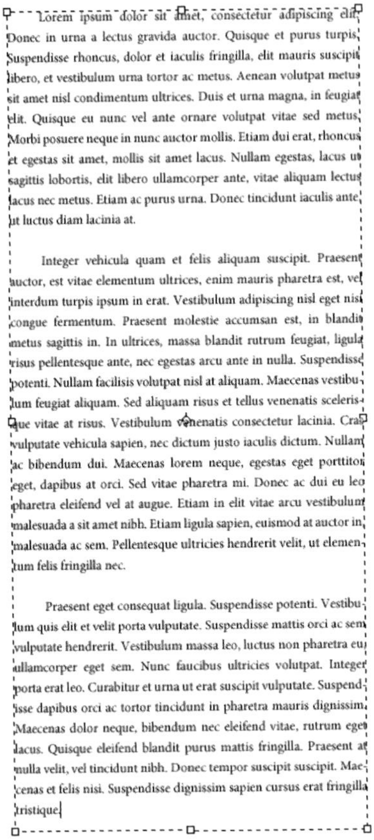

FIGURE 6.17 Formatting body filler text

10. Save your work as Lorem Ipsum.psd. This file is provided on the book's website for your convenience.

ASSIGNING LANGUAGES TO TEXT

Even if you're working with English text, the occasional word from another language can pop up in a spell-check. You can assign a different language to an entire document or just to selected text to check spelling and hyphenation. You can access multiple language dictionaries from the pop-up menu in the bottom corner of the Character panel.

THE ESSENTIALS AND BEYOND

In this chapter you have learned how to write in Photoshop. After reading a primer on typography and gaining experience creating point, mask, and paragraph text, you have learned to write and fine-tune exactly how type appears. You should now have the ability to make text look so good that people might be enticed to actually read what you have to say.

ADDITIONAL EXERCISE

Create a note using the Note tool, which is on the Eyedropper tool's flyout menu. Notes are for your information only and do not print. Use notes to include review comments to your colleagues, to create production notes, or to jot down a to-do list related to the project in question. Notes are saved in the PSD and PDF formats only. Use the Notes panel to read and edit notes.

CHAPTER 7

Selecting Pixels

Selecting pixels is the key to manipulating portions of images. Without selection, any adjustments, filters, or masks you apply would affect the entire image. Photoshop has many different selection tools for use in different situations. In this chapter you'll learn how to choose the right tool for the job by using marquees and lassos, selecting by drawing, painting and by color, and finally, quick selecting and refining for the most efficient results.

▶ **Selecting with marquees**

▶ **Selecting with lassos**

▶ **Drawing selections**

▶ **Painting selections**

▶ **Selecting by color**

▶ **Quick selecting and refining**

Selecting with Marquees

Marquees are windows that you drag across an image to select pixels. Marquees can be square, rectangular, circular, or elliptical. Selection borders appear as a series of dashed lines that slowly migrate along the edge. Selection edges are called *marching ants* because of this uncanny resemblance.

Using the Rectangular Marquee

In the following steps you will create rectangular marquees and use the proportions of a golden rectangle (see Chapter 1, "Design Basics," for more information on this aesthetically pleasing fixed ratio).

1. Go to the book's Downloads page at www.sybex.com /go/photoshopessentials, browse to Chapter 7, get the file Landscape.jpg, and open it.

2. Press M to select the Rectangular Marquee tool. Hold Shift and drag out a square marquee over the photo to frame a composition. Position the cursor inside the selection and drag to move the marching ants to a new location.

3. Hold down Cmd and position the cursor inside the selection. Drag a short distance and observe how the selected pixels are moving (see Figure 7.1). This is just one example of what you can do with a selection.

You can adjust the size of the marquee after you make a selection by choosing Select ➤ Transform Selection.

The keyboard shortcut to Select All is Cmd+A.

FIGURE 7.1 Moving the selection with the Cmd key

4. Press Cmd+Z to undo the previous step. Choose Select ➤ Deselect.

5. Open the Style drop-down on the options bar and select Fixed Ratio. Type 1 in the Width text box and **1.618** in the Height text box. Drag out a selection window. It has portrait orientation.

6. Click the Swaps Height And Width button on the options bar. Drag out another selection window, this time it is in landscape orientation. Position the cursor inside the marching ants and drag the window to frame a tighter composition focusing on the snowy peak in the distance. Choose Image ➤ Crop and press Cmd+D.

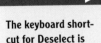

The keyboard shortcut for Deselect is Cmd+D.

The keyboard shortcut to copy a selection to a New Layer via Copy is Cmd+J.

7. Press F twice to enter Full Screen mode. Now you can focus on the entire image and appreciate its proportions. Figure 7.2 shows one possible result.

FIGURE 7.2 Cropping the image with the proportions of a golden rectangle and viewing in Full Screen mode

8. Press F once again to return to Standard Screen mode. Press Cmd+W to close the document and press D to discard the changes.

Using the Elliptical Marquee

In the following steps you will drag out a series of elliptical marquees that add together to form a selection that traces the edge of a geometric dome.

1. Go to the book's Downloads page at www.sybex.com/go /photoshopessentials, browse to Chapter 7, get the file Dome.jpg, and open it.

2. Press F to enter Full Screen with Menu Bar mode. You will need extra space around the canvas to make the selection.

3. Press Shift+M to select the Elliptical Marquee tool. As shown in Figure 7.3, drag from A to B approximately until the edge of the ellipse reaches the edge of the dome.

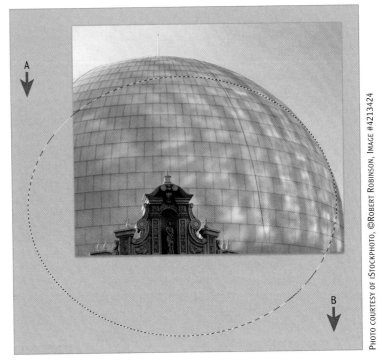

PHOTO COURTESY OF ISTOCKPHOTO, ©ROBERT ROBINSON, IMAGE #4213424

FIGURE 7.3 Creating an elliptical marquee

SINGLE ROW SELECTIONS

There are two specialized marquees for selecting single rows and columns of
pixels. These are good for when you want to shave off contrasting borders.
Drag a single row or column marquee to the edge of the canvas, invert the
selection, and crop the image to shave off one row or column of pixels at a time.

🔳 Single Row Marquee Tool
🔳 Single Column Marquee Tool

4. Select the Add To Selection icon on the options bar. Drag out another
   elliptical marquee from left to right that traces more of the dome's
   outer edge. Continue adding elliptical selections until you have selected
   everything but the sky. You can ignore the mast at the top of the dome.

5. Press Shift+Cmd+I to invert the selection so that the sky is selected.
   Press Shift+Cmd+I again to invert the selection back. Now the

marching ants frame the dome and the edge of the image rather than extending off the canvas. Press Shift+F to return to Standard Screen mode (see Figure 7.4).

FIGURE 7.4 Selecting the dome with additive selections

6. Choose Select ➤ Save Selection. Type **Dome** in the Name text box in the Save Selection dialog box.

7. Save your work as DomeSelection.psd. Make sure Alpha Channels is selected in the Save As dialog box and click Save. You'll come back to this image later in the chapter.

Selections are saved in the form of channels.

Not all file formats support alpha channels, and that is why you are saving in the native Photoshop Document (PSD) format.

REFINE SELECTION

When a selection is active, the Refine Selection button in the option bar is activated which allows fine tuning of the selection's edge. Edge Detection, using Smart Radius, creates an accurate edge based on edge hardness/softness. In Adjust Edge, further changes can be made using Smooth, Feather, Contrast, and Shift Edge. In Output, the Decontaminate Colors option removes color fringe from the image and offers the option of saving the selection as a layer mask, new layer, or new document. You can also use Truer Edge selection for the most difficult components to refine, such as hair.

Selecting with Lassos

Certification Objective

Those outside North America might not be familiar with the word *lasso*; it is a loop of rope a cowboy might throw around a bull to capture it. Thankfully, the type of lassoing we do in Photoshop is far less dangerous. You have three lassos in your toolbox: regular, polygonal, and magnetic.

Using the Lasso

You'll find that it takes a steady hand to use the lasso effectively. As mentioned in Chapter 4, it is much more natural to use a tablet as an input device than a mouse, and this is especially true when using the Lasso tool. In the following steps you'll lasso a hot chili pepper.

1. Go to the book's Downloads page at www.sybex.com/go /photoshopessentials and browse to Chapter 7. Open the file Peppers.jpg.

2. Zoom into the image by pressing Cmd+= a few times.

 3. Press L to select the Lasso tool. Pick a pepper (no need for a peck of pickled, just one will do) and lasso it by carefully tracing its edges. This is much easier said than done. Notice that the pointer is at the tip of the lasso icon. Press the Caps Lock key for the *precise cursor* (a cross) if you prefer. Don't worry if you make a mistake (see Figure 7.5).

PHOTO COURTESY OF ISTOCKPHOTO, ©DOGA YUSUF DOKDOK, IMAGE #10283262

FIGURE 7.5 Lassoing takes a steady hand, but you don't have to get a perfect selection on the first attempt.

4. Hold the spacebar—which temporarily activates the Hand tool—and drag the image to pan while lassoing if the magnified pepper goes off the screen.

5. If you missed some of the pepper, hold down Shift and make another lasso loop to add those pixels to the selection.

6. If you went beyond the edges of the pepper you're tracing with the lasso, hold down Opt and make another lasso loop to remove that area from the selection.

7. Choose Selection ➤ Inverse so that everything but the one pepper is selected.

8. Choose Image ➤ Adjustments ➤ Desaturate.

9. Choose Edit ➤ Fade Desaturate. Drag the Opacity slider down to 80% and click OK. The only time you can fade an adjustment is immediately after its application.

You'll learn more about adjustments in Chapter 11, "Adjusting and Filtering."

10. Save your work as `Highlighted Pepper.psd`. Figure 7.6 shows the result, which was only possible with careful selection.

Selections can be undone with the Undo command (Cmd+Z). You can also revert to a previous selection by using the History panel.

FIGURE 7.6 This play on saturation began with the lasso.

Using the Polygonal Lasso

You can learn more about this sundial at bit.ly/xXvwXW.

The polygonal lasso is good for selecting manufactured objects having straight edges, such as buildings or cut stone. In the following steps you will lasso the obelisk at the center of Europe's largest sundial and make a special effect using the selection.

1. Go to the book's Downloads page at www.sybex.com/go /photoshopessentials, browse to Chapter 7, get the file Sundial .jpg, and open it.

2. Zoom into the image by pressing Cmd+= a few times. Hold the spacebar and drag the image to center the magnified obelisk on screen.

3. Press Shift+Cmd+N to create a new layer, type **Effect** in the New Layer dialog box, and click OK.

4. Press Shift+L to select the Polygonal Lasso tool. Click points around the perimeter of the obelisk to trace its straight edges (see Figure 7.7). Don't worry about the golden ball on top.

PHOTO COURTESY OF ISTOCKPHOTO, © MICHAEL UTECH, IMAGE #3247779

FIGURE 7.7 Selecting with the polygonal lasso

A fill amount of 0% is used to create certain effects.

5. Press Cmd+Delete to fill the selection with the background color. In the Layers panel, drag the fill amount to 0%. Press Cmd+H to hide the selection.

6. Choose Layer ➤ Layer Style ➤ Outer Glow.

7. In the Layer Style dialog box, set Size to 65 pixels (see Figure 7.8). Click OK.

You'll learn much more about layer styles in Chapter 9, "Using Layer Styles and Comps."

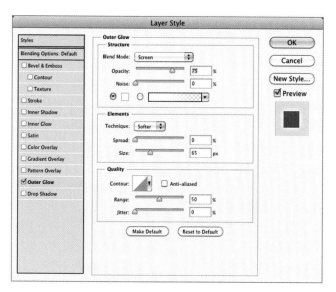

FIGURE 7.8 Creating an outer glow effect

8. Save your work as Glowing Gnomon.jpg. Figure 7.9 shows the result.

FIGURE 7.9 This glowing effect began with the polygonal lasso.

Using the Magnetic Lasso

The Magnetic Lasso tool is something like a cross between the lasso and the polygonal lasso, but with a difference. Like the polygonal lasso, the magnetic lasso lays down tiny straight segments. But like the regular lasso, it lets you work freehand. As you drag the magnetic lasso, Photoshop performs real-time edge detection based upon the contrast between pixels along the edge. In the following steps you will use the Magnetic Lasso tool to subtract from a selection you saved earlier.

1. Reopen the DomeSelection.psd file that you saved earlier or go to the book's Downloads page at www.sybex.com/go/photoshopessentials, browse to Chapter 7, and open that same file.

2. Choose Select ➤ Load Selection. Choose Dome from the Channel drop-down in the Load Selection dialog box (see Figure 7.10). Click OK.

FIGURE 7.10 Loading a saved selection

3. Press Shift+L to select the Magnetic Lasso tool. Set Feather to 0 px, select Anti-Alias, and set Width to 10 px, Contrast to 10%, and Frequency to 100.

4. Select the Subtract From Selection button on the options bar. Press F to switch into Full Screen with Menu Bar mode. Press Cmd+= to zoom into the Baroque architectural element at the bottom of the photo.

5. Carefully trace over the silhouette of the Baroque element, magnetically lassoing its structure to remove it from the selection. You don't have to make a perfect selection: Close is good enough for this tutorial. Double-click when you get to the end of the loop to complete the selection (see Figure 7.11).

Photo courtesy of iStockphoto, ©Robert Robinson, Image #4213424

FIGURE 7.11 Removing the Baroque element with the Magnetic Lasso tool

6. Press Cmd+H to hide the marching ants but keep the selection. Press Cmd+U to invoke the Hue/Saturation adjustment.

7. In the Hue/Saturation dialog box, select Colorize. Drag the Hue slider into the green region with a value in the neighborhood of 122. Drag Saturation to about 36 and Lightness to -35.

8. Press Cmd+H to unhide the selection and then Cmd+D to deselect. Figure 7.12 shows the result that was made possible with careful selection.

9. Press Shift+F to return to Standard Screen mode.

10. Save your work as DomeAdjusted.psd. This file is provided on the book's website for your convenience.

You will learn more about adjustments in Chapter 11, "Adjusting and Filtering."

FIGURE 7.12 Colorized dome

Drawing Selections

Certification
Objective

As you experienced in the previous section, using the lasso to make selections takes a very steady hand. Therefore, the lasso isn't the best tool for hard-edged forms such as those found on manufactured objects. For objects with smooth curves or crisp edges, it is usually preferable to draw the selection using the vector toolset. In the following steps, you will precisely select a wineglass by drawing its silhouette, as you learned in Chapter 5.

1. Go to the book's Downloads page at www.sybex.com/go /photoshopessentials, browse to Chapter 7, get the file Wineglass.jpg, and open it.

2. Press P to select the Pen tool and select Path from the first dropdown menu on the options bar. Draw a path around the silhouette of the wineglass. Drag points to create curves or click without dragging to create corner points. Continue adding points until you come full

circle and click on the first point to close the path. You don't have to get it perfect on the first attempt.

3. Press Shift+A to select the Direct Selection tool. Reposition the anchor points and/or adjust the points' handles to make the path fit the shape of the wineglass (see Figure 7.13).

Use the Convert Point tool underneath the Pen tool if you need to convert between corner points and curved points or vice versa.

PHOTO COURTESY OF ISTOCKPHOTO, ©LUIS ALVAREZ, IMAGE #978869

FIGURE 7.13 Drawing a path around a wineglass

You'll learn more about vector masks in Chapter 8, "Working with Layers and Masks."

4. Press Cmd+J to duplicate the Background layer. Rename the new layer **Wineglass** in the Layers panel.

5. Hold down the Cmd key and click the Add A Layer Mask icon at the bottom of the Layers panel to add a vector mask. The path that you drew will reveal the wineglass and hide everything else in the photo.

6. Click the Create New Fill Or Adjustment Layer icon at the bottom of the Layers panel and select Solid Color from the context menu. Choose pure white in the color picker that appears and click OK.

7. Press Cmd+[to move the Color Fill 1 layer down in the layer stack (see Figure 7.14).

FIGURE 7.14 Creating a solid color layer to obscure the background layer

8. Save your work as Extracted Wineglass.psd. Figure 7.15 shows the result. This file is provided on the book's website for your convenience.

FIGURE 7.15 Extracted wineglass

Painting Selections

Organic shapes are much harder to draw than to paint. Fortunately, Quick Mask mode allows you to select by painting. Unlike drawn selections, painted areas can be partially selected based upon the level of grayscale used in the brush. In the following steps you will paint over all the leaves of a tree to select them in Quick Mask mode.

Certification Objective

1. Go to the book's Downloads page at www.sybex.com/go /photoshopessentials, browse to Chapter 7, get the file Oak.jpg, and open it.

2. Click the Edit In Quick Mask mode icon at the bottom of the Tools panel. Press D to set the default colors so black is in the foreground.

3. Press B to select the Brush tool. Select a soft, round, 15 px brush with the Brush drop-down menu on the options bar.

4. Paint over the leaves of the tree. Decrease the brush size as you get near the tree silhouette by pressing the [key. Increase the brush size by pressing the] key repeatedly to paint over the bulk of the leaves. Photoshop shows the "paint" as a red tinted overlay. Figure 7.16 shows this painting in progress.

You can use the Paint Bucket tool to fill bounded areas in Quick Mask mode.

PHOTO COURTESY OF ISTOCKPHOTO, ©MARTIN BOWKER, IMAGE #4954117

FIGURE 7.16 Painting in Quick Mask mode appears in a red tint

5. Continue painting until all the leaves are covered. If you paint over areas that shouldn't be covered, press X to exchange foreground and background colors and then continue painting to remove the red tinted overlay.

6. Press Q to exit Quick Mask mode (see Figure 7.17).

7. Click the Create New Fill Or Adjustment Layer icon at the bottom of the Layers panel and select Solid Color from the context menu. Choose pure white in the color picker that appears and click OK. The selection turns into a mask on the Color Fill 1 layer that hides everything but the tree (see Figure 7.18).

8. Save your work as Isolated Oak.psd. This file is provided on the book's website for your convenience.

The marching ants reveal what has been selected. Quick Mask mode works in reverse, so everything you painted is *not* selected.

FIGURE 7.17 Painted selection appears as marching ants in standard mode

FIGURE 7.18 Painting a quick mask isolates a tree

Selecting by Color

In addition to all the other selection methods you've learned, you can select by color. You can control how much color is selected using the Color Range dialog box or the Magic Wand tool, both of which you will use in the following steps.

Certification Objective

1. Go to the book's Downloads page at www.sybex.com/go /photoshopessentials, browse to Chapter 7, get the file Windmills.jpg, and open it.

2. Choose Select ➢ Color Range. In the Color Range dialog box, select the Add To Sample mode (the eyedropper icon with a plus sign) and drag across the base of the largest windmill from point A to point B to increase the range of colors that are selected. Drag Fuzziness to 37 and Range to 100 (see Figure 7.19). Click OK.

Choose Skin Tones from the Select menu and/or check Detect Faces when using Color Range on people.

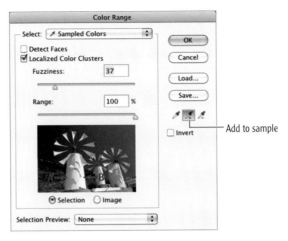

FIGURE 7.19 Selecting a range of colors

3. In one fell swoop you have made what would have been a very difficult selection with other methods. There may be some outlying areas that you can easily remove from the selection. Select the Lasso tool, choose the Subtract From Selection mode on the options bar, and drag loops around any marching ants that aren't part of the windmills or white walls (see Figure 7.20).

FIGURE 7.20 Remove outlying marching ants with the lasso

4. Click the foreground color swatch in the Tools panel, select medium gray (hex color #808080) in the color picker, and click OK. Press Cmd+H to hide the marching ants.

5. Choose Layer ➤ New Adjustment Layer ➤ Gradient Map and click OK to accept the default name in the New Layer dialog box. Select the Foreground To Background gradient in the Gradient drop-down in the Properties panel (see Figure 7.21). The gradient is mapped to the selection, brightening the whites.

FIGURE 7.21 Applying the gradient map adjustment

6. Press Opt+Cmd+Z to step backward through the history and then press Shift+Cmd+Z to step forward. In this way you can compare the image before and after the adjustment. Figure 7.22 shows the resulting luminous windmills.

FIGURE 7.22 Whites brightened through selecting by color

7. Go to the book's Downloads page at www.sybex.com/go /photoshopessentials, browse to Chapter 7, get the file Water.jpg, and open it.

8. Press Shift+W to select the Magic Wand tool. Set Tolerance to 50, select Anti-alias, and deselect Contiguous on the options bar. Click a dark area in the water image. The wand selects a range of dark areas based upon the Tolerance setting.

9. Choose Select ➤ Modify ➤ Feather. Type 3 in the Feather Selection dialog box and click OK. The feathered selection will now fade out in a 3-pixel border.

10. Choose Image ➤ Adjustments ➤ Hue/Saturation. Select Colorize and then drag Hue to 250, Saturation to 48, and Lightness to -14. Click OK. Figure 7.23 shows the result. The water looks more like neurons in the brain due to selection with the Magic Wand and a Hue/Saturation adjustment.

> **Feathering is a means of softening selections for smoother transitions.**

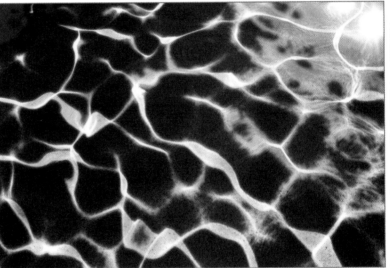

PHOTO COURTESY OF ISTOCKPHOTO, ©RONTECH2000, IMAGE #3547654

FIGURE 7.23 Water adjusted to look like neurons with the Magic Wand

CONTENT AWARE TECHNOLOGY

You can now patch images with greater control using the Content-Aware Patch, where you choose the area that Content-Aware will use to create a patch to repair or replace a portion of the image. You can also use the Content-Aware Move tool to move a selection to another area of the image where it will blend the object seamlessly into the new location.

Quick Selecting and Refining

The newest additions to Photoshop's selection toolset are called the Quick Select tool and the Refine Edge tool. These tools are typically employed together, with Refine Edge cleaning up after the initial quick selection. The Quick Select tool employs real-time processing to make intelligent selections based on brushstrokes that automatically detect color similarity and edges. Quick Select and Refine Edge provide the one-two punch that you will use in the following steps to capture a difficult subject such as hair blowing in the breeze without having to painstakingly lasso every flyaway follicle.

Certification Objective

1. Go to the book's Downloads page at www.sybex.com/go /photoshopessentials, browse to Chapter 7, get the file Woman.jpg, and open it.

2. Select the Quick Select tool by pressing Shift+W. Choose Add To Selection mode on the options bar and select Auto-Enhance. Open the Brush Picker drop-down and select a 13 px hard, round brush.

3. Make a brushstroke over the large region of blue background and observe that the marching ants very quickly adhere to the curves of the figure's body. Continue making strokes above the top of her head and to the right of the figure (see Figure 7.24).

PHOTO COURTESY OF ISTOCKPHOTO, ©HAMMONDOVI, IMAGE #13707719

FIGURE 7.24 Initial quick selection

4. Choose Select ➣ Inverse so that the figure is now selected. Press Cmd+= to zoom in, and decrease the brush size to 5 pixels by pressing the [key repeatedly. Paint over her eyeglasses frame and any windblown hair. Don't worry if you can see some sky within your selection; the important thing is to make sure that you don't leave anything out. If you select too much sky, hold Opt and paint it back out to deselect. Figure 7.25 shows a more careful quick selection.

FIGURE 7.25 Selecting all the hair and eyeglasses

5. Click the Refine Edge button on the options bar. Use the Refine Radius tool in the Refine Edge dialog box to paint over any areas where the figure blends with the background, such as in the eyeglasses and flyaway hair. The Refine Edge tool removes background pixels with each brushstroke.

6. Change the View drop-down to On Black and continue removing light pixels that become visible in her hair. Open the Output To drop-down and select New Layer With Layer Mask (see Figure 7.26). Click OK.

Refine Radius tool

FIGURE 7.26 Using the Refine Edge dialog box

7. Rename the newly created Layer 1 **Woman**.

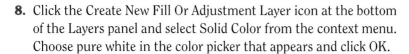

8. Click the Create New Fill Or Adjustment Layer icon at the bottom of the Layers panel and select Solid Color from the context menu. Choose pure white in the color picker that appears and click OK.

9. Press Cmd+[to move the Color Fill 1 layer down in the layer stack. Figure 7.31 shows the result: The woman is now independent from the original photographic background (see Figure 7.27).

FIGURE 7.27 Image of woman extracted from background

Extracted figures can easily be placed on different photographic backgrounds using Smart Objects, which you will learn about in Chapter 10, "Transforming Paths, Layers, and Smart Objects."

10. Save your work as Extracted Woman.psd. This file is provided on the book's website for your convenience.

BATCH-PROCESSING VIA ACTIONS AND DROPLETS

You can apply an Action to an entire group of images at once by selecting File ➢ Automate ➢ Batch. In Play, select an Action, the Source folder, Destination options, and then click OK. File ➢ Automate ➢ Droplet creates an icon that applies an Action to one or more images when the file or folder is dragged onto the droplet icon.

THE ESSENTIALS AND BEYOND

In this chapter you have learned a variety of methods for selecting precisely the pixels you are interested in so that you can alter them. These methods include selecting with marquees and lassos, drawing and painting selections, selecting by color, and finally, quick selecting and refining edges. In subsequent chapters you will learn how to alter selections in many creative ways.

ADDITIONAL EXERCISE

Extract the interior of the building in `Building.jpg` (on the book's website for this chapter) from the exterior, which is seen through the windows, by making a careful selection.

PHOTO COURTESY OF ISTOCKPHOTO, ©ALINA HART, IMAGE #6077114

CHAPTER 8

Working with Layers and Masks

Layers and masks are perhaps the most important features in Photoshop. Amazingly, they weren't invented until Photoshop 3.0, circa 1994, which happened to be when I started using the program. What did people do before layers and masks? Not a lot, I'd wager. In this chapter, you'll learn the essentials of layers and masks, which you must understand to get the most out of Photoshop.

▶ **Understanding layers**

▶ **Managing layers**

▶ **Blending layers**

▶ **Using masks**

Understanding Layers

Using layers is a breakthrough concept that greatly facilitates creativity. Layers allow you to split an image into parts that can be repositioned, protected, managed, and/or blended together in a variety of ways. Layers are at the core of Photoshop's functionality. Figure 8.1 illustrates the concept of layers as a series of stacked translucent sheets. In fact, the concept comes from the traditional practice of drawing on multiple layers of tracing paper that are stacked up to form a composition.

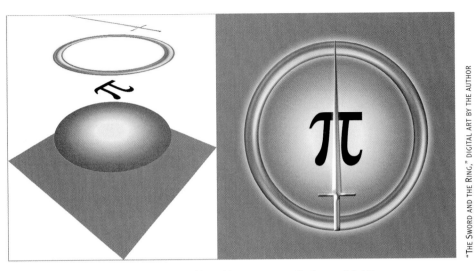

FIGURE 8.1 Concept of layers (left) making up composite image (right)

The Layers panel displays a list of layers that are stacked up from bottom to top (see Figure 8.2). Layers above others can obscure those below, partially mask them, or blend with them in a multiplicity of ways.

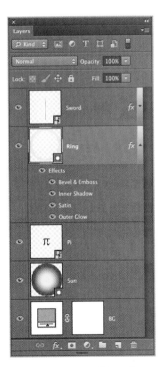

FIGURE 8.2 View of a layered document in the Layers panel

The Background layer is a special layer in Photoshop. Nothing can ever be behind the Background layer. The consequence of this rule is that the Background layer is locked so it can't be moved, have masks, have transparency, or be blended with other layers. However, you can draw or paint on the Background layer without any problems. In the following steps, you will perform some basic layer manipulation.

A Photoshop document does not have to have a Background layer at all.

1. Press Cmd+N and type **Layers** in the Name text box. Choose Pixels in the Width drop-down menu and type 800 in both the Width and Height text boxes. Set Background Contents to White.

2. Open the Swatches panel and click the red swatch to set it as the foreground color. Press B to select the Brush tool. Select a soft round brush and make a brushstroke on the canvas.

3. Select the Rectangle tool and choose Shape from the Tool Mode drop-down on the options bar. Select blue as a solid color fill and set Stroke to None. Drag out a rectangle that partially covers the brushstroke you made in the previous step. A blue rectangle obscures the red brushstroke because the Shape 1 layer is on top of Background in the Layers panel (see Figure 8.3).

FIGURE 8.3 Layers can obscure what is below them in the layer stack

4. Double-click the lock symbol on the Background layer. Type **Brushstroke** in the New Layer dialog box that appears. Click OK. The Background layer is no more and you are left with a "regular" layer.

5. Drag and drop the Brushstroke layer above the Shape 1 layer in the Layers panel. Now you see the red brushstroke but not the blue rectangle. Why? The Brushstroke layer contains a red brushstroke, but it also is filled with white pixels.

You can move layers up or down in the stack by pressing Cmd+] or Cmd+[.

You can adjust the size and opacity of the checkerboard pattern in the application preferences under Transparency & Gamut.

6. Choose the Magic Eraser tool. Set Tolerance to 10 and select Anti-Alias on the options bar. Click once on a white pixel on the canvas. Most of the white pixels are removed up to the point where white pixels mix with the edges of the brushstroke (see Figure 8.4). The checkerboard pattern represents transparency (areas where there are no pixels).

FIGURE 8.4 Using the Magic Eraser to get rid of unwanted white pixels

7. Press Cmd+Z to undo the Magic Eraser. Toggle off the Brushstroke layer by clicking its eye icon in the Layers panel. Select Shape 1 in the Layers panel. Choose Layer ➢ New ➢ Background From Layer. The transparency surrounding the blue rectangle is replaced by white pixels; the layer is locked and renamed Background.

8. Toggle on the Brushstroke layer and select the layer by clicking the word *Brushstroke*. The white pixels on the Brushstroke layer again obscure the new Background layer.

You can toggle a layer's visibility without selecting the layer.

9. Open the blend mode drop-down in the Layers panel and select Multiply (see Figure 8.5). You can now see both the brushstroke and the rectangle through the white pixels on the Brushstroke layer. You'll learn more about blend modes later in this chapter.

FIGURE 8.5 Changing a blend mode to see through the white pixels

10. To get rid of the white border, choose Image ➤ Trim and click OK. Save your work as Layers.psd.

Managing Layers

There is a lot more to layers than simply the order in which they are stacked in the Layers panel. In the following steps. you will learn how to adjust layer properties and how to lock, duplicate, select, reorder, group, link, merge, and flatten layers.

1. Reopen the Layers.psd file that you saved earlier or go to the book's Downloads page at www.sybex.com/go/photoshopessentials, browse to Chapter 8, and open the file with the same name.

2. Choose Layer ➤ New ➤ Layer, type **Spiral** in the Name text box, and select Red from the Color drop-down. You can optionally color-code layers so they are easier to spot in the Layers panel.

 3. Click yellow in the Swatches panel to set the foreground color. Select the Brush tool, and if you have a pressure-sensitive tablet, select Tablet Pressure Controls Size on the options bar. Paint a spiral in the center of the canvas, pressing harder as you spiral outward.

4. Open the Layers panel menu and select Panel Options. Select the medium thumbnail size and deselect Use Default Masks On Fill Layers (see Figure 8.6). Click OK.

Not all file formats support layers. Web formats such as JPG and PNG flatten all layers to reduce file size.

Certification Objective

To change a layer's color, right-click an existing layer and choose Layer Properties.

Multiple layers can be efficiently managed by organizing them into single Layer Groups or Smart Objects. You can also nest up to ten layers within a parent layer.

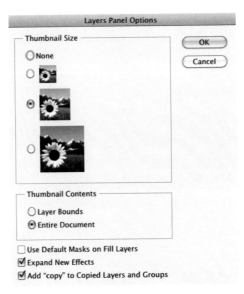

FIGURE 8.6 Configuring Layers Panel Options

5. Click the Transparency Lock icon in the Layers panel (see Figure 8.7). The transparent areas are now protected, so now you can affect only the pixels that are already on the Spiral layer.

You can also lock a layer's position and/or image pixels (so you can't change them).

FIGURE 8.7 Locking a layer's transparency

6. Select green in the Swatches panel. Reduce the brush size and make a series of swipes across the yellow spiral. The only pixels that are affected are those that are yellow because the transparent areas on the Spiral layer are locked (see Figure 8.8).

7. Press Cmd+J to duplicate the current layer. Double-click the new
layer name, type **Reverse Spiral**, and press Return. Choose Edit ➢
Transform ➢ Rotate 180°. Press V to select the Move tool and drag
your rotated spiral so it lines up with the original spiral (see Figure 8.9).
Toggle off the Brushstroke layer.

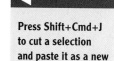

Press Shift+Cmd+J
to cut a selection
and paste it as a new
layer.

FIGURE 8.8 Painting green stripes on the yellow
spiral with transparency locked

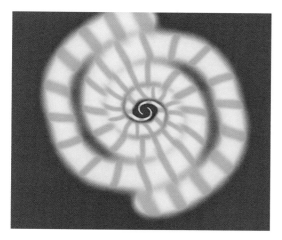

FIGURE 8.9 Duplicating, rotating, and aligning a layer

8. Hold Shift and select both spiral layers. Press Cmd+G to create a
group folder and automatically put the selected layers into it. Double-
click the word *Group* in the Layers panel, type **Spirals**, and press
Return. Press V to select the Move tool and drag to center the spirals
on the canvas. Both spirals move because you are moving the group.

LINKING LAYERS

Multiple layers can be linked together with the link icon at the bottom of the Layers panel. Linked layers are transformed together like multiple selected layers. Linked layers remain linked until you unlink them. (Linking became less important once the ability to select multiple layers was added to Photoshop in CS2.)

9. Press Opt+[to select the Reverse Spiral layer within the Spirals group. Choose Image ➢ Adjustments ➢ Hue/Saturation. Drag the Hue slider to -50 and click OK (see Figure 8.10).

FIGURE 8.10 Color-shifting the Reverse Spiral layer

10. Select the Spirals group and press Cmd+E so you can see how everything in the group merges into one layer. Choose Layer ➢ Flatten Image and click OK when asked whether you want to discard hidden layers. You are left with only a Background layer.

Blending Layers

Certification Objective

Photoshop has a plethora of blend modes offering you many options for compositing images together other than the obvious method of layer opacity. There is also a lesser-known way to blend layers called Blend If that you'll explore in this section.

All this talk reminds me of the hilarious "Will It Blend?" marketing campaign for the Blendtec blender (see www.willitblend.com). With Photoshop, the answer is a definitive, "Yes!" In the following steps you will place two images in one document and experiment with many different methods of blending the two images together.

1. Go to the book's Downloads page at www.sybex.com/go /photoshopessentials, browse to Chapter 8, and download the sample files. Open both Masculine.psd and Feminine.psd; you saw these images in Chapter 1 in the section "Learning Composition Principles." The masculine image is linear, implying strength, logic, efficiency, and mechanism. Diagonal lines imply motion toward a goal. The feminine image of the rose is soft and curvilinear with subtle tonality. There should be alchemy in the blending of these two archetypes. Figure 8.11 shows both images.

PHOTO COURTESY OF ISTOCKPHOTO, ©TOMOGRAF, IMAGE #4823532

PHOTO COURTESY OF ISTOCKPHOTO, ©KEVIN DAVIDSON, IMAGE #12076591

FIGURE 8.11 Masculine.psd (top) and Feminine.psd (bottom) images

2. Choose Window ➢ Arrange ➢ Float All In Windows if they are not already floating.

3. Press V to select the Move tool. Hold Shift and drag the Masculine image into the Feminine image. Close `Masculine.psd` without saving and then save `Feminine.psd` as `Blending.psd`.

4. In the Layers panel, slowly decrease the opacity of Layer 1 by dragging over the word *Opacity* toward the left. You will progressively see more of the rose. Press 0 to restore the opacity of Layer 1 to 100%. Opacity is the simplest type of blend.

5. Open the blend mode drop-down in the Layers panel. Blend modes are separated into groups in the menu by horizontal lines (see Figure 8.12).

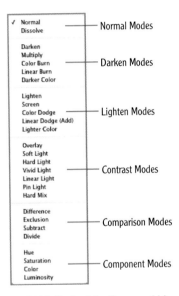

FIGURE 8.12 Groups of blend modes

ABOUT PHOTOSHOP'S BLEND MODES

Here are brief descriptions of the blend modes.

Normal modes   Normal mode is used by default, so it's the most commonly used blend mode. I've never seen anyone use Dissolve mode. (Perhaps it is grouped with Normal because opposites attract?) Layer groups (folder icons in the Layers panel) also have a Pass-Through blend mode appearing with the normal modes.

You'll learn about Pass-Through in Chapter 11, "Adjusting and Filtering."

(Continues)

ABOUT PHOTOSHOP'S BLEND MODES *(Continued)*

Darken modes   As the name suggests, this group of blend modes makes images darker by dropping out the highlights. Multiply is the most popular.

Lighten modes   These modes drop out shadows, thereby making the blend appear lighter. The most commonly used blend mode in this group is Screen.

Contrast modes   These modes drop out some of the mid-tones, so the image appears to have more contrast. Overlay is the most common mode in this group, along with Soft Light (shines a diffused light on the image), and Hard Light (shines a harsh spotlight on the image).

Comparison modes   These modes, such as Difference, do radical things to images with Boolean logic and are not often used except for special effects.

Component modes   These modes allow you to blend specific image channels such as color or luminosity in Lab color mode. Color and luminosity are the most commonly used component modes. They can do things as diverse as colorizing a black-and-white photo or sharpening an image's luminosity only.

6. Hold Shift and press the = key. Each time you do this, you select the next blend mode. Continue pressing these shortcut keys until you get to Color Burn. (The result is shown in Figure 8.13).

FIGURE 8.13 Blending Layer 1 with Color Burn

7. Select Lighten, Overlay, and Subtract (see Figure 8.14). Each blend mode presents different aesthetic qualities.

FIGURE 8.14 Experimenting with the following blend modes: Lighten (top), Overlay (middle), and Subtract (bottom)

8. Chose Layer ➤ Layer Style ➤ Blending Options. Open the blend mode drop-down in the Layer Style dialog box and select Normal. Open the Blend If drop-down and select Blue. Drag the This Layer highlight slider (white slider on the right) to the left until it reads 182. Hold Opt and drag the left half of this slider farther to the left until it reads 53 (see Figure 8.15). You are now blending the blue highlights of Layer 1 with the Background layer. Splitting the one slider into two parts creates a gradient that ramps up until it is fully blended. Click OK.

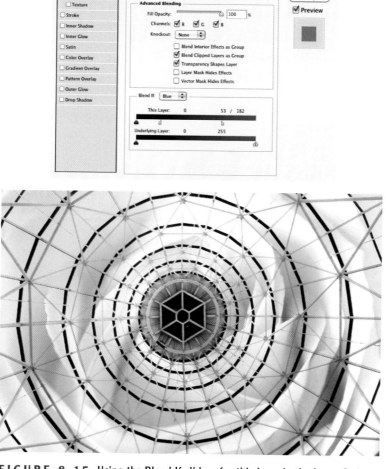

FIGURE 8.15 Using the Blend If sliders for this layer in the Layer Style dialog box (top) and the resulting image (bottom)

9. Press Cmd+Z to undo. Double-click just to the right of the name Layer 1 to reopen the Layer Style dialog box. You can blend the underlying layer with Layer 1 in much the same way you did in the previous step. Drag the highlight slider for the underlying layer to the left until it reads 218. Hold Opt and drag the left half of the highlight slider to the left until it reads 208 (see Figure 8.16). Click OK.

10. Press Cmd+W and press D to close the window without saving.

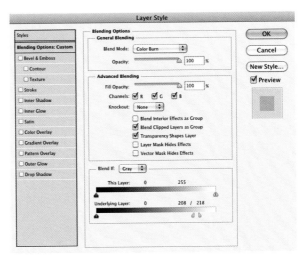

FIGURE 8.16 Using the Blend If underlying layer slider (top) to produce the resulting image (bottom)

Using Masks

Certification
Objective

You've seen how to use the mysterious Blend If controls to blend two images globally using various blend modes and according to tonal range. You might be pleased to use a more direct method called layer masks. As the name suggests, masks allow you to hide pixels. Just which pixels you mask is up to you to indicate by either painting or drawing. In the following steps you will explore pixel, vector, and clipping masks.

1. Reopen the Blending.psd file you saved in the previous section or go to the book's Downloads page at www.sybex.com/go /photoshopessentials, browse to Chapter 8, download the sample files, and open Blending.psd.

2. Click the Add Layer Mask icon at the bottom of the Layers panel. Layer 1 now has an additional thumbnail representing the pixel layer mask. The black corners framing the thumbnail indicate that the layer mask is selected by default (see Figure 8.17).

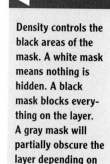

Density controls the black areas of the mask. A white mask means nothing is hidden. A black mask blocks everything on the layer. A gray mask will partially obscure the layer depending on its tonal value.

FIGURE 8.17 Creating a pixel layer mask

3. Press B to select the Brush tool. Select a medium round brush with 50% hardness from the brush picker drop-down on the options bar. Press X to exchange foreground and background colors so that black is in the foreground. Paint over the central part of the dome image to mask these pixels and reveal the rose on the Background layer. Open the Masks panel and drag the Feather slider to 20 px. Pixel masks allow you to create soft edges (see Figure 8.18).

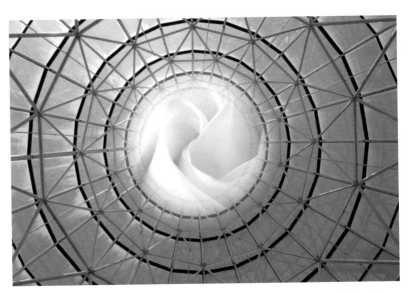

FIGURE 8.18 Painting in black on a pixel mask reveals the underlying layer; feathering softens the transition.

4. Click the link icon in between the layer thumbnail and the pixel mask thumbnail to unlink the mask from the layer. Press V to select the Move tool. Put the cursor on the canvas and drag the mask. The portion of the Background layer that is revealed moves and you can dynamically understand what the mask is doing. The black spot you painted on the pixel thumbnail moves with the cursor.

> **Applied masks permanently remove pixels from their associated layers.**

5. Choose Image Duplicate and click OK to accept the default name in the Duplicate Image dialog box. Drag the pixel mask thumbnail into the Trash icon at the bottom of the Layers panel. When prompted whether to apply the layer mask to the layer before removing, choose Delete.

6. Hold Cmd and click the same icon you clicked in step 2. Now this icon's tooltip reads Add Vector Mask. A similar white thumbnail appears linked to the layer thumbnail, but this is a different kind of mask that you must draw rather than paint.

> **Holding Opt when creating a mask creates a black pixel mask that hides everything.**

7. Select the Ellipse tool. Make sure that Path mode is selected from the first drop-down on the options bar. Start dragging from the center of the image and then hold Shift+Opt so that the shape will be a circle coming from the center. Release the mouse button when you have framed the central part of the dome image.

8. Press A to select the Path Selection tool. Click the circle you drew in the previous step. Select Subtract Front Shape from the Path Operations menu on the options bar and witness the mask reverse. Select Combine Shapes to have it flip back again (see Figure 8.19). Vector masks provide a clean crisp edge.

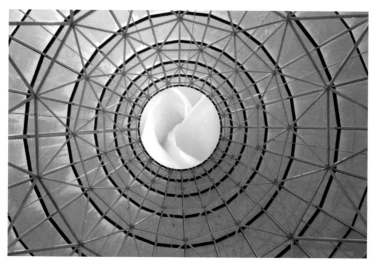

FIGURE 8.19 Toggling the mode of a shape on a vector mask reverses the effect: Subtract Front Shape mode (top) and Combine Shapes mode (bottom).

9. Switch to the duplicate image you created in step 5 that still contains the pixel mask. Open the Adjustments panel and click the Hue/Saturation icon. In the Properties panel, select Colorize and drag the Saturation slider to 69. The entire image is saturated in red because adjustment layers normally affect all the layers below them in the stack. Click the first icon on the left at the bottom of the Properties panel (see Figure 8.20). The adjustment layer is indented in the Layers panel, clipping to Layer 1, so that only this layer is tinted red. Clipped layers affect the pixels on the underlined layer only.

FIGURE 8.20 Adding an adjustment layer that clips to Layer 1

10. Save your work as Clipped and Masked.psd. This file is provided on the book's website for your convenience. Figure 8.21 shows the result.

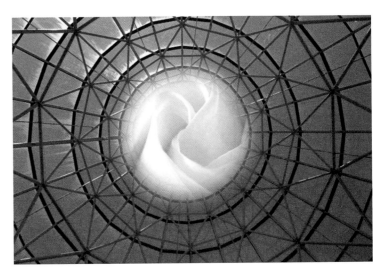

FIGURE 8.21 A red adjustment layer is clipped to Layer 1, which itself has a pixel mask revealing the white rose.

THE ESSENTIALS AND BEYOND

From understanding layers in general to managing and blending layers and working with pixel, vector, and clipping masks, you have learned all the skills you will need to work effectively with layers and masks.

ADDITIONAL EXERCISE

Add both a pixel mask and a vector mask to the Blending.psd file you created in this chapter. Give the pixel mask a feathered edge to contrast with the vector mask that will always appear clean and crisp.

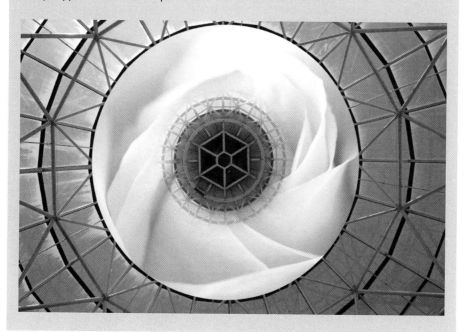

CHAPTER 9

Using Layer Styles and Comps

Layer styles allow you to manage layer effects and layer-blending options through a dialog-box-based interface. Layer effects offer you tremendous creative possibilities, and everyone from graphic and web designers to illustrators and digital artists use them every day. Layer comps can record all the layers' styles, positions, and visibility settings; you'll learn to use comps to explore design variations. In this chapter, you will re-create a piece of my digital art from a line drawing and in the process explore layer effects, styles, and comps.

▶ **Applying layer effects**

▶ **Working with layer styles**

▶ **Using layer comps**

Applying Layer Effects

Certification
Objective

Photoshop has a dozen layer effects, including various shadows, glows, and overlays plus bevel and emboss, satin, and stroke. You will learn to use each of these effects by creating a series of layers and layer groups in the following exercise.

1. Go to the book's Downloads page at www.sybex.com/go /photoshopessentials, browse to Chapter 9, download the sample files, and open Line-Drawing.png. Figure 9.1 shows this drawing.

2. The image is currently in grayscale color mode. You will need to change the mode in order to create layer effects in color. Choose Image ➢ Mode ➢ RGB Color.

3. Save the file as Digital-Art.psd and leave the file open as you work through the remainder of this exercise.

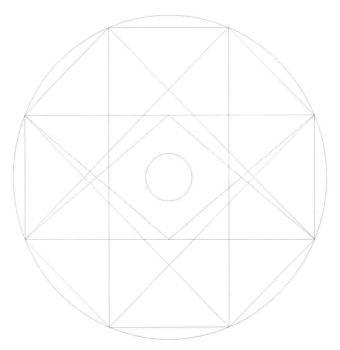

FIGURE 9.1 Line drawing you will enhance with layer effects

Enhancing Drawings with Layer Effects

If you are interested in more advanced techniques for enhancing drawings with layer effects, please refer to my book *Enhancing Architectural Drawings and Models with Photoshop* (Sybex, 2010).

Octagram Layer

Layer effects affect pixels on the layer to which they are assigned. It doesn't matter what color the pixels are, it's where they are on the layer that's important. In this exercise, you will use the Paint Bucket tool to fill in pixels between the lines of the sample file. In the following steps you will fill specific bounded areas with black and then change their color with the Color Overlay effect. You will also create shadows within each bounded area using the Inner Shadow effect.

Digital-Art.psd is also available on the book's Downloads page.

1. Continue using Digital-Art.psd. Create a new layer by pressing Shift+Cmd+N, type **Octagram** in the New Layer dialog box, and click OK.

2. Press D to set the default colors so black is in the foreground.

3. Select the Paint Bucket tool and set the Source For Fill Area drop-down to Foreground. Mode should be left as the default Normal and Opacity should be at 100%. Set Tolerance to 0 because this is a line drawing (in a photograph, you might want to use a higher tolerance setting so the paint would fill more than one color). Select Anti-alias, Contiguous, and All Layers so that you can fill in between the lines of the underlying layer.

4. Click inside the bounded areas, filling each with black to match Figure 9.2.

◄

The fill goes on the Octagram layer, not the Background layer.

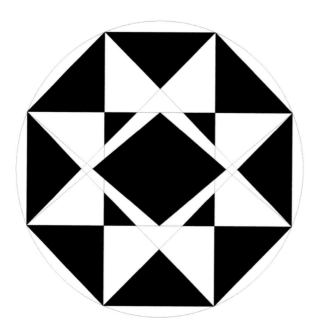

FIGURE 9.2 Use the paint bucket to fill in areas as shown

5. Choose Layer ➢ Layer Style ➢ Color Overlay. Click the color swatch in the Layer Style dialog box that appears, type **555555** in the # text box (# indicates hex color), and click OK to close the Select Overlay color picker. One advantage to setting the fill color with the Color Overlay effect is that you can change your mind at a later date and/or explore different options using Layer Comps, which you'll learn more about in the section "Using Layer Comps" later in this chapter. Figure 9.3 shows the Layer Style dialog box displaying the Color Overlay effect page. Click OK to close the Layer Style dialog box.

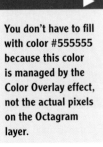

Drag the Layer Style dialog box out of the middle of the screen so you can see the design on the canvas.

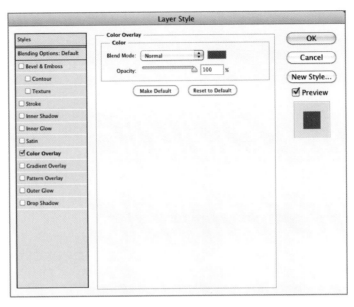

FIGURE 9.3 Applying a Color Overlay effect in the Layer Style dialog box

6. Toggle off the Background layer containing the black line drawing and the white background pixels. The areas you filled went inside the lines by one pixel. Hold the Cmd key and click the Octagram layer thumbnail to select all the pixels on this layer.

7. Choose Select ➢ Modify ➢ Expand. Type **1** in the Expand Selection dialog box and click OK.

8. Choose Edit ➢ Fill, select Black from the Use drop-down in the Fill dialog box, and click OK. Press Cmd+D to deselect all.

You don't have to fill with color #555555 because this color is managed by the Color Overlay effect, not the actual pixels on the Octagram layer.

9. Double-click just to the right of the word *Octagram* in the Layers panel. (This is a shortcut to open the Layer Style dialog box.) Select the words *Inner Shadow* (rather than their check box) to simultaneously enable the effect and switch to the effect's page within the Layer Style dialog box. Drag the Distance slider to 15 px and the Size slider to 35 px. Select Use Global Light and set the angle by dragging the circular control to 123° (see Figure 9.4). Click OK.

10. Save the file as Digital-Art-1.psd and leave it open as you work through the remainder of this exercise. Figure 9.5 shows the Octagram layer's Color Overlay and Inner Shadow effects. The inner shadow makes it seem like the affected areas are cut into the canvas.

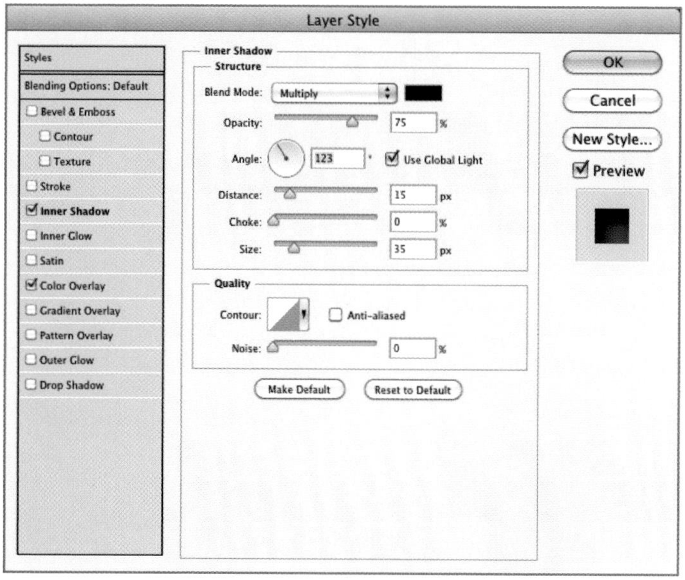

FIGURE 9.4 Creating an Inner Shadow effect

FIGURE 9.5 Color Overlay and Inner Shadow Effects on
the Octagram layer

Rays Layer

In the following steps you will create and fill a Rays layer and apply Gradient Overlay, Inner Glow, and Outer Glow effects.

1. Continue using Digital-Art-1.psd. Create a new layer by clicking the Create A New Layer icon ▣ at the bottom of the Layers panel. Double-click the name Layer 1, type **Rays**, and press Enter.

2. Toggle off the Octagram layer and toggle on the Background layer. Press G to select the Paint Bucket tool. Click within each of the rays of the star (a total of eight clicks) as shown in Figure 9.6.

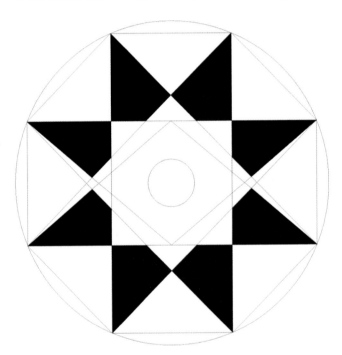

FIGURE 9.6 Filling in the rays with black pixels

3. Toggle off the Background layer and Cmd+click the thumbnail of the Rays layer to select the black pixels you created in the previous step.

4. Choose Select ➤ Modify ➤ Expand and click OK in the Expand Selection dialog box to accept the value of 1 pixel. Press Opt+Delete to fill the selection with the foreground color (black) and Cmd+D to deselect all.

5. Position the cursor over the Octagram layer's eye icon 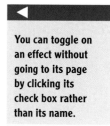 and drag down the column to also toggle on the Background layer in one fluid motion.

6. Click the Add A Layer Style icon ▣ at the bottom of the Layers panel and select Gradient Overlay from the menu that pops up. Open the gradient picker in the Layer Style dialog box and select the Orange, Yellow, Orange gradient. Change the Style drop-down to Radial (see Figure 9.7).

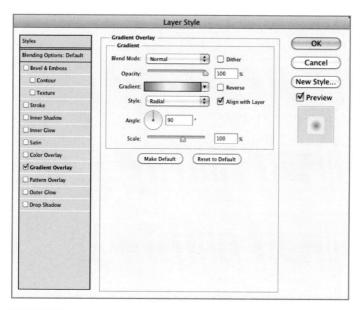

FIGURE 9.7 Creating a Gradient Overlay layer effect

7. Click the words *Inner Glow* to toggle on this effect and switch to its page within the Layer Style dialog box. Click the color swatch in the Structure category, pick pure white, and click OK to close the color picker. Select Precise from the Technique drop-down. Drag the Size slider to 45 px (see Figure 9.8).

8. Click the words *Outer Glow* to toggle on this effect and switch to its page. Click the color swatch in the Structure category, pick pure white, and click OK to close the color picker. Drag the Size slider to 30 px (see Figure 9.9). Click OK.

> You can toggle on an effect without going to its page by clicking its check box rather than its name.

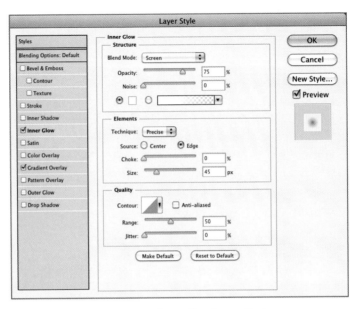

FIGURE 9.8 Creating an Inner Glow layer effect

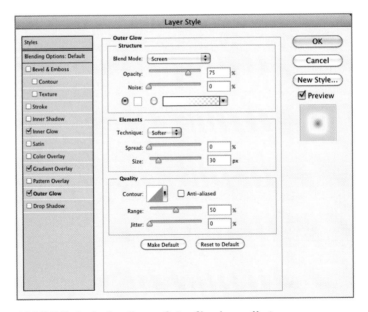

FIGURE 9.9 Creating an Outer Glow layer effect

9. Press Cmd+[to move the Rays layer below Octagram. The Outer Glow effect creates pixels outside the boundaries of the pixels on the Rays layer. These pixels are now obscured by the pixels on the Octagram layer. Press Cmd+] to move Rays back above Octagram so the outer glow is visible.

10. Save the file as Digital-Art-2.psd and leave it open as you work through the remainder of this exercise. Figure 9.10 shows the Rays layer's inner and outer glows highlighting the Gradient Overlay effect.

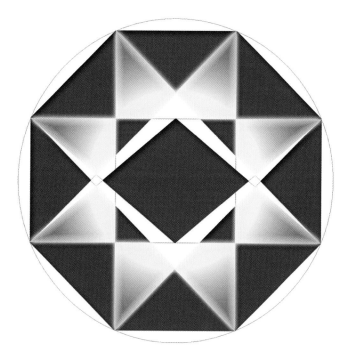

FIGURE 9.10 Inner Glow, Outer Glow, and Gradient Overlay effects on the Rays layer

Outer and Circle Layers

In the following steps you will create and fill the Outer layer and apply Inner Glow and Stroke effects. In addition, you will draw a large circle and create a drop shadow, giving dimensionality to the entire design.

1. Continue using Digital-Art-2.psd. Create a new layer by clicking the Create A New Layer icon at the bottom of the Layers panel. Double click the name Layer 1, type **Outer**, and press Enter.

2. Toggle off the Rays layer because its Outer Glow effect creates pixels that overlap the eight outer areas you need to fill in this section.

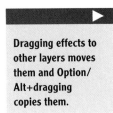

3. Press G to select the Paint Bucket tool. Click inside each of the eight outer areas to fill them with black.

4. Hold down the Opt key, then drag the Inner Glow effect from the Rays layer and drop it on the Outer layer (see Figure 9.11).

Dragging effects to other layers moves them and Option/ Alt+dragging copies them.

FIGURE 9.11 Copying the Inner Glow effect to the Outer layer

The parameters of copied layer styles are not connected to their original styles.

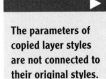

5. Double-click the words *Inner Glow* under the Outer layer to open the Layer Style dialog box to that page. Select the Center radio button and drag the Size slider to 35 px. Click OK.

6. Press Cmd+R to toggle on the rulers. Right-click a ruler and choose Percent if it is not already selected. Press V for the Move tool and drag out horizontal and vertical guides to 50% on the ruler.

7. Select the Ellipse tool and Shape tool mode on the options bar. Position the cursor at the intersection of the two guides and start

dragging out an ellipse. Hold down Shift+Opt to create a circle from the center and keep dragging until the circle perfectly covers the entire design. You should be left with a large black circle that obscures everything.

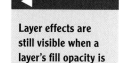

8. Double-click the term *Shape 1* and rename it **Circle**. Double-click to the right of the word *Circle* in the Layers panel to open the Layer Style dialog box on the Blending Options page. Drag the Fill Opacity slider to 0%. The black circle disappears.

Layer effects are still visible when a layer's fill opacity is set to 0%.

9. Click the words *Drop Shadow* in the Layer Style dialog box. Drag the Distance slider to 25 px and the Size slider to 32 px (see Figure 9.12). Click OK.

Drop shadows create pixels beyond the fill defining the effect.

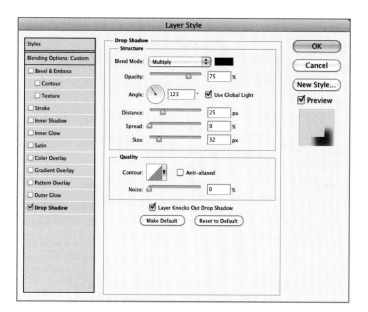

FIGURE 9.12 Creating a Drop Shadow layer effect

10. Press Cmd+R to toggle off the rulers. Toggle on the Rays layer. Save the file as `Digital-Art-3.psd` and leave it open as you work through the remainder of this exercise. Figure 9.13 shows the Circle layer's drop shadow in the lower right (opposite the light source at 123°).

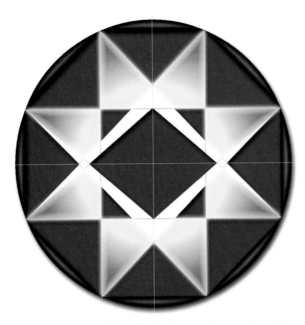

FIGURE 9.13 Drop Shadow layer effect created with a solid circle having no fill opacity

Circled Dot Layer Group

In the following steps you will create a layer group containing the central "circled dot" part of the design. In the process you will use the Bevel and Emboss layer effect as well as many of the effects you've already used.

Digital-Art-3
.psd is also avail-
able on the book's
Downloads page.

1. Continue using Digital-Art-3.psd. Double-click the word *Background* in the Layers panel, type **Linework** in the New Layer dialog box, and click OK. Drag the Linework layer to the top of the layer stack and change its blend mode to Multiply so you can see the black lines above all the other layers.

2. Select the Ellipse tool and Path tool mode on the options bar. Position the cursor at the intersection of the guides, hold down Shift+Opt, and drag out a circle path the same size as the circle on the Linework layer.

3. Press Shift+Cmd+N, type **Ring** in the New Layer dialog box, and click OK. Press B for the Brush tool and press [or] until the brush size is 10 px. Click the Stroke Path With Brush icon at the bottom of the Paths panel. Press the Delete key to get rid of the work path.

4. Click the Add A Layer Style icon at the bottom of the Layers panel, choose Bevel & Emboss from the context menu, and drag the Size

slider to 5 px (see Figure 9.14). The ring has highlights that make it appear almost three-dimensional.

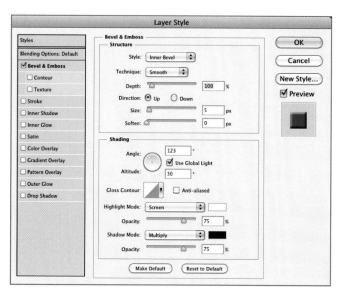

FIGURE 9.14 Creating a Bevel & Emboss layer effect

5. Click the words *Outer Glow* to enable this effect. Drag the Spread slider to 10% and the Size slider to 45 px. (see Figure 9.15). Click OK to close the Layer Style dialog box.

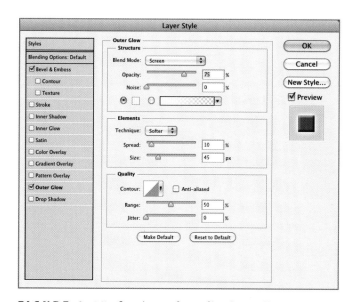

FIGURE 9.15 Creating an Outer Glow layer effect

6. Select the Ellipse tool, choose Shape tool mode, and drag out a small circle to act as a dot within the ring. Press Cmd+; to toggle off the guides. Change the name of layer Shape 1 to **Dot**.

7. Select the Add A Layer Style icon ![fx] at the bottom of the Layers panel and choose Stroke from the context menu. Click the color swatch in the Layer Style dialog box and click an orange hue on the Rays layer in the canvas. Click OK to close the color picker. Drag the Size slider to 4 px (see Figure 9.16).

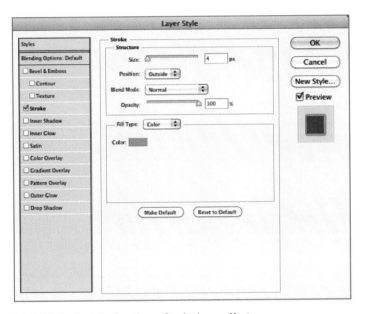

FIGURE 9.16 Creating a Stroke layer effect

8. Select Bevel & Emboss in the Layer Style dialog box and drag the Size slider to 27 px. Select Outer Glow and drag Noise to 30% and Size to 100 px. Click OK to close the Layer Style dialog box.

9. Shift+select the Ring and Dot layers. Press Cmd+G to create a layer group containing the selected layers. Change the name of Group 1 to **Circled Dot** (see Figure 9.17).

10. Save the file as `Digital-Art-4.psd` and leave it open as you work through the remainder of this exercise. Figure 9.18 shows the Circled Dot layer group in the center of the canvas.

FIGURE 9.17 Creating a layer group containing the Ring and Dot layers

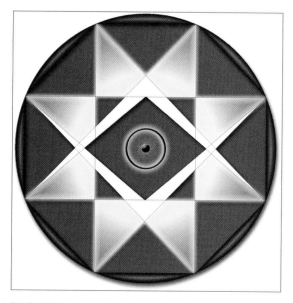

FIGURE 9.18 The Circled Dot layer group uses many effects to enhance two circles.

Dividers Layer

The Dividers layer is the most complex you will create in this exercise, utilizing multiple layer effects. In the following steps you will simulate gold using the Pattern Overlay, Color Overlay, Satin, Bevel & Emboss, and Contour layer effects.

Digital-Art-4 .psd is also available on the book's Downloads page.

1. Continue using Digital-Art-4.psd. Select the Linework layer. Right-click the eye icon 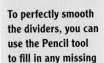 on the Linework layer and choose Show/Hide All Other Layers from the context menu. Press Shift+Cmd+N, type **Dividers** in the New Layer dialog box, and click OK.

2. Select the Paint Bucket tool and click nine points in between the lines defining the upper divider (see Figure 9.19).

To perfectly smooth the dividers, you can use the Pencil tool to fill in any missing pixels.

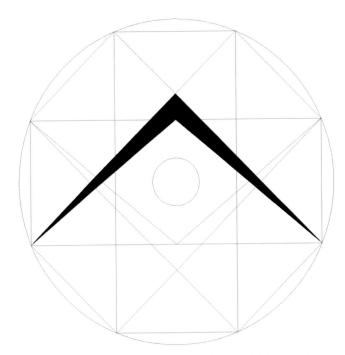

FIGURE 9.19 Filling the Dividers layer with black pixels in between the lines

3. Toggle off the Linework layer. Cmd+click the Dividers layer thumbnail to select everything on this layer. Choose Select ➢ Modify ➢ Expand and click OK in the Expand Selection dialog box to accept the value of 1 pixel. Press Opt+Delete to fill the selection with the foreground color (black) and Cmd+D to deselect all.

4. Right-click the eye icon 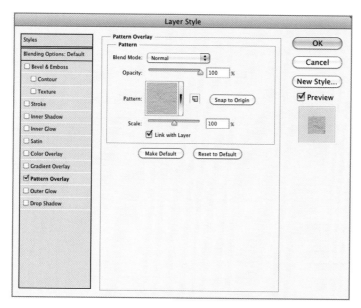 on the Dividers layer and choose Show/ Hide All Other Layers from the context menu. Double-click just to the right of the word *Dividers* in the Layers panel to open the Layer Style dialog box.

5. Select Pattern Overlay and open the pattern picker. Open the menu on the pattern picker, select Colored Paper, and click OK when asked whether you want to replace the current patterns. Select Buff Textured (see Figure 9.20).

FIGURE 9.20 Selecting a specific pattern from a pattern library in the Pattern Overlay layer effect

6. We don't want the color from this texture, just the pattern. Set Blend Mode to Luminosity and drag the Opacity slider to 70%. Select Color

Overlay and click the color swatch. Type **ffde00** in the # text box and click OK to close the color picker. Drag the Opacity slider of the Color Overlay effect to 75%.

7. Select Bevel & Emboss. Set Technique to Chisel Hard, Depth to 250%, Size to 75 px, Soften to 10 px, and Altitude to 60°. Select Rounded Slope as the Cove – Deep Contour (names are in tooltips). Set Highlight Mode to Linear Dodge (Add) with color **fffbd9** and 100% opacity. Set Shadow Mode to Linear Burn with color **2a2716** and 75% opacity (see Figure 9.21).

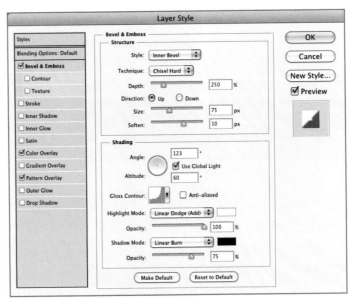

FIGURE 9.21 Configuring Bevel & Emboss

 8. Select the Contour sub-effect, which is indented under Bevel & Emboss in the Layer Style dialog box. Select Half Round from the contour picker and select Anti-Alias.

9. To deepen the overall effect, select Satin. Click the color swatch, type **a99b50** in the # text box, and click OK to close the color picker. Set Angle to 9°, Distance to 22 px, and Size to 24 px. Select Gaussian Slope and deselect Invert if it is already selected.

10. Satin has left the gold a bit too dark. Select Color Overlay, drag the Opacity slider up to 100%, and change the Blend Mode setting to Overlay. Click OK to close the Layer Style dialog box.

11. Save the file as `Digital-Art-5.psd` and leave it open as you work through the remainder of this exercise. Figure 9.22 shows the Dividers layer looking much like gold.

CONVERTING LAYER EFFECTS TO LAYERS

Layer effects can be converted to layers that become members of a clipping group. A clipping group is a special arrangement where one or more layers are clipped (masked) by the pixels on a base layer. To do this, right-click the word *Effects* under the Dividers layer and choose Create Layers from the context menu. Warning: This action is not reversible and you will lose the ability to edit the effects in the Layer Style dialog box. In some cases you might want to do this to go beyond what is possible with layer effects (for example, reorienting a pattern). The individual layer effects are transformed into raster layers that are clipped by the base Dividers layer.

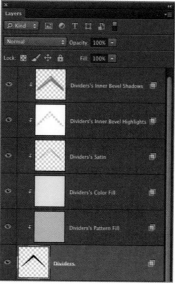

FIGURE 9.22 Creating gold dividers with multiple layer effects

Working with Layer Styles

Layer Styles can also be applied to text layers.

Digital-Art-5 .psd is also available on the book's Downloads page.

Because you went to a lot of trouble creating the effects that produced the gold dividers in the previous section, you'll be pleased to know all this work can be easily reused with layer styles. Layer styles store everything that you have configured in the Layer Style dialog box, including layer effects and/or layer blending options. In the following steps you will save a layer style, apply it to another layer, change some of its parameters, and save it as another layer style.

1. Continue using Digital-Art-5.psd. Perform the same actions that you did in step 1 in the section "Dividers Layer" earlier in this chapter, but name the layer **Lower Dividers**.

2. On the Lower Dividers layer, perform the tasks described in steps 2 and 3 of the previous section, "Dividers Layer."

3. Right-click the eye icon  on the Lower Dividers layer and choose Show/Hide All Other Layers from the context menu.

4. Double-click the word *Effects* under the Dividers layer to open the Layer Style dialog box. Click the New Style button, type **Gold** in the Name box, and select Include Layer Effects. Click OK.

5. Open the Styles panel, and with the Lower Dividers layer selected, click the Gold style icon, which is the last icon in the list. The lower dividers now appear gold.

6. Double-click the words *Color Overlay* under the Lower Dividers layer. Change Blend Mode to Luminosity. Select Satin and change its Blend Mode setting to Luminosity also. Select Bevel & Emboss and click the color swatch for Highlight Mode. Drag the color picker to the upper-left corner to select color #ffffff (pure white) and click OK to close the color picker.

7. Click the New Style button, type **Silver** in the Name box, select Include Layer Effects, and click OK. Click OK once more to close the Layer Style dialog box.

8. Toggle off the Linework layer. Click the Create New Fill Or Adjustment Layer icon at the bottom of the Layers panel and select Solid Color. Type 808080 in the # text box in the color text box and click OK. Change the name of Color Fill 1 to **Backdrop**. Drag the Backdrop layer to the bottom of the layer stack.

9. Save the file as Digital-Art-6.psd and leave it open for work in the next section. Figure 9.23 shows the completed artwork.

FIGURE 9.23 Completed artwork made entirely with layer effects and layer styles

Using Layer Comps

Layer comps can store a series of layers' visibility settings (whether on or off), positions, and/or layer styles. This makes layer comps great for exploring design variations. In the following steps you will store a layer comp of the design as it is, adjust a number of layer style parameters, and then save another layer style. You'll be able to toggle between comps with a single click. This can be just the ticket for making onscreen presentations.

1. Continue using `Digital-Art-6.psd`. Choose Window ➤ Layer Comps.

2. Click the Create New Layer Comp icon ▣ at the bottom of the Layer Comps panel. Deselect Visibility and Position and select Appearance (Layer Style) in the New Layer Comp dialog box. Click OK to accept the default name Layer Comp 1.

3. Double-click the word *Effects* under the Rays layer to open the Layer Style dialog box. Click the New Style button, type **Sun** in the New Style dialog box, and click OK. Click OK again to close the Layer Style dialog box.

4. Drag the word *Effects* from the Octagram layer to the Rays layer to overwrite the effects that you saved in the previous step as a style.

5. Select the Octagram layer in the Layers panel and click the Sun style in the Styles panel to assign it to this layer.

6. Toggle off all the layer effects under the Lower Dividers layer by clicking the eye icon next to the word *Effects* (not the layer's eye icon). Figure 9.24 shows the result.

7. Click the Create New Layer Comp icon ▣ at the bottom of the Layer Comps panel. Click OK to accept the default name Layer Comp 2.

8. Click the Layer Comp icon next to Layer Comp 1 in the Layer Comps panel. The canvas changes back to the way it was when you saved Layer Comp 1 in step 2.

9. Click the Layer Comp icon next to Layer Comp 2 in the Layer Comps panel. The canvas changes to the way it was in step 7. You can switch among any number of layer comps in this way to explore design alternatives.

10. Save the file as `Digital-Art-7.psd`.

◀

`Digital-Art-7`
`.psd` is also available on the book's download page.

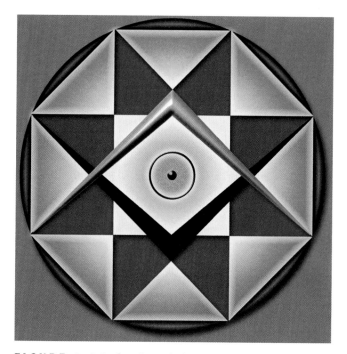

FIGURE 9.24 Creating a design alternative by altering layer styles

THE ESSENTIALS AND BEYOND

You have learned how to create all of the layer effects in the exercise running throughout this chapter. You now have a taste of the creative power that layer effects offer. You have created and applied layer styles and layer comps and should now be able to explore design alternatives in an efficient manner.

(Continues)

THE ESSENTIALS AND BEYOND *(Continued)*

ADDITIONAL EXERCISE

Open the file Digital-Art-7.psd that you created, or download the file of the same name from the book's Downloads page. Significantly alter layer effects in the file and then save your changes as Layer Comp 3. Choose File ➢ Scripts ➢ Layer Comps To Files and output three JPEG images. This workflow is the most efficient way to share design alternatives by email.

Layer Comps To Files	
Destination:	
Desktop Browse...	Run
File Name Prefix:	Cancel
Digital-Art	
☐ Selected Layer Comps Only	
┌ **File Type:**	
JPEG ▼	
☐ Include ICC Profile	
┌ JPEG Options:	
Quality: 8	

Please specify the format and location for saving each layer comp as a file.

CHAPTER 10

Transforming Paths, Layers, and Smart Objects

Transforming layers and paths is a fundamental graphic design skill. Photoshop's tools for transformation are simple yet quite powerful once you learn how to use them to position, orient, scale, align, distribute, and deform layers and paths. You'll also learn how to encapsulate layers in Smart Objects and transform them all together in a nondestructive container.

▶ **Using rulers and guides**

▶ **Moving, aligning, and distributing**

▶ **Free transforming**

▶ **Deforming**

▶ **Transforming smart objects**

Using Rulers and Guides

Certification Objective

Rulers and guides are aids that give you straight edges with which to align layers and paths. In the following exercise you will change the rulers' units, create horizontal and vertical guides, and reposition the origin point of the rulers to the guides' intersection point.

1. Create a new document by pressing Cmd+N. In the New dialog box, change the Width drop-down menu to pixels. Type 800 in Width text box, press Tab, and type 800 in the Height text box. Click OK.

2. Press Cmd+R to toggle on the rulers.

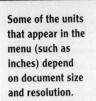

Some of the units that appear in the menu (such as inches) depend on document size and resolution.

3. Right-click either one of the rulers at the edges of the document window and choose Percent from the context menu that appears (see Figure 10.1).

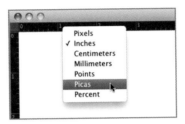

FIGURE 10.1 Changing the units of the rulers

4. Press M to select the Move tool. Position the cursor over the vertical ruler and drag to the right to pull out a vertical guide. Drop the guide when the mark on the *horizontal* ruler reads 50%. It will snap into place.

Press Cmd+; if you don't see the guide.

5. Position the cursor over the horizontal ruler and drag down to pull out a horizontal guide. Drop the guide when the mark on the *vertical* ruler reads 50%. The intersection of guides marks the center of the image.

CREATING AND REPOSITIONING GUIDES

Guides can be dragged out from the rulers with whatever tool you are working with, but you need to use the Move tool to reposition existing guides. Create as many guides as your design requires; eliminate unwanted guides by dragging them back to either edge.

You can also lock or clear guidelines by clicking View ➢ Lock Guides or Clear Guides.

6. Drag the origin point from point A to point B as shown in Figure 10.2. As the origin point snaps to the intersection of the guides, the center of the image becomes the new origin.

7. Save the file as Setup.psd and leave it open for work in the next section.

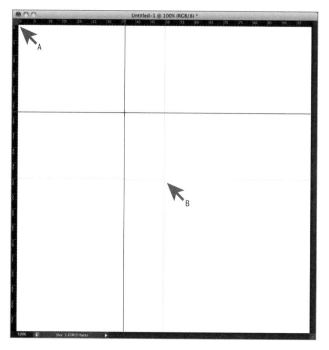

FIGURE 10.2 Drag the origin point of the rulers from A to B

THE RULER TOOL IS NOT THE RULERS

You can use the Ruler tool to measure distances and angles, but it is most useful for straightening crooked images. Here's how it works:

Select the Ruler tool (under the eyedropper icon) and drag out a line along an edge that is nearly horizontal or vertical. Click the Straighten button on the options bar. Voilà, you are left with a straightened image. The straightened image is cropped in the process and you'll lose more or less of the border, depending on how crooked the original image was.

PHOTO COURTESY OF ISTOCKPHOTO, ©MLENNY PHOTOGRAPHY, IMAGE #1000006

Moving, Aligning, and Distributing

Certification
Objective

Layers and paths can be repositioned, aligned, and distributed using the Move tool and/or Path Selection tool. In the following steps you will create a few basic shapes and experiment with moving, aligning, and distributing both layers and paths.

1. Open Setup.psd.

2. Select the Rectangle tool, Shape tool mode, red solid color fill, and no stroke on the options bar. Hold down the Shift key, and at an arbitrary location, drag out a square whose edge length measures 10% on the rulers.

3. Deselect the Rectangle 1 layer so that you can create another shape layer with a different color. Select the blue solid color fill on the options bar and drag out a rectangle with width and height proportions of 20% to 2%.

4. Press T to select the Text tool. Select Zapfino from the Font Family drop-down and type **100 pt** in the Font Size text box on the options bar. Click an arbitrary point on the canvas, type **Text**, and click the Commit Any Current Edits button on the options bar.

5. Press V to select the Move tool and select Auto-Select on the options bar. Drag each one of the objects to align with a guide. Figure 10.3 shows one possible result.

6. Choose View ➢ Show ➢ Smart Guides if this menu item is not already checked. Drag the red square so that its lower edge aligns with the lower edge of the text object; you will see a purple smart guide appear, indicating this alignment (see Figure 10.4).

7. Press A to select the Path Selection tool. Select the blue rectangle. Press Cmd+C and Cmd+V to copy and paste a path in place. Position the cursor inside the path and drag it off to the side to some arbitrary location; two blue rectangles are now visible on the canvas. Press Cmd+C and Cmd+V to make another copy. Drag the second copy off to the side. Figure 10.5 shows one possible result.

Setup.psd is also available on the book's Downloads page at www.sybex .com/go/photo shopessentials.

If the objects do not snap to align to the guides, choose View ➢ Snap to toggle on this feature.

Every object has six invisible smart guides you can snap to: top middle, bottom, left, center, and right. Go to View ➢ Snap To to snap guides to Guides, Grids, Layers, Slices, Pixels, Objects, or Document Bounds.

FIGURE 10.3 Aligning layers with the guides

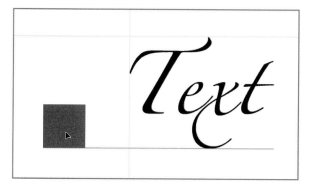

FIGURE 10.4 Using smart guides to align objects

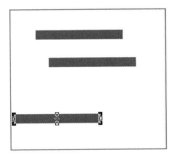

FIGURE 10.5 Copying paths on a shape layer

8. Drag a selection window around all three blue rectangles to select three paths. Open the Path Alignment menu on the options bar and select Left Edges (see Figure 10.6). All three rectangles line up horizontally, but there is still an arbitrary vertical distance between each rectangle.

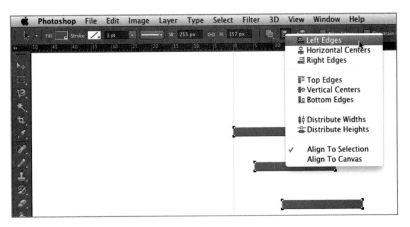

FIGURE 10.6 Alignment and distribution tools

You can combine subpaths into a single path with Merge Shape Components in the Path Operations menu on the options bar.

9. Select Distribute Heights from the Path Alignment menu on the options bar. The rectangles are distributed so there is an equal distance between them along the vertical axis.

10. Save your work as Move-Align-Distribute.psd. Press Ctrl+W to close the file.

Free Transforming

When you *free transform* layers, paths, and Smart Objects in Photoshop, you can change their position, orientation, and scale and/or deform them (change their shapes). In the following steps you will perform some free transformations on paths to create a logo design.

Certification
Objective

1. Open Setup.psd. Open the Swatches panel and select the red swatch to set the foreground color.

Setup.psd is
also available
on the book's
Downloads page.

2. Select the Rectangle tool and Shape tool mode, red solid color fill, and no stroke on the options bar. Hold down the Shift and Opt keys and drag out a square from the intersection of the guides whose edge length measures approximately 10% on the rulers.

3. Choose Edit ➢ Free Transform Path. Position the cursor outside the shape and drag up or down to rotate the square; hold down Shift as you drag to constrain rotation to 45 degree increments. Continue dragging until the square appears as a diamond (see Figure 10.7). Click Commit Transform (check mark icon) on the options bar.

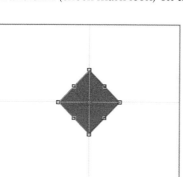

FIGURE 10.7 Rotating the box
45 degrees by Shift-dragging

4. Press Cmd+T to invoke Free Transform Path mode again. Position the cursor inside the shape and drag the diamond upward; hold down Shift to constrain the movement vertically until the horizontal axis of the diamond is approximately 20% from the top of the vertical ruler. Click Commit Transform.

Moving an object
with Free Transform
is different from
translating it with
the Move tool; you
can repeat displace-
ments only with free
transform.

5. Press A to select the Path Selection tool. Select the diamond shape, and press Cmd+C and Cmd+V to copy and paste the shape in place.

Press Cmd+T to enter Free Transform Path mode. Drag the reference point in the center of the diamond to the intersection of the guides; this point marks the center of the transformation (see Figure 10.8). Type 30 in the Set Rotation text box. Press Enter to commit the transform.

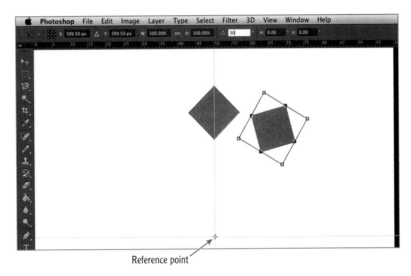

Reference point

FIGURE 10.8 Rotating a box about a user-specified center of rotation

6. Press Cmd+C and Cmd+V to make another copy. Choose Edit ➤ Transform Path ➤ Again. Press Cmd+C and Cmd+V to make yet another copy and press Shift+Cmd+T to transform again. Figure 10.9 shows the result.

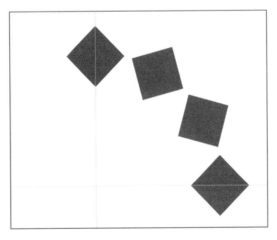

FIGURE 10.9 Transforming copies of the shape again and again

7. Double-click the top box, then hold Shift and select the next two boxes, leaving the fourth box unselected. Press Cmd+C and Cmd+V to make a copy of the three boxes in place. Drag the reference point at the center of the selection to the intersection of the guides and type **100%** in the Width box and **-100%** in the Height box. Figure 10.10 shows the result. Press Enter twice to exit Free Transform Path mode and to dismiss the paths.

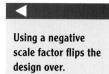

Using a negative scale factor flips the design over.

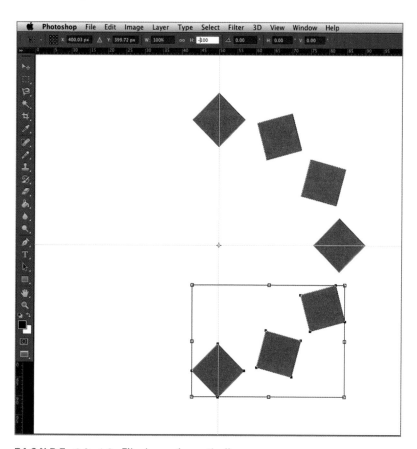

FIGURE 10.10 Flipping paths vertically

8. Drag a window around the five rightmost boxes (excluding the top and bottom boxes) to select them. Press Cmd+C, Cmd+V, and Cmd+T to duplicate the boxes and enter Free Transform Path mode. Drag the reference point to the intersection of the guides. Type **-100%** in the Width box and **100%** in the Height box and press Enter. Figure 10.11 shows the resulting symmetrical design. Deselect the Rectangle 1 layer.

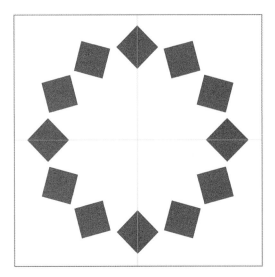

FIGURE 10.11 Symmetrical design created with
a variety of transformation techniques

9. Select the Custom Shape tool and then select green solid color fill.
Open the Custom Shape Picker drop-down, open the picker menu,
select Shapes, and click OK. Select the crescent moon icon, position
the cursor at the intersection of guides, hold down Shift+Opt, and
drag out a moon shape that is approximately 20% in height as measured along the vertical ruler (see Figure 10.12).

FIGURE 10.12 Drawing a custom shape at the
center of the design

10. Save your work as Design.psd. Leave the file open if you are continuing directly to the next section.

Deforming

You can use advanced free transform modes to deform paths by nonuniformly scaling, skewing, distorting, warping, and altering perspective. In the following steps you will experiment with each of these modes.

Certification
Objective

1. Open Design.psd or continue with the file you created in the previous section.

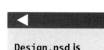

Design.psd is
also available
on the book's
Downloads page.

2. Select the Shape 1 layer containing the green moon custom shape. Press Cmd+T to enter Free Transform Path mode. Position the cursor outside the moon shape and drag until both points of the crescent point downward, about -118 degrees. Drag the moon so that its reference point is centered on the intersection of guides (see Figure 10.13). Press Enter.

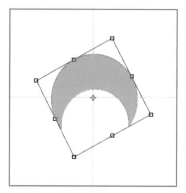

FIGURE 10.13 Rotating and moving the crescent shape

3. Press Cmd+T, hold Opt to scale symmetrically about the reference point, and drag the top middle handle of the transform controls upward until the Height value on the canvas reads approximately 150% (see Figure 10.14). Press Enter.

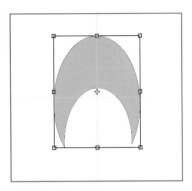

FIGURE 10.14 Nonuniformly scaling a path

Skew is a set of constraints placed on the handles of the transform controls.

4. Press Cmd+T and right click on the canvas. Choose Skew from the context menu. Drag the lower-right handle and you will see that you can only drag it left, right, up, or down. Right-click and choose Distort. Drag the lower-right handle and you will see that you can drag it in any direction. Distort releases all constraints. After experimenting with distortion, press Esc to cancel.

Perspective transforms opposite handles equally.

5. Press Cmd+T, right-click again, and choose Perspective. Drag the upper-right handle to the right and observe that the upper-left handle automatically moves to the left. Drag the lower-right handle to the left and see the lower-left handle move to the right (see Figure 10.15). Press Enter.

Use Edit ➢ Puppet Warp to modify the shape of select portions of graphic elements and images. You can also use Puppet Warp to move entire portions of an image, such as someone's arm or head in a photo.

FIGURE 10.15 Using the Perspective transformation mode

6. Save the file as Design-final.psd, but do not close it.

7. Open Flag.psd. Choose Window ➤ Arrange ➤ Float All In Windows.

8. Select the Design-final document window, hold Shift, and select the Rectangle 1 layer so that the Shape 1 and Rectangle 1 layers are both selected. Keep holding Shift and drag these layer thumbnails into the Flag document window.

9. Choose Edit ➤ Free Transform to scale both of these layers down to fit the flag. Select the Maintain Aspect Ratio button 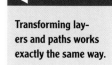 on the options bar, click in the Width box, hold Shift, and press the down arrow five times to reduce the scale uniformly to 50%. Press Enter.

Transforming layers and paths works exactly the same way.

10. Press Cmd+G to create a layer group containing the Shape 1 and Rectangle 1 layers. Change the blend mode of Group 1 to Color. The result is shown in Figure 10.16.

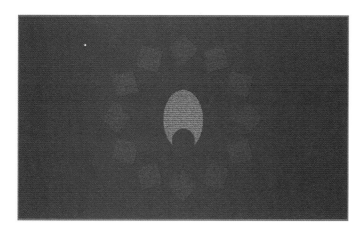

FIGURE 10.16 Blending a layer group by color

11. Hold Shift and select the Flag layer so that both Group 1 and Flag are selected. Press Cmd+E to merge the visible layers, which results in a single layer. Press Cmd+T and click the Warp toggle. 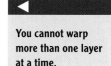 Open the Warp drop-down on the options bar, choose Flag, type 15 in the Bend text box, and press Enter. Press Cmd+; to hide the guides. Figure 10.17 shows the result.

You cannot warp more than one layer at a time.

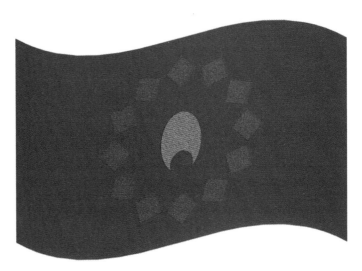

FIGURE 10.17 Warping with the flag deformation

12. Save as `Flag-final.psd`. Press Cmd+W to close this file but leave `Design-final.psd` open if you are continuing directly to the next section.

Transforming Smart Objects

Certification Objective

▶

You can use smart objects as templates for creating many Photoshop effects.

▶

`Design-final.psd` is also available on the book's Downloads page.

When you convert any number of layers into a smart object, they are placed into a container, if you will. You can transform this container as one layer. Transformations are applied to smart object layers in nondestructive (vector) fashion, so you don't damage image quality with each transformation as you do with raster layers. As the name suggests, using Smart Objects is the intelligent way to manage layers through multiple transformations because the sum total of transformations is applied all at once. In the following steps you will convert layers into a smart object, place it in another file, and deform the result.

1. Open `Design-final.psd` or continue with the file you created in the previous section.

2. Shift+select the Shape 1 and Rectangle 1 layers. Right-click one of the layer names and select Convert To Smart Object from the context menu that appears. Rename the resulting smart object **Design**.

3. Open `Flag-photo.psd` (see Figure 10.18). Open the Channels panel, hold down the Cmd key, and click the Alpha 1 thumbnail to load it as a selection.

PHOTO COURTESY OF ISTOCKPHOTO, ©BLACKRED, IMAGE #1620584

FIGURE 10.18 Blank
white flag photo

4. Open the Adjustments panel and select the Hue/Saturation icon. The selection automatically becomes a layer mask (switch to the Layers panel to see this). In the Properties panel, select Colorize and drag the Hue slider into the blue region at 239. Set Saturation to 50 and Lightness to -36 (see Figure 10.19).

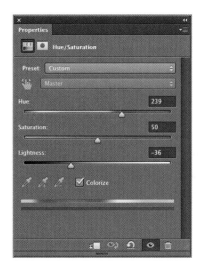

FIGURE 10.19 Colorizing the
white flag with a Hue/Saturation adjustment

5. Select the Design-final document window. Choose Window ➢ Arrange ➢ Float All In Windows if they are not already floating. Open the Layers panel and drag the Design smart object into the Flag-photo document window.

6. In the Layers panel, decrease the opacity of layer Design to 80% to make it blend better with the flag.

7. Press Cmd+T to transform the Design smart object layer. Click the Maintain Aspect Ratio icon ⊜ on the options bar. Position the cursor over the word *Width* on the options bar and drag to the left to reduce the scale of the design until it fits on the flag. Move the cursor inside the design and drag to reposition the design over the center of the flag.

8. Right-click in the canvas and select Warp from the shortcut menu. A grid appears over the object with dots at each of the outer intersections. Drag some of these dots to warp the grid and thus deform the contents of the smart object. Position the cursor inside the grid and drag to bend the grid until you are satisfied that the design looks like it belongs on the flag that is rippling in the wind (see Figure 10.20).

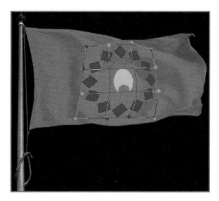

FIGURE 10.20 Warping the design to look like it is part of the flag

The .psb filename extension is automatically used for smart objects.

9. Double-click the Design layer thumbnail to open the contents of the smart object in another window. In the Shape 2.psb document window, double-click the Shape 2 layer thumbnail and select an orange color in the picker that appears; click OK. Double-click the Shape 1

layer thumbnail, pick a cyan color, and click OK. Press Cmd+W and press Enter to close and save Shape 2.psb.

10. Save Flag-photo-design.psd. Figure 10.21 shows the final result.

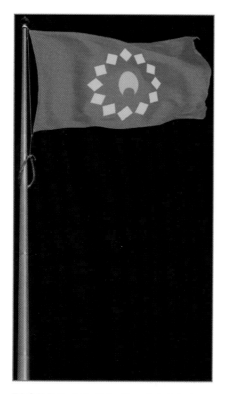

FIGURE 10.21 Completed design transformed as a smart object

THE ESSENTIALS AND BEYOND

In this chapter, you have learned how to transform paths, layers, and smart objects. You have gained the skills to transform simple designs into real world applications, from simple repositioning to complex rotations. You have learned skills such as flipping over shapes, nonuniform scaling, skewing, distorting, warping, and changing perspective.

(Continues)

THE ESSENTIALS AND BEYOND *(Continued)*

ADDITIONAL EXERCISE

Convert all the layers in Flag-photo-design.psd into a smart object. Extract the flag from the background by selecting all the black pixels, inverting the selection, and converting this selection into a layer mask for the smart object. Place the extracted photographic flag smart object into the photo of your choosing. Transform the smart object as necessary to make it fit your scene.

BACKGROUND PHOTO COURTESY RICHARD TRUEMAN

Flag-photo
-design
-extracted.psd
is also available
on the book's
Downloads page.

CHAPTER 11

Adjusting and Filtering

Photoshop has a plethora of algorithms used for altering images. In the days of film photography, adjustments were done in the darkroom, and filters were attached to the camera lens. However, the distinction between adjustments and filters in Photoshop is somewhat arbitrary; you'll use both tools interchangeably to improve digital images.

▶ **Applying adjustments and filters**

▶ **Working with smart filters**

▶ **Creating fill and adjustment layers**

Applying Adjustments and Filters

There are dozens of adjustments and filters in Photoshop, so I won't try to cover them all, just the essentials. Once you get the hang of applying adjustments and filters you should have the confidence to try other algorithms on your own to see what they can do for you. In the following steps you will apply a few adjustments and filters to give a piece of traditional artwork much more punch.

Certification Objective

1. Open David-and-Goliath.psd (see Figure 11.1).

2. Choose Image ➢ Duplicate and click OK in the Duplicate Image dialog box that appears, accepting the default name that appends the word *copy* to the document title. Choose Window ➢ Arrange ➢ Float All In Windows so you can compare the original with the copy side-by-side if they are not already.

3. Choose Window ➢ Histogram. The graph represents the distribution of pixels across the tonal range. Figure 11.2 shows that the washed-out artwork does not fill the available tonal range, having no pixels in the shadows or highlights.

David-and-Goliath.psd is available on the book's Downloads page at www.sybex.com/go/photoshopessentials.

Duplicating the image allows you to compare before-and-after images.

FIGURE 11.1 Original color lithograph *David and Goliath* by Osmar Schindler (1888)

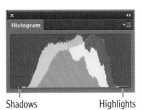

Shadows   Highlights

FIGURE 11.2 The image's histogram shows how it fills the available tonal range

4. Choose Image ➢ Adjustments ➢ Levels (or press Cmd+L). The histogram takes the center stage of the Levels dialog box. Drag the shadow input slider to the right until it reaches the graph (a value of 31 in this case). Drag the highlight input slider to the left until it reaches the graph (a value of 222 in this case). The image now has much more contrast. Drag the gamma slider to the right so that more of the pixels in the graph are on the left of the slider, thereby darkening the image (see Figure 11.3). Click OK.

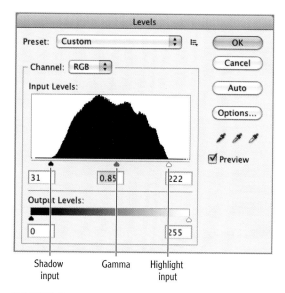

Shadow input   Gamma   Highlight input

FIGURE 11.3 Remapping the tones to take advantage of the full range available in the image

Keep in mind that 8-bit images such as the example have 2^8, or 256, possible values of luminosity from black up to white.

5. Click the yellow warning triangle icon in the Histogram panel to recalculate the graph. The recalculated graph is shown in Figure 11.4. The pixels are now distributed across the full tonal range. The gaps represent missing data; every adjustment partially destroys some of the original tone data in the mathematical transformations. You'll learn later in this chapter how to work nondestructively with smart filters and adjustment layers.

FIGURE 11.4 Histogram after the Levels adjustment

6. Choose Image ➢ Adjustments ➢ Vibrance. Drag the Vibrance slider to the right, to around +44, to increase mid-tones color saturation. Click OK.

7. Choose Image ➢ Adjustments ➢ Color Balance. Drag the Yellow/Blue slider toward Blue (+20). Select the Highlights radio button and type -15, -10, and +10 in the three Color Levels text boxes. Select the Shadows radio button and type -12, 0, and +14 in the Color Levels text boxes (see Figure 11.5). Click OK.

FIGURE 11.5 Shifting the color balance in shadows, mid-tones, and highlights

8. Choose Filter ➢ Sharpen ➢ Smart Sharpen. Drag the Amount slider to 66% and Radius to 2.0 px. Choose Lens Blur from the Remove drop-down menu (see Figure 11.6). Drag the Smart Sharpen dialog box out of the way and toggle preview off and on by pressing P several times so you can see what it is doing in the David and Goliath copy window. Click OK.

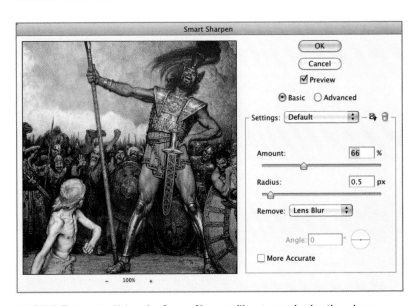

FIGURE 11.6 Using the Smart Sharpen filter to emphasize the edges

9. Maybe the sharpening was too strong? Choose Edit ➤ Fade Smart Sharpen. Drag the Opacity slider down to 50% and click OK.

10. Save your work as David-and-Goliath-Final.psd. Figure 11.7 shows the result.

You can fade the previous adjustment or filter only immediately after applying it.

If you want Photoshop to automatically correct the image, you can use the Auto button in any adjustment dialog box—or Image ➤ Auto Tone, Auto Contrast, and Auto Color.

FIGURE 11.7 The David and Goliath image after adjusting and filtering (compare with Figure 11.1)

Working with Smart Filters

In Chapter 10, "Transforming Paths, Layers, and Smart Objects," you learned how smart objects allow you to transform any number of layers

Certification
Objective

nondestructively. In much the same way, filters applied to smart objects (called smart filters) remain editable and are part of a nondestructive workflow. All the smart filters you assign are applied simultaneously to minimize the amount of data loss that unavoidably occurs when altering pixels. In the following steps you will create a texture from scratch using a sequence of smart filters. The following technique can be used to create innumerable textures by varying the smart filters used.

1. Press Cmd+N to create a new document. Type **Texture** as the name in the New dialog box. Open the Width unit drop-down and select Pixels. Type **800** in the Width text box and **800** in the Height text box. Select Transparent from the Background Contents drop-down and click OK.

2. Choose Edit ➢ Fill. Select 50% Gray from the Use drop-down in the Fill dialog box and click OK.

3. Rename Layer 1 **Base**. Choose Filter ➢ Convert For Smart Filters. (If you see a message that the layer will be converted into a smart object, select Don't Show Again.)

4. Choose Filter ➢ Noise ➢ Add Noise. Set Amount to 20% and select Gaussian and Monochromatic (see Figure 11.8). Click OK.

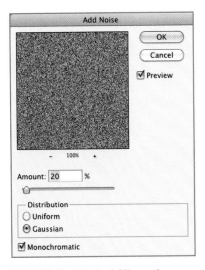

FIGURE 11.8 Adding noise as a smart filter

5. Choose Filter ➤ Render ➤ Clouds. There are no configurable parameters with this filter, and it completely obscures the noise filter, which appears below Clouds in the Layers panel (see Figure 11.9).

FIGURE 11.9 Stacking smart filters

6. Double-click the filter blending options for Clouds in the Layers panel. Decrease the opacity of the Clouds smart filter to 75% (see Figure 11.10) and click OK. Now noise is mixed with clouds.

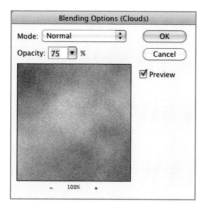

FIGURE 11.10 Adjusting filter blending options

7. Choose Filter ➤ Filter Gallery. Expand the Sketch category and select Note Paper. Set Image Balance to 24, Graininess to 0 , and Relief to 4 (see Figure 11.11). Click OK.

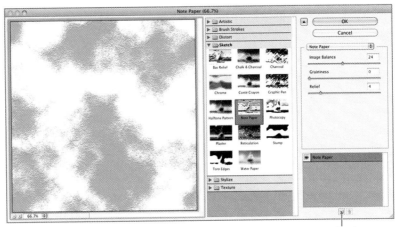

New effect layer

FIGURE 11.11 Selecting a filter in the gallery interface

8. Double-click the words *Filter Gallery* in the Layers panel to reopen the dialog box interface. Click New Effect Layer at the bottom, expand the Artistic category, and select Cutout. Set Number Of Levels to 8, Edge Simplicity to 3, and Edge Fidelity to 2 (see Figure 11.12).

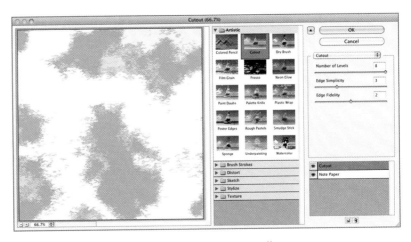

FIGURE 11.12 Layering effects in the filter gallery

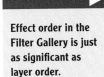

Effect order in the Filter Gallery is just as significant as layer order.

9. Click New Effect Layer. Select Poster Edges in the Artistic category. Set Edge Thickness to 2, Edge Intensity to 1, and Posterization to 2. Drag the Poster Edges effect down the stack and drop it below Cutout (see Figure 11.13). Click OK.

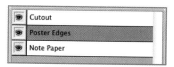

FIGURE 11.13 Reordering effects in the Filter Gallery by dragging

10. Save your work as Texture.psd. Leave this file open if you are continuing directly to the next section.

Creating Fill and Adjustment Layers

Just as smart filters allow you to reedit your filters at a later date, fill and adjustment layers offer similar parametric editability. For this reason it is almost always preferable to create fill and adjustment layers rather than directly filling or applying single adjustments. In the following steps you will create both fill and adjustment layers and control their scope with clipping groups.

1. Open Texture.psd if it is not already open.

2. Choose Layer ➤ New Fill Layer ➤ Solid Color. Type **Green** as the name in the New Layer dialog box and click OK. Select a deep forest-green color in the picker and click OK. Drag the Green layer below the Base layer in the Layers panel.

3. You cannot see the green hue because the pixels on the Base layer obscure the fill layer underneath. Double-click just to the right of the word *Base* in the Layers panel to open the Layer Style dialog box's Blending Options page. Drag the slider labeled This Layer to the left until the value reads 190 (see Figure 11.14). Click OK.

Certification
Objective

◄

**Texture.psd
is also available
on the book's
Downloads page.**

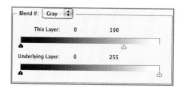

FIGURE 11.14 Using a Blend If slider to mix the Base layer with the color fill layer

4. Choose Layer ➤ New Adjustment Layer ➤ Hue/Saturation. Open the Adjustments panel if it is not already visible. Select Colorize, and in the Properties panel, drag the Hue slider to 240, Saturation to 43, and Lightness to +33 (see Figure 11.15).

Clipping group toggle

FIGURE 11.15 Configuring a Hue/Saturation adjustment layer

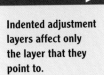

Indented adjustment layers affect only the layer that they point to.

5. At this point the blue hue obscures the green color fill layer that you could see prior to step 4 because adjustment layers affect all the layers below them in the layer stack by default. Click the clipping group toggle icon. ▦ The Hue/Saturation 1 layer becomes indented and the Base layer becomes underlined, indicating that they are part of a clipping group (see Figure 11.16). The Base layer clips (masks) the effect of the indented adjustment layer. Figure 11.17 shows the resulting texture.

6. Double-click the Filter Gallery smart filter under the Base layer to reopen its dialog box. Toggle off the Poster Edges effect and click OK. Toggle off the Add Noise smart layer in the Layers panel.

By combining smart layers and adjustment layers, you can create myriad textures.

7. Select the Hue/Saturation layer and drag the Saturation slider to 73 and Lightness to -10 in the Adjustments panel. The result looks more like a map.

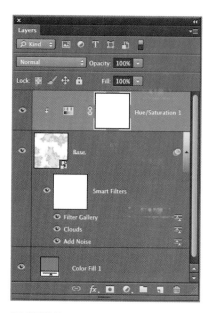

FIGURE 11.16 Making an adjustment clip to a layer

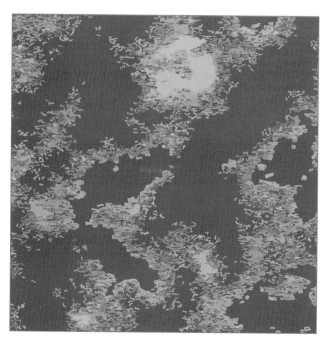

FIGURE 11.17 Complex texture created with smart filters, fill, and adjustment layers

8. Double-click Filter Gallery in the Layers panel. Click the Add Effect Layer icon at the bottom of the Filter Gallery. Select Smudge Stick in the Artistic category. Set Stroke Length to 5, Highlight Area to 6, and Intensity to 4 (see Figure 11.18). Click OK.

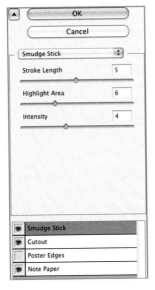

FIGURE 11.18 Creating another effect layer in the Filter Gallery

9. Change the blend mode of the Base layer to Linear Dodge (Add). The water gets much more punch with this blend mode. Figure 11.19 shows the resulting texture.

10. Save your work as Texture-Final.psd.

Texture-Final .psd is also available on the book's Downloads page.

USING ADVANCED ADJUSTMENTS FOR EFFECTS

There may be some instances where you want to manually adjust your images for certain effects or improvements. You can use the Channel Mixer adjustment to convert a color image to black-and-white photo. Simply choose one of the presets or create a tinted version by selecting, then deselecting, the Monochrome option and adjusting the Output Channels to create a slight tint or color cast. The Posterize adjustment enables you to apply levels of a graphic posterization effect ranging from 2 (heavy) to 255 (none). See Chapter 12, "Developing Photos," for more information on adjusting images in raw format.

CHAPTER 12

Developing Photos

Adobe replaces the traditional lightbox and darkroom with a trio of programs: Bridge, Adobe Camera Raw (ACR), and Photoshop. You'll use Bridge as a digital lightbox to review and tag your shots, ACR to develop individual photos, and Photoshop to do more advanced work involving layers, filters, and more.

▶ **Using Adobe Bridge**

▶ **Making development decisions in ACR**

▶ **Making local adjustments in ACR**

Using Adobe Bridge

Adobe Bridge is a separate program that comes free with Photoshop and many other Adobe products. As its name suggests, Bridge serves as a media browser that links different Adobe programs. More than just a way to see multiple thumbnails of your photos, Bridge allows you to *tag* your shots with metadata. As you shoot more and more photos, finding particular photos becomes a significant issue. With metadata, you add searchable keywords to photos. In the following steps you will use Bridge to visualize the samples provided with this chapter, tag a photo with keywords, and explore the Mini Bridge feature within Photoshop.

1. Download the sample files for Chapter 12 from the book's Downloads page (www.sybex.com/go/photoshopessentials) and place them in a memorable location on your hard drive.

2. Launch Photoshop. Select File ➤ Browse In Bridge to launch the program.

3. In Bridge, locate the Folders panel and navigate to the folder where you saved the sample files in step 1. The Folders panel is organized in a tree structure that you can expand, much like the Mac Finder and Windows Explorer.

> You can rate photos from none to five stars using the Label menu or the dots underneath each thumbnail.

4. Bridge is organized into workspaces just like Photoshop. Select the Essentials workspace if it is not already selected. Select the second photo, called 7D-0808.cr2. Figure 12.1 shows the Adobe Bridge interface with the photo selected.

FIGURE 12.1 Adobe Bridge interface

5. Select the Keywords panel. Click the New Keyword icon , type Objects, and press Enter.

> Once you create keywords, you can assign them to any number of photos with a single click.

6. Click the New Sub Keyword icon , type **Flowers**, and press Enter. Check Flowers to assign this new sub-keyword to the selected photo.

7. Click the New Keyword icon , type **POV**, and press Enter.

8. Click the New Sub Keyword icon, type **Worms Eye Perspective**, and press Enter. Check Worms Eye Perspective to assign this second keyword (see Figure 12.2).

> Use the Keywords section of the Filter panel to locate specific photos quickly.

9. Switch back to Photoshop by pressing Cmd+Tab on the Mac or Alt+Tab on Windows. Choose Window ➢ Extensions ➢ Mini Bridge. Select Browse Photos and navigate to the folder where you saved the sample files in step 1. Mini Bridge (see Figure 12.3) allows you to visually access photos but is not for tagging as you do in the full-fledged Bridge application.

FIGURE 12.2 Creating and assigning keywords to the selected photo

FIGURE 12.3 Mini Bridge panel

10. Right-click 7D-0808.cr2 and choose Open In Camera Raw in either Mini Bridge or Bridge.

Making Development Decisions in ACR

Every digital camera captures raw sensor data. This raw data is recorded without any processing only in "prosumer," or professional-level, cameras. In lower-end cameras, the raw data is typically processed into JPEG format with the in-camera circuitry, and much of the data is discarded in exchange for smaller file size. Adobe Camera Raw (ACR) was designed to handle the raw data, which you can think of as the digital equivalent of film negatives. ACR exists in a workflow between Bridge (or the Mini Bridge) and Photoshop. ACR is where you will make almost all of your photographic development decisions.

Certification Objective

PHOTOSHOP LIGHTROOM

Adobe sells another product called Photoshop Lightroom that integrates the functionality of Bridge and ACR into one streamlined program optimized for photographers. Many Lightroom users still use Photoshop for activities such as layered blending, effects, filters, and much more.

For more information about Photoshop Lightroom, see `www.adobe.com/products/photoshoplightroom/`.

Basic Parameters

In the following steps, you will use the parameters on the Basic tab to develop the photo you opened in the previous section.

7D-0808.cr2 is available on the book's Downloads page.

1. Open `7D-0808.cr2` if it is not already open in ACR. Because CR2 (the second version of Canon raw) is a raw format, ACR will automatically open when you choose File ➢ Open In Photoshop.

2. Select the Basic tab if it is not already selected. The histogram is color-coded by component, including RGB and CMYK. Black (K) is actually shown in white. As you can see in Figure 12.4, the photo is underexposed—the histogram shows all the peaks in the shadows.

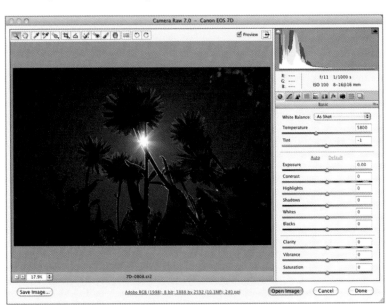

FIGURE 12.4 Opening a raw file in Adobe Camera Raw

IMAGE COURTESY OF RICHARD TRUEMAN

CAMERA RAW PREFERENCES

You can access Camera Raw preferences from Bridge or from the toolbar in ACR. From there you decide whether you want to save image settings in separate sidecar files (.xmp) that you can see in the file system or as part of the (invisible) Camera Raw database.

ACR can also be used to develop JPEG and TIFF images. You can choose whether to open such files in ACR always, only if they already have image settings, or never.

3. Press O and U to toggle on the highlight and shadow clipping warnings, respectively. Blown out highlights are shown in red, and underexposed areas that have gone completely black are shown in blue. Drag the Exposure slider to +2.00, representing opening up the lens aperture two full stops (simulating four times as much light on the sensor). The histogram is now spread out across the tonal range, but we are getting a fair amount of highlight clipping and a tiny bit of shadow clipping (see Figure 12.5).

Data in the red and blue areas is not lost in ACR as it would be in Photoshop. Raw data exists beyond the mathematical limits of the tonal range.

FIGURE 12.5 Adjusting exposure and previewing highlight (red) and shadow (blue) clipping

4. To recover the blown highlights, drag the Highlights slider to -44. To push the tonal range out of the shadows, increase Blacks to +33. Click the two arrow buttons at the top corners of the histogram within the ACR dialog box to toggle off highlight and shadow clipping warnings.

5. Increase Contrast to +22, Clarity to +32, and Vibrance to +44.

6. To push the sky more into the blue range, shift the white balance by dragging the (color) Temperature slider to 5200 (see Figure 12.6).

Think of Clarity as mid-tone sharpening and Vibrance as mid-tone saturation.

FIGURE 12.6 Developing a photo with basic parameters

7. Press P twice to toggle the preview off and then back on. In this way you can see how dramatic the changes are that you've made in the development process. Click Open Image to open the developed file in Photoshop.

8. Open the Histogram panel and see that there are no gaps or thin spikes in the distribution of pixels across the tonal range (see Figure 12.7).

Once it is in Photoshop, the image is no longer considered a raw file.

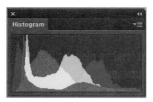

FIGURE 12.7 Resulting
tonal distribution in Photoshop

9. Save your developed image as Worms eye flowers.psd.

10. Switch back to Bridge by pressing Cmd+Tab on the Mac or Alt+Tab on Windows. Notice that a settings icon is above the 7D-0808.cr2 thumbnail; this indicates that the image has been developed in ACR. Right-click the settings icon and choose Develop Settings ➢ Clear Settings from the context menu. The thumbnail updates with its original underexposed appearance (see Figure 12.8). This should prove to you that ACR doesn't ever *bake in* any of its settings; the raw data always remains unaltered on disk, even when there are image settings.

FIGURE 12.8 Image settings have been removed
from a thumbnail in Bridge

Advanced Parameters

ACR has numerous tabs that contain advanced parameters. In the process of developing photos in the following steps, you will explore the Tone Curve, Detail, HSL/Grayscale, Lens Correction, and Camera Calibration tabs.

1. Switch to Bridge by pressing Cmd+Tab on the Mac and Alt+Tab on Windows. Right-click 7D-7591.jpg, and choose Open In Camera Raw. Figure 12.9 shows the file opened in the ACR interface.

FIGURE 12.9 Opening a JPEG file in Adobe Camera Raw

2. You should always start with basic adjustments. On the Basic tab, click the Auto button to have ACR calculate values for the Exposure through Blacks sliders. The tonal range isn't being fully realized, so drag the Blacks slider to -45. Drag Clarity to +100 and Vibrance to +57 to give the image some tropical punch (the shot was taken in Mexico). Figure 12.10 shows the results.

3. Switch to the Tone Curve tab. The interface is similar to the Curves adjustment; here you can affect specific regions within the tonal range by adjusting the sliders (see Figure 12.11). Boost the highlights by dragging the Highlights slider to +33. Press P to toggle off the preview for this tab. Press P again to toggle it back on so you can see the effect of boosting the highlights.

FIGURE 12.10 Making basic adjustments

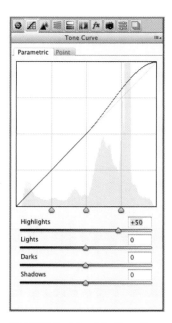

FIGURE 12.11 Boosting
highlights on the tone curve

4. Switch to the Detail tab. Click the plus icon in the lower-left corner of the Camera Raw dialog box until the zoom magnification is at 100%. It is important to view the image at full size when adjusting detail. Make the following Sharpening adjustments:

Amount	65
Radius	0.5
Detail	19
Masking	65

Try holding down Opt when you drag the sliders to get grayscale previews of what you are doing. The most informative grayscale preview is Masking, which shows in white which edges will be sharpened. Press P repeatedly to toggle on and off the preview for this tab to see what the sharpening is doing. All of the adjustments are subjective and the values will be different on every image. Figure 12.12 shows the result.

FIGURE 12.12 Making detailed adjustments with sharpening and noise reduction

5. Make the following Noise Reduction adjustments:

Luminance	50
Luminance Detail	100
Luminance Contrast	0
Color	7
Color Detail	50

> Sharpening and noise reduction can also be accomplished in Photoshop with individual filters; see Chapter 11, "Adjusting and Filtering."

6. Click the minus icon until the whole image fits within the Camera Raw dialog box (33.3% magnification in this case). Select the HSL/Grayscale tab and then click the Saturation subtab. To make the sky appear more saturated, drag the Blues slider to +80. Select the Luminance subtab. Darken the sky by dragging the Blues slider to -66. Figure 12.13 shows the result. Click Done. Image settings are saved with the JPEG and the preview is updated in Bridge.

FIGURE 12.13 Saturating and darkening blues on the HSL / Grayscale tab

7. Right click 5D2-1524.cr2 and choose Open In Camera Raw. Figure 12.14 shows the undeveloped shot.

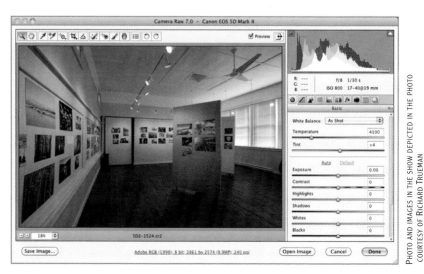

FIGURE 12.14 Opening another raw file in Camera Raw

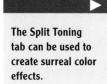

The Split Toning tab can be used to create surreal color effects.

8. Select the Lens Corrections tab. 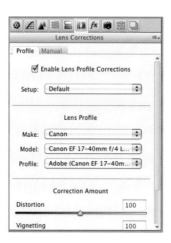 Select Enable Lens Profile Corrections (see Figure 12.15). The lens used is already stored in the file's metadata and Photoshop automatically corrects for lens distortion, vignetting (darkening in the outer corners), and chromatic aberration (color problems) associated with that particular lens. Press P repeatedly to toggle on and off the preview for this tab.

FIGURE 12.15 Using the lens profile to correct vignetting and chromatic aberrations

9. Select the Camera Calibration tab. Try each one of the Camera Profile choices. For this image I chose Camera Portrait; the choices you make on this tab are quite subjective. Make the following slider adjustments:

Shadows	-15
Red Primary Hue	0
Red Primary Saturation	-10
Green Primary Hue	+15
Green Primary Saturation	0
Blue Primary Hue	+15
Blue Primary Saturation	-10

Switch to the Basic tab and increase Exposure to +0.50. Figure 12.16 shows the result.

FIGURE 12.16 Final developed gallery image

10. Hold down Shift and the Open Image button changes to Open Object. Click Open Object. The layer thumbnail indicates that you have a Smart Object (see Figure 12.17). Double-click the layer thumbnail. The Camera

Raw dialog box reopens—you can make additional development decisions at any time. Click OK. Close the document without saving.

FIGURE 12.17 The developed photo is editable as a Smart Object.

Making Local Adjustments in ACR

So far all the development decisions you have made in ACR are global; that is, they affect the entire image. It is also possible to make local adjustments that affect only a portion of the image in ACR. It might seem like a paradox, but you can create adjustments that fade with a gradient or even paint in adjustments with a brush, all the while having them remain parametric. In other words, these targeted adjustments in ACR are stored as image settings and do not permanently alter the actual pixels. In the following steps, you will make several targeted adjustments.

1. Switch to Bridge by pressing Cmd+Tab and Alt+Tab on Windows. Right-click 7D-7591.jpg, and choose Open In Camera Raw.

2. Select the Straighten tool in the Camera Raw dialog box. Drag a line along the horizon. The new orientation is suggested by the crop border (see Figure 12.18). Press Enter to complete the operation and click Done.

3. Switch to Bridge by pressing Cmd+Tab on the Mac and Alt+Tab on Windows. Right-click 7D-7161.jpg, and choose Open In Camera Raw. Click the Auto button on the Basic tab.

FIGURE 12.18 Straightening in Camera Raw

4. Open the menu under the Crop tool inside the Camera Raw dialog box and choose Show Overlay. Drag a window around the entire document; the rule of thirds grid appears. Hold Shift and drag the lower-right handle up to the left, as shown in Figure 12.19, so that the white-peaked mountain is aligned with a vertical grid line. Press Enter to complete the operation and click Done.

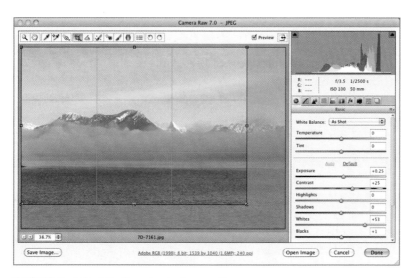

FIGURE 12.19 Cropping in Camera Raw

5. Switch to Bridge by pressing Cmd+Tab on the Mac and Alt+Tab on Windows. Right-click 7D-9239.jpg, and choose Open In Camera Raw.

6. Select the Targeted Adjustment tool, open its flyout menu, and choose Saturation. Position the cursor over the sky and drag to the right to increase blue saturation. Watch the slider move as you drag and stop dragging when it gets to +77 (see Figure 12.20).

FIGURE 12.20 Making a targeted adjustment to increase blue saturation in the sky

7. Select the Graduated Filter tool in the Camera Raw dialog box. Drag from the top middle of the image, hold down Shift to constrain vertically, and continue dragging to the horizon. Drag the Exposure slider to -0.70 to darken the sky. The darkness gradually fades away toward the horizon. Repeatedly press P to toggle the effect on and off and back on again (see Figure 12.21).

8. Click the New radio button in the Graduated Filter parameters. Drag the Exposure slider back to 0, and drag the Clarity slider to +100. Drag from the middle of the image, hold Shift, and stop at the bottom. Now objects at and below the horizon have fading levels of clarity to compensate for naturally diminishing clarity with distance; this brings more of the landscape into sharp focus (see Figure 12.22).

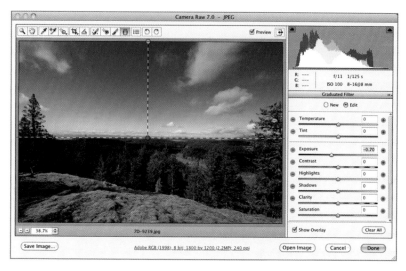

FIGURE 12.21 Applying a graduated filter to darken the sky

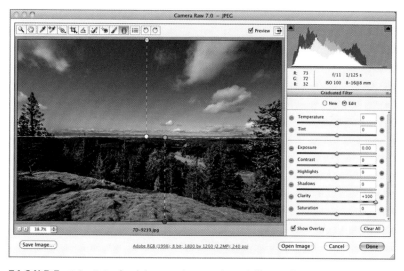

FIGURE 12.22 Applying another graduated filter to boost clarity in the distance

    9. The tree on the right foreground received too much clarity (midtones sharpening), especially near the horizon. Select the Adjustment Brush tool in the Camera Raw dialog box. Drag the Clarity slider to -100. Paint over the tree on the right. Hover your cursor over the green pin to reveal the area you've painted (see Figure 12.23).

10. Click Done to close ACR.

FIGURE 12.23 Painting with the Adjustment Brush tool

REUSING IMAGES

You can use images, graphics, and video files over multiple Adobe software products. For example, templates, scripts, and presets can be used to create items in Photoshop that can be used later when creating videos in Adobe Premiere or graphics with Adobe Illustrator.

THE ESSENTIALS AND BEYOND

In this chapter you have learned the essentials of Adobe Camera Raw and how to use it to develop photos. You should now have the knowledge of parameters, from basic to advanced, to use ACR as your digital darkroom and develop your shots the way you see fit.

ADDITIONAL EXERCISE

Shoot a "roll" of your own photos and import them into Bridge by choosing File ➢ Get Photos From Camera. Select your three best photos in Bridge and develop them in ACR.

CHAPTER 13

Retouching Photos

Retouching is the art of manipulating the contents of photos. Reasons for retouching include selectively controlling exposure, removing blemishes, adding special effects, and even outright deception. Ethics aside, photo manipulation is as old as photography itself. What used to require an airbrush is now easily accomplished in Photoshop.

▶ **Using retouching tools**

▶ **Replacing textures in perspective**

▶ **Changing focus**

Using Retouching Tools

Certification Objective

There is no one-click solution to retouching, and each photo presents its own challenges, depending on what you want to alter. Fortunately, there are several specialized retouching tools that aid in the art of photo manipulation.

Developing the Photo

7D-9856.jpg is available on the book's Downloads page at www .sybex.com/go/ photoshop essentials.

You will start with an unprocessed JPEG image of the tiny church (open on Easter only) that's near where I live in British Columbia and develop it using some of the skills you learned in Chapter 12, "Developing Photos."

1. Launch Adobe Bridge directly or by choosing File ➢ Browse In Bridge from Photoshop. Navigate to this chapter's sample files in the Folders panel.

2. Right click 7D-9856.jpg and choose Open In Camera Raw. Figure 13.1 shows the original image.

FIGURE 13.1 Original JPEG image prior to development

3. Make the following adjustments on the Basic tab of Adobe Camera Raw:

Exposure	+1.00
Highlights	-40
Blacks	-40
Clarity	+50

4. Select the Crop tool within the Camera Raw dialog box and crop out the picket fence on the left (see Figure 13.2).

5. Hold down Shift and click Open Object. The image is transferred from Camera Raw to Photoshop as a Smart Object. You can now quit Bridge.

6. In Photoshop, choose Layer ➢ New ➢ Layer Via Copy. Rename the new layer **Retouching**.

7. Right-click the Retouching layer and choose Rasterize Layer from the context menu. Figure 13.3 shows the result.

8. Save your work as Church.psd, making sure Layers is selected in the Save As dialog box (or it would be flattened and the Smart Object destroyed).

You cannot retouch Smart Objects. Rasterizing instead of flattening allows you to make a before and after comparison.

▶

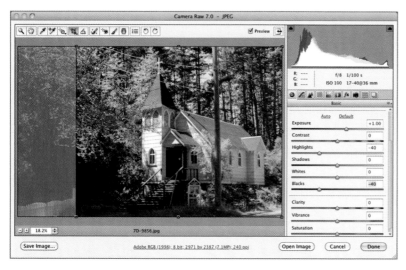

FIGURE 13.2 Cropping the photo in Camera Raw

FIGURE 13.3 Rasterizing a copy of the Smart Object in preparation for retouching

Removing the Telephone Pole and Wires

In the following steps you will use the Spot Healing Brush, Content-Aware Fill, and Clone Stamp tools to remove the unsightly telephone pole and its wires.

1. Open Church.psd in Photoshop.

2. Select the Spot Healing Brush tool and select the Content-Aware radio button on the options bar. Open the brush picker and set Size to 10 px and Hardness to 100%. Carefully trace over the bright wires and watch as they are magically blended into the surrounding image.

Church.psd is also available on the book's download page.

The content-aware algorithm makes up new pixels based on those surrounding the wires.

Spot healing works best on small spots or thin lines.

3. Increase the zoom magnification by pressing Cmd+= if the wires are too small for you to trace by hand. Select the Rotate View tool (under the Hand tool in the toolbox) and drag to rotate the view to match the natural arc of your hand's motion (see Figure 13.4). This will make it easier to trace thin lines.

FIGURE 13.4 Rotating the view can make tracing lines more comfortable.

When spot healing, use the smallest brush possible for the best result.

4. Press J to continue using the Spot Healing Brush tool. Remove all the dark wires using this technique. Do not attempt to spot-heal the telephone box marked 1892; you would end up with a blurry smudge if you did because the box is too big. Figure 13.5 shows the wires removed.

5. Select the Patch tool and select Content-Aware from the Patch drop-down on the options bar. Lasso a loop around the telephone box. Position the cursor inside the lassoed area and drag upward to the point indicated in Figure 13.6. As you drag, the contents of the lasso change. Release the cursor when you have found a good replacement patch.

FIGURE 13.5 Wires removed with the Spot Healing Brush tool

—— Lasso telephone box

FIGURE 13.6 Patching the telephone box with another area

6. Select the Polygonal Lasso tool. Click four points surrounding the telephone pole as closely as possible; the last point should be over the first point to close the selection. Choose Edit ➢ Fill. Select Content-Aware from the Use drop-down menu. Click OK.

Content-aware fill is not perfect but it's 90 percent of the way to a convincing illusion.

7. Press Cmd+D to deselect. Figure 13.7 identifies two problem areas that aren't of acceptable quality to maintain the illusion.

Problem areas

FIGURE 13.7 Identifying problem areas that require further retouching

8. Select the Clone Stamp tool. Open the brush picker on the options bar and set Size to 50 px and Hardness to 75%. Hold the Opt key and click point A to set this as your clone source. Release the Opt key and paint over point B (see Figure 13.8). The pixels from A are stamped to B as you paint.
   The success of a clone stamp operation lies in how carefully you match the clone source to the stamp target.

9. Continue cloning and stamping any problem areas you find. Try to avoid repeating similar areas close to each other because the eye will spot this as an illusion more readily.

10. Toggle the Retouched layer off and on to see how far you've come. Save your work as `Church-Retouched.psd`. Figure 13.9 shows the picturesque church the way it was intended to look.

Clone stamping is much more of an art than a science. Your skills will improve with practice.

FIGURE 13.8 Clone stamping the missing tree trunk

FIGURE 13.9 Retouched church

Replacing Textures In Perspective

Now that you've learned how to use a few of the retouching tools, you might
think you can apply them successfully to any surface. But that's not always
the case. Surfaces that recede from the viewer diminish in size in perspective,
making retouching architectural surfaces much more challenging. To solve
this problem Adobe invented the Vanishing Point filter, its name referencing
the lines of perspective that converge at one or more vanishing points in the
distance. In the following exercises, you will create perspective grids and replace
the siding of a stucco building with brick.

Mapping Perspective Grids

In the first stage, you will map perspective grids onto building surfaces to give
the Vanishing Point filter an idea of the 3D space that you naturally understand
and is implied in the photo.

Commercial-
Building.jpg
is available on
the book's
Downloads page.

1. Open Commercial-Building.jpg in Photoshop. Figure 13.10 shows
   the original image.

FIGURE 13.10 Original photo

2. Choose Filter ➢ Vanishing Point. Click four points along horizontal and vertical lines in the photo to define a perspective surface, as shown in Figure 13.11.

Perspective grid

FIGURE 13.11 Draw a surface along horizontal and vertical edges in the photo.

3. Press Cmd+= a couple of times to zoom in. Hold the spacebar and drag the image to pan so the surface you drew is centered in the Vanishing Point dialog box.

 4. Select the Edit Plane tool and drag each of the four corner handles to adjust them so they are exactly in their architectural reveals (in this case, the grooves) to perfect the perspective of the surface.

   The surface will turn yellow or red to warn you if the perspective isn't quite right. Keep adjusting until the plane is blue.

5. Press Cmd+- a couple of times to zoom out. Drag the side handles so the plane covers the entire right surface of the building (see Figure 13.12).

6. Position the cursor over the middle left handle of the single perspective grid. Hold the Cmd key and drag the handle to the left to create a perpendicular plane (see Figure 13.13).

FIGURE 13.12 Extending the plane to cover one side of the building

FIGURE 13.13 Creating a perpendicular plane

7. Hold the Opt key and drag the middle-left handle of the perpendicular plane to rotate it. Keep dragging the plane until it matches the orientation of the building surface it covers.

8. Drag the upper-middle handle down so the plane fits the stucco but doesn't cover the white cornice. Drag the middle-left handle so the plane stops at the edge of the building. Adjust the middle-bottom handles on both planes if necessary to match them to the stucco area to be replaced with brick (see Figure 13.14).

FIGURE 13.14 Adjusting the planes to match the building surfaces

9. Click OK to close the Vanishing Point dialog box.

10. Save your work as Commercial-Building-Mapped.psd.

The work you spent creating planes in Vanishing Point is not lost when you click OK.

Copying a Texture onto Surfaces in Perspective

In the following steps you will replace the original stucco with a brick texture using the perspective grids you created in the Vanishing Point filter.

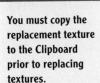

1. Open Commercial-Building-Mapped.psd and then open Brick.jpg (see Figure 13.15). In the Brick.jpg window, press Cmd+A, Cmd+C, and Cmd+W to select all, copy it to the Clipboard, and close the file without saving.

FIGURE 13.15 Brick texture

2. Choose Layer ➢ New ➢ Layer. Type **Brick** in the New Layer dialog box and click OK.

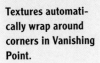

3. Choose Filter ➢ Vanishing Point and press Cmd+V to paste the brick texture into the Vanishing Point grid. Position the cursor inside the selection and drag it to the left plane (see Figure 13.16).

FIGURE 13.16 Pasting brick into the Vanishing Point filter

4. The bricks are too large. Press Cmd+T to free transform the selection. Hold Shift to maintain the aspect ratio and drag the lower-right handle up and to the left to make the pattern smaller until it fits entirely on the left surface (see Figure 13.17).

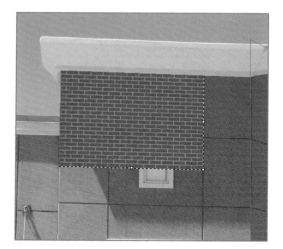

FIGURE 13.17 Transforming a selection in Vanishing Point

5. Position the cursor inside the selection, hold Cmd, and drag down to create a copy of the selection. Release Cmd and hold Shift to constrain the selection as you drag it down vertically. Stop dragging when the brick courses match up (see Figure 13.18).

FIGURE 13.18 Copying a texture vertically

▶

Press Cmd+Z if you make a mistake in Vanishing Point; it takes you back one step.

6. Position the cursor inside the selection, hold Cmd, and drag to create a copy of the selection. Continue in this way, copying the brick texture to cover both perspective planes. Hold Shift whenever you need to constrain the transform operation horizontally or vertically. Figure 13.19 shows the result. Click OK to close the Vanishing Point dialog box; the textures you've copied and pasted in Vanishing Point are now placed on the Brick layer.

FIGURE 13.19 Copying a texture to cover perspective planes

 7. Toggle off the Brick layer and target the Background layer. Select the Quick Selection tool. Drag over the stucco to make a quick selection. Hold Opt and remove areas from the selection that don't belong. When you are satisfied that you have a good rough selection, click Refine Edge on the options bar.

8. In the Refine Edge dialog box, select Smart Radius and drag the Radius slider to 2.0 px. Figure 13.20 shows the preview in Refine Edge. Click OK.

▶

Soft Light is another nice blend mode in this scenario.

9. Toggle on the Brick layer and select it in the Layers panel. Click Add Layer Mask at the bottom of the Layers panel to convert the selection into a mask. ▣ Change the blend mode of the Brick layer to Multiply to the darken the image and reduce its opacity to 75%. Figure 13.21 shows the result.

FIGURE 13.20 Refining the selection edge with the Smart Radius feature

FIGURE 13.21 Final image showing new brick texture

10. Save your work as Commercial-Building-Final.psd.

This technique is a great way to explore design alternatives in renovation projects. If you've ever wondered how your house would look with new siding, find out with Vanishing Point.

If you're interested in the architectural application of Photoshop, check out my book *Enhancing Architectural Drawings and Models with Photoshop* (Sybex, 2010).

FIXING WIDE ANGLE PROBLEMS

Imperfections from wide angle lens use can be corrected in the Filter section. For example, the Adaptive Wide Angle filter allows you to correct distorted horizontal and vertical planes, and Lens Correction uses the manufacturer's camera and lens data to correct geometric distortion, vignetting, and chromatic aberrations.

Changing Focus

The eye is naturally drawn to areas that are in sharp focus. You can use this fact to draw the viewer's attention to the area of interest in a photo by narrowing depth of field. In the following steps you will draw attention to the middle ground by selectively defocusing (blurring) the foreground and background. Photoshop CS6 has a new blur filter called Tilt-Shift that makes changing focus a snap.

1. Open `St-Peters-Square.jpg` in Photoshop. Figure 13.22 shows the original image.

`St-Peters-Square.jpg` is available on the book's Downloads page.

PHOTO COURTESY OF ISTOCKPHOTO, ©TRAVELIF, IMAGE #16027514

FIGURE 13.22 Original photo

2. Choose Filter ➢ Blur ➢ Tilt-Shift. In-canvas controls appear, including a series of dashed and continuous horizontal lines and a ring that controls the amount of blur (see Figure 13.23). The solid lines indicate where the blur begins and the dashed lines indicate where the blur reaches full intensity. The blur ramps up in smooth gradients from the solid to the dashed lines.

FIGURE 13.23 Tilt-Shift in-canvas controls

You can also use Iris Blur to sharpen a single focal point in a blurred image, or use Field Blur to create a variable blurriness between multiple focal points.

3. Drag the central circle to the tip of the obelisk. Drag the bars as shown in Figure 10.24 so that St. Peter's Square is the only area in sharp focus. Drag the central ring to 10 px or use the slider in the Blur Tools panel. Increase Light Bokeh to 30% in the Blur Effects panel. Click OK on the options bar.

Bokeh is a Japanese term referring to the aesthetic quality of blur.

4. Click the Brightness/Contrast icon in the Adjustments panel. Drag the Contrast slider to +40 in the Properties panel. Increasing contrast accentuates the toy effect. The people and cars in St. Peter's Square now look like architectural miniatures.

FIGURE 13.24 Adjusting blur controls on the canvas

5. Select the Crop tool and crop out the burned-out region of sky. Figure 13.25 shows the final result. Save your work as St-Peters-Square-Focused.psd.

FIGURE 13.25 Focused image draws attention to St. Peter's Square.

REMOVING RED EYE

The Red Eye tool is designed specifically to remove unsightly red eye in portraits caused by direct flash. Simply select the Red Eye tool (Cmd+J) and use to draw a selection around the red portion of the eye. Photoshop will replace it with a dark tone that matches the subject's pupil.

THE ESSENTIALS AND BEYOND

In this chapter you have learned some of the skills that people refer to when they say that an image must have been manipulated with Photoshop. However, if the photo manipulation is well done, people are not conscious of it. Having the ability to deceive isn't license to perform unethical acts. You must rely on your own moral compass to decide if a particular photo manipulation enhances the visual story you are trying to tell or if it goes too far. That said, you now have the basic skills to retouch, replace textures in perspective, and change focus to direct viewer attention.

ADDITIONAL EXERCISE

Go outside and take some photos that are marred by something unsightly such as a telephone pole, wires, advertisements, fences, or the like. Retouch them to remove unwanted elements, replace some of their textures in perspective, or change the focus to draw the viewer's eye where you want it to go. Alternatively, find some photos online and create a photo montage using the retouching skills you've learned in this chapter. It's amazing what you can do with Photoshop!

IMAGE COURTESY OF MMXX UNDER THE CREATIVE COMMONS ATTRIBUTION-SHARE ALIKE 3.0 UNPORTED LICENSE.

CHAPTER 14

Merging Photos

Many interesting creative possibilities open up in Photoshop when you merge multiple photos together into single forms of output. For example, you can create images with greater dynamic range than is possible with single exposures, merge multiple adjacent overlapping photos into a seamless panorama, and remove moving objects from a sequence of stills taken from the same vantage point. In this chapter, you'll learn how to composite images with several handy tools.

▶ **Making high dynamic range imagery**

▶ **Working with panoramas**

▶ **Processing images in stacks**

Making High Dynamic Range Imagery

Dynamic range refers to the intensity difference between the brightest whites and darkest blacks in a photo. Our eyes can perceive a much larger dynamic range than any single camera exposure. High dynamic range (HDR) images are popular these days, and Photoshop has two ways to create the HDR look. The first is to create a true HDR image from multiple exposures in a semi-automated process called Merge To HDR Pro, and the second is essentially a trick called HDR Toning that gives a single image the super-detailed HDR look (but without actually having an increased dynamic range). We will explore them both.

Using Merge to HDR Pro

By bracketing multiple exposures at different shutter speeds, you can capture detail in the highlights, mid-tones, and shadows. You can use Photoshop to merge these multiple exposures into a single HDR picture. Although it is possible to bracket by adjusting the lens aperture, this should be avoided because doing so changes the depth of field (the area that remains in focus). Many higher-end cameras have bracketing modes in which the camera takes multiple pictures every time you press the shutter release.

In the following exercise you will merge a series of bracketed photos that are part of a panoramic photo shoot. Here you'll be creating one of the HDR photos for use in the next section, where you will be merging 12 photos into a wrap-around HDR panorama.

▶

The images used in this exercise are available on the book's Downloads page at www .sybex.com/ go/photoshop essentials.

1. Open the first three files in this chapter's `Panoramic Photo Shoot` folder (`IMG_2241.jpg`, `IMG_2242.jpg`, and `IMG2243.jpg`). Figure 14.1 shows the three images side by side. The images were created in the camera's automatic bracketing mode at three different shutter speeds: 1/250, 1/60, and 1/15 second, all at f/8.

PHOTOS COURTESY OF RICHARD TRUEMAN

FIGURE 14.1 Three shots taken from a tripod bracketed by shutter speed

▶

Bracket shots with a tripod for the best results.

2. Choose File ➢ Automate ➢ Merge To HDR Pro. Click Browse and select the three images you just opened. Select Attempt To Automatically Align Source Images (see Figure 14.2). This step is necessary because even though the images were shot on a tripod, there were subtle vibrations caused by wind or even the shutter itself that moved the frame a few pixels between each shot. Click OK and Photoshop goes to work merging the photos.

3. In the larger Merge To HDR Pro dialog box (see Figure 14.3), you will see the three source images at the lower left with exposure values (EV) from +1.91 to -2.06, offering a high dynamic range of almost 4 stops. Begin by selecting Photorealistic High Contrast from the Preset drop-down as a starting point.

4. To improve the look of the HDR preview image in the Merge To HDR Pro dialog box, set Gamma to 0.50, Exposure to +1.00, and Detail to +100%. When you make these changes, the name in the Preset menu changes to Custom.

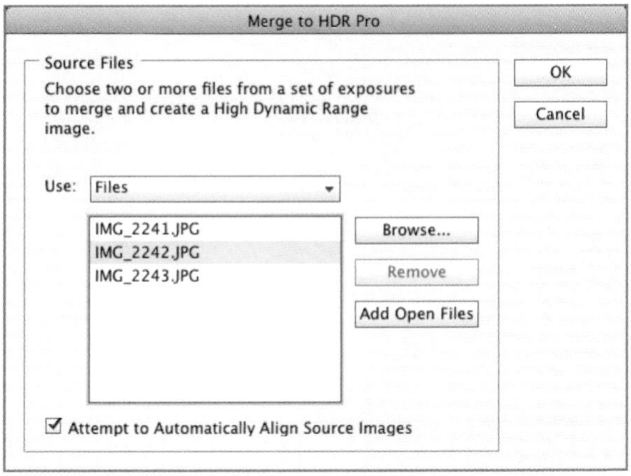

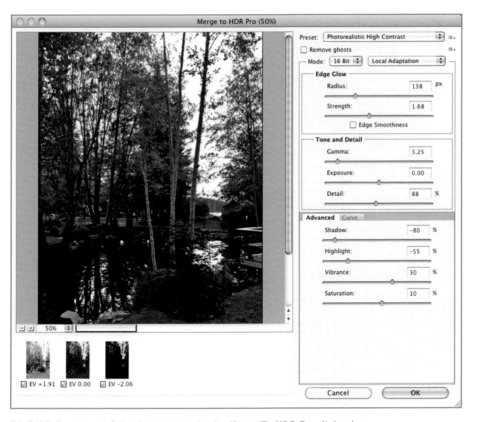

FIGURE 14.2 Selecting files and an option in preparation for merging

FIGURE 14.3 Selecting a preset in the Merge To HDR Pro dialog box

5. Select the menu icon on the right of the Preset drop-down and select Save Preset. Type **My HDR.hdt** in the Save dialog box and click OK. Click OK again to complete the Merge To HDR Pro operation. After a delay for additional processing, the final HDR image appears in a document window (see Figure 14.4).

FIGURE 14.4 HDR image created from merging the three bracketed images shown in Figure 14.1

6. Choose File ➤ Save For Web. Select JPEG High from the Preset drop-down. Type 800 in the Width text box under Image Size and press Tab. Select Bicubic Sharper from the Quality drop-down (see Figure 14.5). Click Save.

7. Save the image as HDR01.jpg.

Bicubic Sharper is the best resampling algorithm for reduction.

FIGURE 14.5 Saving the HDR as a JPEG and reducing the image size

To gain practice, you can optionally create the 11 remaining HDR images by merging each sequential set of 3 images from the `Panoramic Photo Shoot` folder to HDR images using the My HDR preset, or you can use the sample files provided for the section "Working With Panoramas" later in this chapter.

Applying HDR Toning To A Single Image

If you don't have a camera that can manually vary shutter speed for bracketing, you can create a faux HDR image with the HDR Toning adjustment. Although it doesn't actually increase the dynamic range (so burned-out or underexposed areas still lack detail), HDR Toning can give your photos the popular hyperreal *HDR look*. In the following steps you will adjust a single exposure to look like it is almost an HDR image.

IMG_2242.jpg
is available on
the book's
Downloads page.

1. Open `IMG_2242.jpg` from this chapter's `Panoramic Photo Shoot` folder (it's the middle exposure in Figure 14.1, earlier in this chapter).

2. Choose Image ➢ Adjustments ➢ HDR Toning. Select Photorealistic High Contrast from the Preset drop-down in the HDR Toning dialog box as a starting point.

HDR Toning works
only on flattened
images.

3. To improve the look of the image in the HDR Toning dialog box, set Gamma to 0.50, Exposure to +1.00, and Detail to +100%. and select Smooth Edges (see Figure 14.6).

Presets saved in
Merge To HDR Pro
are available in
HDR Toning and
vice versa.

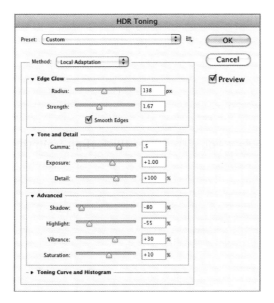

FIGURE 14.6 Adjusting the sliders in the HDR Toning dialog box

4. Choose File ➢ Save For Web & Devices. Select JPEG High from the Preset drop-down. Type 800 in the Width text box under Image Size and press Tab. Select Bicubic Sharper from the Quality drop-down. Click Save.

5. Save the image as Faux-HDR.jpg.

6. Open the file HDR01.jpg that you saved in the previous section or open the copy in the HDR Panoramic Photos folder if you didn't save your own copy.

7. HDR01.jpg is a stop darker than Faux-HDR.jpg. To make a fair comparison, select HDR01.jpg and choose Image ➢ Adjustments ➢ Exposure. Open the Adjustments panel and drag the Exposure slider to +1.

8. Choose Window ➢ Arrange ➢ Float All In Windows. Position Faux-HDR.jpg and HDR01.jpg side by side to make an onscreen comparison. Figure 14.7 shows these images. The true HDR image has detail in the bright sky and dark shadows; these parts of the photo are burned out or underexposed in the faux HDR image.

9. Close all open windows without saving.

FIGURE 14.7 Comparing the true HDR image (left) and the HDR toned image (right)

Working with Panoramas

You can create a variety of panoramic images with Photoshop—starting from two side-by-side photos all the way to a wraparound 360-degree panorama that's viewable on the Web. Photoshop doesn't include an interactive wraparound panoramic web exporter, but I'll direct you to third-party software that makes this optional step easy. Panoramas, whether for the Web or for print, can be impressive ways to visualize anything from a room to a city.

Using Photomerge

In the following steps you will merge 12 HDR photos into a super-wide panorama.

1. Locate and view the HDR Panoramic Photos folder among this chapter downloads. The folder contains 12 overlapping images shot on a tripod. Figure 14.8 shows this assortment of photos. When you are shooting overlapping images, plan for about 40 percent overlap for best results.

Shooting overlapping photos in portrait orientation captures a larger vertical swath.

FIGURE 14.8 Overlapping HDR photos shot every 30 degrees on a tripod

PHOTOS COURTESY OF RICHARD TRUEMAN

2. Choose File ➤ Automate ➤ Photomerge. Select the Browse button and navigate to the HDR Panoramic Photos folder. Shift+select all 12 photos with sequential names HDR01.jpg through HDR12.jpg and click OK. Select Blend Images Together, Vignette Removal, and Geometric Distortion Correction. Select Auto in the Layout panel (see Figure 14.9). Click OK and Photoshop begins an automated process that results in a single panoramic image.

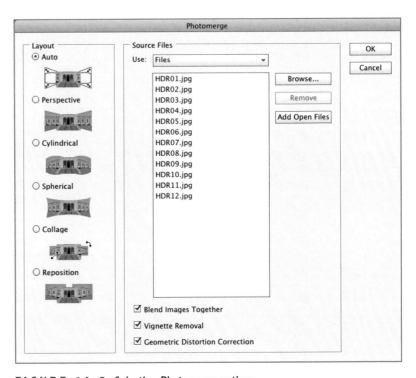

FIGURE 14.9 Selecting Photomerge options

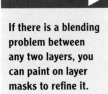

If there is a blending problem between any two layers, you can paint on layer masks to refine it.

3. Open the Layers panel and see that you are left with 12 layers, each with a mask that blends it with its surrounding layers (see Figure 14.10). Press Cmd+E to merge the visible layers.

4. The border is ragged after Photomerge. You could either crop this away or see if you can fill some of it in; here you'll end up doing a little of both. Cmd+click the single remaining layer's thumbnail to select all of its pixels.

5. Press Shift+Cmd+I to invert the selection so that the transparent border pixels are selected (see Figure 14.11).

FIGURE 14.10 Layers with masks result after running Photomerge with the Blend Images Together option

FIGURE 14.11 Selecting the ragged border around the panorama

6. Choose Edit ➢ Fill. Select Content-Aware from the Use drop-down in the Fill dialog box (see Figure 14.12). Click OK.

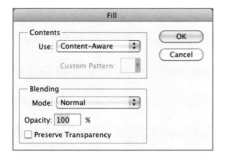

FIGURE 14.12 Using Content-Aware to fill in the missing pixels

7. Content-Aware did a nearly perfect job along the bottom edge but it leaves something to be desired in the treetops. Increase the size of the document window by dragging its handle down and to the right. Select the Crop tool and drag out a window covering the entire panorama. Drag the top-middle handle down until you crop out the tops of the trees where Content-Aware was less than perfect (see Figure 14.13). Press Enter.

FIGURE 14.13 Cropping away less than perfect content-aware fill

8. The image is a bit dark. Open the Adjustments panel and select the Exposure icon ▣. Drag the Exposure slider to +1.00. Select Layer ➢ Flatten Image. Figure 14.14 shows the resulting panorama.

FIGURE 14.14 Final HDR panorama

9. Save your work as HDR-Panorama.psd. You can leave this file open if you are continuing directly in the next section.

Making A Seamless 360-Degree Panorama

The panorama you created in the previous section was seamless in between the individual photos but a seam remains between the left and right edges. If you look closely at Figure 14.14, you will see the same trees on the extreme left and right sides. In this section you will blend this outer edge to create a fully seamless 360 degree panorama that can be exported to a third-party program for posting on the Web as an interactive wraparound panorama.

1. Open HDR-Panorama.psd if it is not already open.

2. Press Cmd+A to select all. Choose Select ➢ Transform Selection. Select the middle-left reference point on the options bar, make sure the aspect ratio is unlocked, and type **50%** in the Width text box (see Figure 14.15). Press Enter to select exactly the left half of the panorama.

HDR-Panorama
.jpg is avail-
able on the book's
Downloads page.

FIGURE 14.15 Transforming the selection to precisely select half of the panorama

3. Press Cmd+J to copy the selection to Layer 1. Press Opt+[to select the Background layer. Cmd+click the Layer 1 thumbnail to reselect what you selected in step 2. Press Shift+Cmd+I to invert the selection and thus select the right half of the panorama. Press Cmd+J to copy the selection to Layer 2. Figure 14.16 shows the resulting layers.

FIGURE 14.16 Copying each half of the panorama to separate layers

4. Toggle off the Background layer and look for a vertical seam, one pixel wide, between Layers 1 and 2. Zoom into this seam until you can see individual pixels (see Figure 14.17).

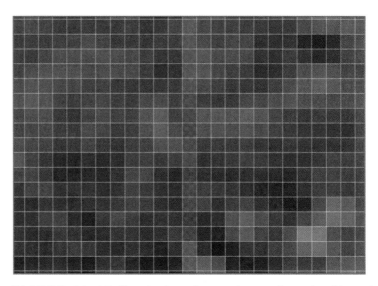

FIGURE 14.17 Zooming in on the seam between Layer 1 and Layer 2

5. Select the Single Column Marquee tool and select the partially transparent column of pixels between Layer 1 and Layer 2. Select the Background layer in the Layers panel. Press Cmd+J to copy the single column of pixels to Layer 3. Shift+select Layers 2 and 3 and press Cmd+E to merge them. Select the Background layer and press Delete to get rid of it. You are left with the panorama split perfectly into two equal parts.

6. Double-click the Hand tool to fit the image on the screen. Press V to select the Move tool and uncheck Auto-Select on the options bar if it is already selected. Hold Shift to constrain the motion horizontally and drag Layer 2 all the way to the left edge. Select Layer 1 and drag its contents all the way to the right. The outer seam has become an inner seam.

7. Drag Layer 1 to the left until you can see that it aligns with the underlying Layer 2. Zoom in and nudge one pixel at a time using the arrow keys to get it as close as possible. Shift+select Layers 1 and 2. Choose Edit ➢ Auto-Blend Layers. Select Panorama as the blend method, select Seamless Tones And Colors (see Figure 14.18), and click OK.

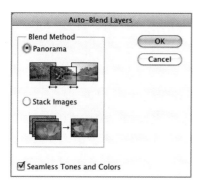

FIGURE 14.18 Blending the last seam

8. Select Edit ≻ Trim, select Transparent Pixels in the Trim dialog box, and click OK. Press Cmd+E to merge Layers 1 and 2.

9. Choose Filter ≻ Other ≻ Offset. Drag the Horizontal slider and see that the panorama is seamless. Use a value of -1765 to center the pond on the screen (see Figure 14.19).

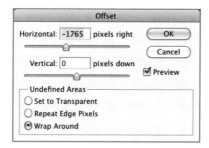

FIGURE 14.19 Offsetting the panorama

10. Save your work as Seamless-HDR-Panorama.psd. Figure 14.20 shows the final result.

FIGURE 14.20 Final seamless HDR 360-degree panorama

CREATING INTERACTIVE PANORAMAS ON THE WEB

There are many third-party programs that can take a seamless panorama as input and output an interactive web format using technologies such as Java, Quicktime VR, Flash, and/or HTML5. My favorite program in this class is Garden Gnome's Pano2VR (gardengnomesoftware.com). It can export in Quicktime VR and Flash, and it outputs all the necessary HTML files and JavaScript to make it a turnkey solution. The result can be viewed on a web page, full screen, or in a viewer such as the QuickTime Player. Simply drag to navigate within the panorama. The Quicktime VR file Seamless-HDR-Panorama.mov has been provided as an example of Pano2VR output.

Processing Images in Stacks

A series of images taken from the same vantage point can be loaded into a *stack*, or as layers in a single document, where processing can be performed across the entire dataset. A selection of algorithms called *stack modes* are available expressly for this purpose. The most popular stack mode is called Median—it effectively removes all moving objects from a stack. In the following steps you will load a series of images into a stack, clean them up, and get rid of the walking pedestrians with Median stack mode (and no other time-consuming retouching). It's a great way to rid architectural spaces of tourists and moving cars in a way that is not possible in the real world without incurring huge expense.

1. Locate and view the Stack folder among this chapter's downloads. The folder contains 20 handheld still images shot every few seconds. Figure 14.21 shows this assortment of photos. Every photo contains moving people.

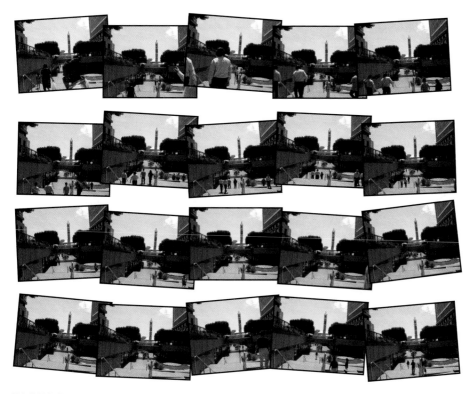

FIGURE 14.21 Series of handheld still images taken in succession

2. Choose File ➢ Scripts ➢ Load Files Into Stack. Click the Browse button, Shift+select all the files in the Stack folder, and click Open. Select Attempt To Automatically Align Source Images (because the shots were handheld) and Create Smart Object After Loading Layers (see Figure 14.22). Click OK.

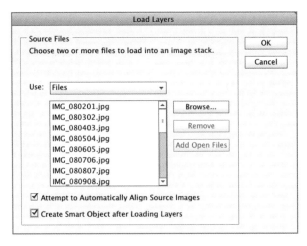

<figure>**FIGURE 14.22** Configuring options for loading files into a stack</figure>

3. The stack of images has a ragged border, like a bunch of photos stacked loosely on a table. It has this appearance because the photographer's slight movements between shots created this slight variance between the photos and you requested Photoshop to align the images. Select the Crop tool and drag out a window that crops out the ragged border (see Figure 14.23). Press Enter.

<figure>**FIGURE 14.23** Cropping ragged border resulting from aligning the stack of images</figure>

4. The image appears to have too much contrast. Choose Image ➢ Adjustments ➢ Shadows/Highlights. Drag the Shadows Amount slider to 50% to lighten the shadows. Drag the Highlights Amount slider to 16% darken the highlights slightly (see Figure 14.24). This adjustment appears as a smart filter in the Layers panel because you applied it to a Smart Object.

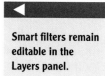

Smart filters remain editable in the Layers panel.

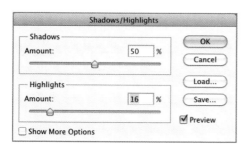

FIGURE 14.24 Brightening the shadows and dimming the highlights

5. Choose Layer ➢ Smart Objects ➢ Stack Mode ➢ Median. This algorithm analyzes the entire stack of images and returns pixels that are present more than half the time in all the images. The effect is the removal of all moving objects and the reduction of image noise (random variation is also eliminated). Figure 14.25 shows the result.

FIGURE 14.25 Applying Median stack mode eliminates all the moving people.

6. Save your work as Stack.psd.

THE ESSENTIALS AND BEYOND

In this chapter you have learned how to create both true and faux HDR images, how to create panoramas, how to heal the outer seam so that you have a 360-degree panorama suitable for creating interactive experiences on the Web, and how to remove moving objects from a stack of photos.

ADDITIONAL EXERCISE

Open Stack.psd and try out the other stack modes to explore the artistic options processing stacks of images offers.

PHOTOS COURTESY OF RICHARD TRUEMAN

CHAPTER 15

Working with Color

Color is a complex subject, and this chapter will help you work successfully with it. You'll manage color workflows, starting with input from digital cameras to display on your computer monitor, then representation in Photoshop, and ultimately output made by printers. Sometimes the pictures you take will have color casts. You'll learn how to use curves to correct color and employ various adjustments to alter color for artistic effect. Finally, you'll soft proof color onscreen to get a sense of how it will look prior to professional CMYK printing.

▶ **Managing color**

▶ **Correcting color**

▶ **Adjusting color**

▶ **Proofing color**

Managing Color

Certification Objective

Without color management, it is very likely that the color you see on your camera's LCD will be different from both the color on your computer monitor and the color of printed output. The reason we need color management is because every device handles color a bit differently. Recall from Chapter 3, "Digital Imaging Fundamentals," how color is stored in grayscale channels. Color is therefore something that must always be interpreted. The absolute color is never actually recorded, only intensities in three different wavelengths of light corresponding to the red, green, and blue primaries.

The range of visible light is called the full color *gamut*. Computers cannot display, and printers cannot print, the full dynamic range or color gamut that our eyes perceive. Instead, various color spaces have been standardized to represent the most common colors. Figure 15.1 shows the full gamut outlined in the graph and the Adobe 1998 color space defined within the triangle. Daylight standard D65 is also indicated.

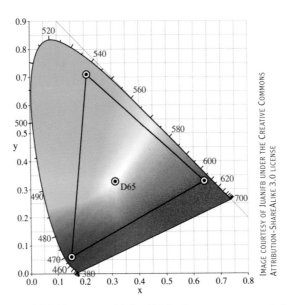

FIGURE 15.1 Adobe 1998 color space represented on graph of full color gamut

Adobe published the color space that bears its name in 1998 in an effort to encompass most of the colors that professional CMYK printers are able to output.

Figure 15.2 shows the sRGB color space, which has a narrower gamut than the Adobe RGB 1998 color space.

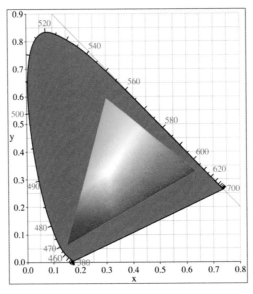

FIGURE 15.2 sRGB color space, which has a narrow gamut

The sRGB (standard RGB) color space is the de facto standard on the Web. If a camera doesn't support color profiles, or if an image lacks a color profile, or if the browser doesn't support color profiles, one can assume that the image will be in the sRGB space. Think of sRGB as the lowest common denominator and narrowest of color spaces.

Both Adobe RGB 1998 and sRGB were designed to be viewed under D65 lights. D65 lights have a color temperature of 6500 degrees above absolute zero, which most closely simulates the light of the sun through Earth's atmosphere. If you don't use D65 daylight bulbs in your environment, then the colors you see will be shifted from these standards.

There are many other color spaces in addition to Adobe RGB 1998 and sRGB; ColorMatch and ProPhoto are two popular examples. Figure 15.3 shows the subtle differences in viewing the same data in different color spaces.

The sRGB color space was designed to be viewed under typical home and office viewing lighting conditions rather than the much darker environment specified in the Adobe RGB color space.

A   B

PHOTO COURTESY OF ISTOCKPHOTO, ©CRISMA, IMAGE #7224544

C   D

FIGURE 15.3 Color profiles: Adobe 1998 (A), ColorMatch (B), ProPhoto (C), and sRGB (D)

Both Mac OS X and Windows 7 manage color at the operating system level. Printer drivers also try to manage color at the level of hardware. These layers of management occur on top of the color management that Photoshop automatically performs. If you set up Photoshop to use sRGB, the colors will shift again at the operating system level before being displayed on your screen, so what you see onscreen won't actually be in sRGB.

Configuring Color Settings

If you are creating graphics for the Web or mobile devices, the best solution I have found is to disable color management in Photoshop. If, on the other hand, you are creating graphics for print, you should use Photoshop's color management system with your chosen working color space. In the following steps you will specify color settings for both situations and then synchronize all your color settings across the applications in the Creative Suite (if you own more Adobe applications in addition to Photoshop).

> **Check out spyder .datacolor.com and www.xrite .com for color calibration hardware.**

1. The first step is to create a color profile. How you do this depends on what equipment you have and what computer operating system you use. If you own a colorimeter or a (more expensive) spectrophotometer, you can measure the light emitted from your monitor and use the software included with your device to create an accurate color profile of your monitor. If not, you can use the color profile or color calibration utilities that come with your operating system to "eyeball" a profile. (Keep in mind that this is far less accurate than using a meter.)

   ▶ To eyeball a color profile on the Mac, from the Apple menu choose System Preferences ➢ Displays and click the Color tab (see Figure 15.4). Click the Calibrate button and follow the onscreen instructions.

   ▶ On Windows, click the Start button and choose Control Panel ➢ Calibrate Display Color and follow the onscreen instructions.

   Save a profile with the name of your computer followed by the word *Calibrated* (i.e., iMac Calibrated).

2. Launch Photoshop and choose Edit ➢ Color Settings. Select the profile you just created for the RGB working space in the previous step. I chose Monitor RGB—iMac Calibrated because I produce web graphics rather than images printed on a desktop printer. If you produce

printed matter on a desktop printer, you might choose Adobe RGB (1998) or the color space of your choice. Figure 15.5 shows the Color Settings dialog box.

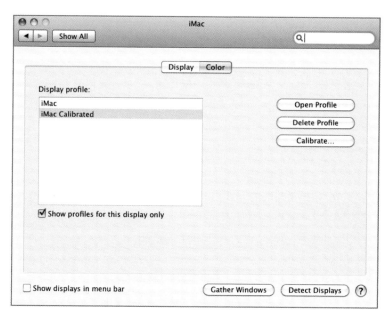

FIGURE 15.4 Selecting a color profile on the Mac

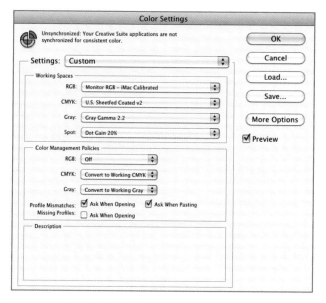

FIGURE 15.5 Specifying color settings for your color workflow

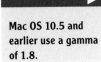

Mac OS 10.5 and earlier use a gamma of 1.8.

3. Contact the professional printing company you use for offset printing and select the CMYK working space they specify. For example, you might select U.S. Sheetfed Coated v2. Select Gray Gamma 2.2 if you are using any version of Windows or Mac OS 10.6 (Snow Leopard) or later. Select Dot Gain 20% or whatever your professional printing company specifies for spot color.

4. Select a color management policy:

   ▶ Select Off as your RGB color management policy if you intend to create output for the Web.

   ▶ Select Preserve Embedded Profile to leave existing profiles alone.

   ▶ Select Convert To Working RGB if you want Photoshop to convert to your chosen print color space.

   I select Convert To Working CMYK and Convert To Working Gray if I ever open documents in CMYK or Grayscale color modes.

5. Select whether you want to be informed of profile mismatches and/or missing profiles.

   I prefer not to be queried every time I open an image. so I deselect the Missing Profiles check box.

6. Click Save, type **My Color Settings.csf**, and click Save. Figure 15.6 shows the resulting settings, which are now saved as a preset. Click OK to close the Color Settings dialog box.

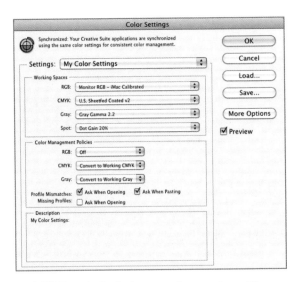

FIGURE 15.6 Saving your chosen color settings as a preset called My Color Settings

7. Select File ➤ Browse In Bridge. In Bridge, select Edit ➤ Creative Suite Color Settings. Select My Color Settings and click Apply (see Figure 15.7).

FIGURE 15.7 Selecting color settings for the Creative Suite in Bridge

8. Close Bridge and switch back to Photoshop.

9. Choose Edit ➤ Color Settings. The top of the dialog box shows that your chosen settings are synchronized across the Creative Suite (see Figure 15.8).

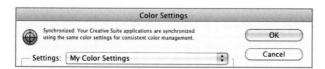

FIGURE 15.8 Synchronizing color settings across the Creative Suite

Assigning and Converting Color Profiles

There is an important difference between assigning color profiles and converting color profiles. Assigning profiles is nondestructive, meaning it does not change the underlying pixel data. Different profiles affect only the delivery of that information to the screen. On the other hand, converting profiles alters the pixel data while keeping the colors as close as possible to how they are represented in the current profile. In the following steps you will both assign and convert profiles.

1. Open Leaves.jpg from the book's Download page at www.sybex .com/go/photoshopessentials. Depending on what you chose in step 5 in the previous section, you might be asked what to do because of the mismatch between the embedded and working profiles (see Figure 15.9). Assuming you want to use this image for Web output, select Discard The Embedded Profile (Don't Color Manage) and click OK. The document now lacks a color profile.

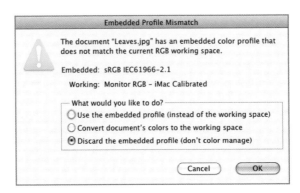

FIGURE 15.9 Selecting what to do with a profile mismatch

2. To view the image correctly in Photoshop, you should assign your monitor's calibrated profile to the image. Select Edit ➢ Assign Profile. Select Working RGB, which was set to iMac Calibrated (or whatever you named your color profile in step 1 of the previous section, "Configuring Color Settings"). See Figure 15.10.

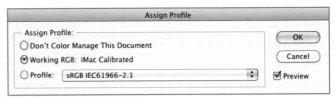

FIGURE 15.10 Assigning the working color profile to an image

3. Suppose you decided to prepare this image for professional printing on a four-color printing press. Choose Edit ➢ Convert Profile. The destination space is set to the profile you set up as your working

CMYK space in the previous section (U.S. Sheetfed Coated v2 in the example shown in Figure 15.11). Click OK.

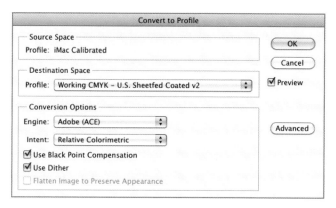

FIGURE 15.11 Converting the color profile and changing modes

4. The title bar now says CMYK/8, meaning you now have a four-channel document with 8 bits per channel. Select the right-facing arrow at the bottom of the document window and select Document Profile from the menu that appears. The color profile is now shown at a glance (see Figure 15.12).

5. Close the document without saving.

FIGURE 15.12 Showing the color profile in the document window

Correcting Color

**Certification
Objective**

When you take photos under artificial lighting, they can be left with a notice-able color cast that can negatively influence the feeling. In other cases, natural light might appear too warm or too cool for your taste and you might want to intentionally create a color cast to shift the subtle balance of color.

Using Curves to Set Black, Gray, and White Points

In the following steps you will remove an undesirable yellow color cast using the Threshold and Curves adjustments.

1. Open Man.jpg (see Figure 15.13). This image has a yellow cast from the artificial lighting.

FIGURE 15.13 This photo suffers from a yellow color cast.

2. Press Cmd+J to duplicate the Background layer so you can make a before-and-after comparison onscreen.

3. Choose Layer ➤ New Adjustment Layer ➤ Threshold to help you identify the black, gray, and white points on the image. Click OK when prompted to name the layer Threshold 1. Drag the slider in the Properties panel all the way to the left and then slowly drag it to the right until you start to see some black in the document window (see Figure 15.14). The first places you see black are the darkest pixels in the image.

4. Select the Color Sampler tool. Click one point inside the darkest part of the image as indicated by the Threshold adjustment layer to place marker #1.

FIGURE 15.14 Adjusting the Threshold slider

5. Drag the Threshold slider in the Properties panel all the way to the right. Then back the slider off slightly to the left until you see some white appear in the document window; this represents the brightest part of the image. Click inside the white area to place color sampler marker #2.

6. Drag the Threshold slider to the left and observe which pixels change color from black to white near the middle of the histogram. Click once more in the document window (in this case in the lower-right corner) to set marker #3. Figure 15.15 shows the location of the three markers.

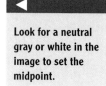

Look for a neutral gray or white in the image to set the midpoint.

7. Press Delete to get rid of the Threshold 1 layer because it is no longer needed.

FIGURE 15.15 Placing color sampler markers at the brightest and darkest parts of the image and midpoint as indicated by the Threshold adjustment

> You can shape each channel's curves manually as you gain more experience.

8. Choose Image ➢ Adjustments ➢ Curves. Select the Sample In Image To Set Black Point tool in the Curves dialog box and click sampler marker #1 in the document window. Select the Sample In Image To Set White Point tool and click sampler marker #2. Select the Sample In Image To Set Gray Point tool and click color sampler marker #3 (see Figure 15.16).

9. Click the Clear button on the options bar to remove the color sampler markers. Figure 15.17 shows the result.

10. Save your work as Man-color-corrected.psd. Toggle Layer 1 off and on to see before-and-after views.

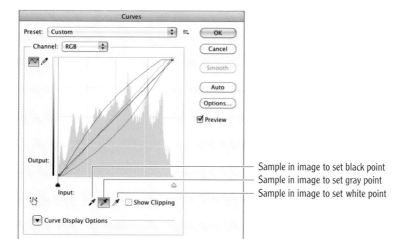

FIGURE 15.16 Sampling black, gray, and white points with Curves

Use the Eye Dropper tool and press the Shift key to determine exact RGB and CMYK values of specific areas of the image. The color values can be viewed in the Info panel and used as a guide for correction.

FIGURE 15.17 Color-corrected photo

You can also diminish or remove an unwanted color cast by using the sampling tool in Hue and Saturation then desaturating that specific color by moving the Saturation slider to the left.

Creating a Color Cast with the Photo Filter

Photo Filter is not a filter but an adjustment (and adjustment layer) that allows you to introduce a digital color cast, which works much like a color filter screwed onto a physical lens. In the following steps you will cool a hot summer day with a blue photo filter in Photoshop.

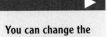

Landscape.jpg is available on the book's Downloads page.

1. Open Landscape.jpg (see Figure 15.18). This image has a yellow cast from haze in the warm air.

IMAGE COURTESY OF RICHARD TRUEMAN

FIGURE 15.18 Landscape in natural light

You can change the amount of filtering by dragging the Density slider.

2. Choose Layer ➤ New Adjustment Layer ➤ Photo Filter. Experiment by selecting different filters from the Filter drop-down in the Properties panel. I like Cooling Filter (80), but the choice is very subjective (see Figure 15.19).

FIGURE 15.19 Selecting a photo filter

3. Save your work as Landscape-with-photo-filter.psd. Figure 15.20 shows the result. Toggle the Photo Filter 1 layer off and on to see before-and-after views.

FIGURE 15.20 Landscape with cooling photo filter

Adjusting Color

You have complete control over color in Photoshop. If you don't like how a color looks, adjust it! You are limited only by your creativity and your skill with selection (covered in Chapter 7, "Selecting Pixels"). In the following steps you will draw attention to a model by desaturating the color of the background. Then you will adjust the color of her coat. These are just two examples of what you can do with color and adjustment layers.

Certification
Objective

1. Open Woman.psd (see Figure 15.21).

Woman.jpg is available on the book's Downloads page.

PHOTO COURTESY OF ISTOCKPHOTO,
©DMITRY MORDVINTSEV, IMAGE #11052046

FIGURE 15.21 Original photo

2. Choose the Quick Select tool and select Auto-Enhance on the options bar if it is not already selected. Drag over the woman to select her. Hold down Opt and drag over anything selected that is not part of her body or clothing.

3. Press Shift+Cmd+I to select the inverse (everything but the woman).

4. Click the Black & White icon ▣ in the Create panel. The current selection automatically becomes a layer mask on a Black & White adjustment layer. Drag the Reds slider to -110 and the Yellows slider to +166 (see Figure 15.22).

> Cmd+click the "not woman" channel to load it as a selection if you are having trouble getting a clean selection.

FIGURE 15.22 Adjusting the grayscale values of reds and yellows in the color image

5. Select the woman's white coat with Quick Select. Again, hold down Opt and remove any areas you unintentionally select. Use any of the selection techniques you learned in Chapter 7 to refine the selection so that only her coat is selected and not her hands, face, or hair (see Figure 15.23).

> Cmd+click the coat channel to load it as a selection if you are having trouble getting a clean selection.

6. Click the Hue/Saturation icon ▦ in the Create panel. In the Properties panel, select Colorize. Drag the Saturation slider to 51 and the Lightness slider to -62. If you wanted to change the hue, it would be as simple as dragging the Hue slider, but in this case I like red (see Figure 15.24).

7. Save your work as Woman-adjusted.psd. Figure 15.25 shows the result.

FIGURE 15.23 Selecting the coat in preparation for color adjustment

FIGURE 15.24 Applying a Hue/Saturation adjustment layer

FIGURE 15.25 Final image

Proofing Color

Certification
Objective

Before you print a hard proof on paper, it is always a good idea to view a soft proof onscreen because you can save valuable paper and ink this way. Most printer manufacturers offer International Color Consortium (ICC) files for output created with specific combinations of specialty papers, printers, and driver software. I recommend that you search your printer manufacturer's website and download not only the drivers but any ICC files they offer (the filename extension is .icc). In the following steps you will download specific ICC files, set up a custom soft proof, and then color-correct the print prior to creating a hard proof. (Hard proofs, also known as printed output, are covered in Chapter 16, "Creating Output.")

1. Download the premium glossy ICC profiles for the Epson Stylus Photo 2200 printer, which as of this book's publication date are here:
   `http://www.epson.com/cgi-bin/Store/EditorialAnnouncement`
   `.jsp?oid=42114986`

   If these are not available, search for the ICC files for your own printer and paper.

2. Install these drivers according to the manufacturer's instructions. Mac ICC files go in `/Library/ColorSync/Profiles`, and Windows ICC files go in `C:\Windows\system32\spool\drivers\color`.

3. Open `Rowboat.jpg`. If asked, choose Use The Embedded Profile (sRGB).

4. Choose Image ➢ Duplicate. Accept the default name Rowboat copy and click OK in the Duplicate Image dialog box. Choose Window ➢ Arrange ➢ 2-Up Vertical.

5. In `Rowboat copy`, choose View ➢ Proof Setup ➢ Custom. Select SP2200 Prem.Glossy 2880.icc from the Device To Simulate drop-down. Deselect Preserve RGB Numbers and select Perceptual from the Rendering Intent drop-down. Select Black Point Compensation and Simulate Paper Color (see Figure 15.26). Click OK. The colors in `Rowboat copy` now look as close as they can on-screen to how they will look when printed by the specific device on the specific paper.

   Rowboat copy looks different from the original appearance of the image in Photoshop. If you want to maintain the original look in the print, you can perform some color adjustment to try to make the soft-proofed Rowboat copy more closely match Rowboat onscreen.

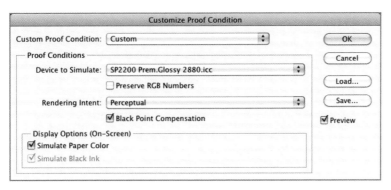

FIGURE 15.26 Customizing a soft proof

6. The soft proof version looks washed out compared to the original. To compensate, select the Brightness/Contrast icon in the Create panel. In the Properties panel, drag the Brightness slider to 11 and Contrast to 26.

7. The water in the soft proof still doesn't look anywhere near as dark as in the original. Select the Selective Color icon in the Create panel. In the Properties panel, select Green from the Color drop-down (to affect the water). Drag the Black slider all the way to +100% (see Figure 15.27).

FIGURE 15.27 Affecting the water with Selective Color

In most cases you won't be able to create a perfect match because paper has much less dynamic range than the screen.

8. Save your work as Rowboat-soft-proofed.psd. Figure 15.28 shows the side-by-side comparison. The adjusted image will now print close to how the original appears onscreen.

FIGURE 15.28 Left image shows the original and the right image shows soft-proofed and adjusted image.

THE ESSENTIALS AND BEYOND

In this chapter you learned how to work with color, including assigning and converting profiles to management workflows, correcting color casts with curves, shifting color with adjustments, and finally, soft-proofing color prior to committing to output.

ADDITIONAL EXERCISE

Go outside and take some pictures. After you review, develop, and retouch the best photo from the shoot, soft-proof the photo onscreen. Finally, shift its color using any of the following adjustments to make it stand out: Brightness/Contrast, Curves, Vibrance, Hue/Saturation/Color Balance, Photo Filter, and/or Selective Color.

IMAGE COURTESY RICHARD TRUEMAN

CHAPTER 16

Creating Output

For every project, you must eventually create some form of output. In this chapter you will learn how to print on an ink-jet printer in a way that maintains the colors you see onscreen as faithfully as possible on the printed page. In addition, you will learn how to create optimized web graphics if the screen is the ultimate destination for your output.

▶ **Printing**

▶ **Saving for the web**

▶ **Rendering images to video**

Printing

Certification Objective

There is a lot more to printing in Photoshop that pressing Cmd+P as you might in a word processing program. Photoshop itself, your printer manufacturer's driver software, and the operating system all play a part in the color management workflow. In the following steps you will see how to print using Photoshop for color management.

You need to install your printer manufacturer's driver software prior to printing.

1. Open Dock.psd from the book's Downloads page at www.sybex.com/go/photoshopessentials. Soft-proof this image for your specific printer and paper combination according to the instructions in Chapter 15, "Working with Color." In this example I am using an Epson Stylus Photo 1280 printer with premium glossy photo paper.

2. Choose File ➢ Print. In the Photoshop Print Settings dialog box, the first thing you need to do is select your printer driver from the Printer drop-down (see Figure 16.1). In this case I will select Epson Stylus Photo 1280. Select the Landscape layout button.

Ideal file formats for creating prints: JPG, TIFF, PDF, DCS, EPS, and PSD.

FIGURE 16.1 Selecting a printer driver in the Photoshop Print Settings dialog box

The list of paper sizes changes depending on which printer driver you have selected.

3. Click the Print Settings button next to the Copies text box to open a dialog box specific to your operating system.

4. Open the paper size drop-down and select your chosen paper size, which is specific to your device. In this case I will select US Letter (Sheet Feeder Borderless).

5. Open the fourth drop-down menu and select Print Settings. This drop-down's choices change the information that appears below the horizontal bar. Under Print Settings it says Page Setup: Sheet Feeder—Borderless, echoing the selected paper size. Select Premium Photo Paper Glossy from the Media Type drop-down.

Media types are specific to the selected sheet feeder. If you don't see a particular media type listed, choose the correct sheet feeder as a paper size.

6. Select Color Matching from the same drop-down you used in step 5 in the Print dialog box and select the Off (No Color Adjustment) radio button to disable color management within the printer.

Windows users should select ICM and select Off (No Color Adjustment).

7. Select the Advanced Settings radio button and select Photo—1440dpi from the Print Quality drop-down. Deselect High Speed for highest print quality (but twice the print time). Figure 16.2 shows the Print dialog box with the specific information selected for this device and paper selection. Click Save to close the Print dialog box.

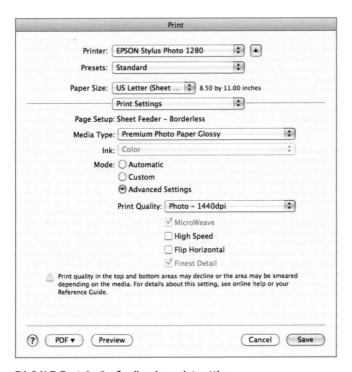

Dots Per Inch (dpi) determines the amount of ink that is dispersed on a print. *Pixels Per Inch (ppi)* determines the image file's resolution. *Lines Per Inch (lpi)* measures a printer's resolution of halftone patterns.

Print settings are specific to each image. Save a preset if you want to use the same settings on another image.

FIGURE 16.2 Configuring print settings

8. In the Photoshop Print Settings dialog box, make sure the Color Management section is expanded. Select Photoshop Manages Colors in the Color Handling drop-down.

9. Open the Printer Profile drop-down in the Color Management section and select your chosen profile. In this case I will choose Epson Stylus Photo 1280 Premium Glossy Photo Paper. Select Send 16-bit Data. Under Normal Printing, select your rendering intent. In this case I will select Perceptual and leave Black Point Compensation unchecked. Figure 16.3 shows these selections.

Printer profiles are specific to the device and paper type (they are ICC files, as discussed in Chapter 15).

10. Expand the Position And Size section and select Scale To Fit Media. The preview image should now fill the page because the image's aspect ratio matches the output size (see Figure 16.4). Click Print and the print job is handed to your operating system and then printer.

Not all printers allow you to print borderless prints.

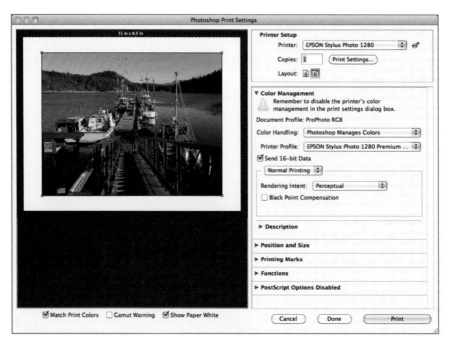

FIGURE 16.3 Making color management decisions

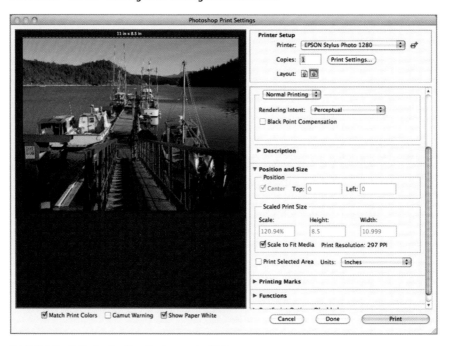

FIGURE 16.4 Scaling the image to fit the page

Saving for the Web

If you are preparing images for the Web, then file size must be taken into account. Nobody wants to wait for large images to download on a web page, and if you make people wait, chances are you will lose your audience. In the following steps, you will learn options for optimizing image file size within the Save For Web dialog box.

Certification Objective

1. Open Painting.psd from this book's Downloads page at www.sybex .com/go/photoshopessentials (see Figure 16.5). The original is a 2.22 MB file.

This painting was made with the Oil Paint filter.

FIGURE 16.5 Original digital painting of the author's house

2. Choose File ➤ Save For The Web. Select the Optimized tab and select WBMP from the Optimized File Format drop-down (second from the top of the Save For Web dialog box). Figure 16.6 shows an image made of exactly two colors: black and white. Notice that the file size in the lower-left corner, 94.93 KB, is just 4 percent of the original size. This is the maximum compression that is possible at a constant image size. However, we have lost all color and tonal information, so WBMP is really only practical for newsprint and faxes.

Ideal image file formats for the web: JPG, GIF, BMP, and PNG.

FIGURE 16.6 Previewing the Windows Bitmap file format in Save For Web

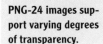

PNG-24 images support varying degrees of transparency.

PNG-8 images are often used for logos on the Web. They are best for representing contiguous areas of solid color with binary (on or off) transparency.

JPEG is a lossy format; the level of compression is inversely related to image quality.

3. Change the File Format drop-down to PNG-24 (24-bit or 8 bits per channel). This format is non-lossy, meaning none of the visual information is lost or compromised in the compression process. The optimized preview looks identical to Figure 16.6. The file size of the PNG-24 image is 1.205 MB, almost a 50 percent reduction compared to the original.

4. Change the File Format drop-down to PNG-8 (8 bits in one indexed channel). The file size is down to 432.7 KB (19 percent of the original). To achieve this reduction in file size, the number of colors was reduced to 256 (8-bits). You can perceive a graininess that comes from this color dithering. PNG-8 images are not good at representing gradients because of the reduced number of colors. Open the Colors drop-down and reduce the number to 64. The file size goes down to 301 KB but with unacceptable dithering (see Figure 16.7).

5. Change the File Format drop-down to JPEG. Select Very High from the Compression Quality drop-down underneath the File Format drop-down. The file size is 384 KB and the quality is excellent (see Figure 16.8).

FIGURE 16.7 Previewing PNG-8 format in Save For Web

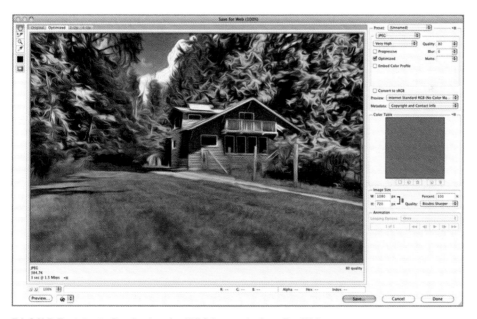

FIGURE 16.8 Previewing the JPEG format in Save For Web

6. You can probably reduce the file size even more while still maintaining an acceptable level of quality. Select the 4-Up tab in the Save For Web dialog box. You'll see four previews: the original and JPEGs of varying quality levels, including 80, 40, and 20 (see Figure 16.9).

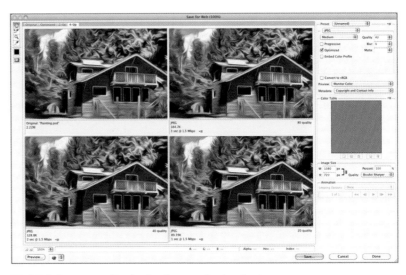

FIGURE 16.9 Previewing four quality levels at once

7. Select the 40 Quality preview, which seems acceptable. Its file size is only 128 KB. You can make the file smaller by reducing the number of pixels (making the image smaller). Type **600** in the Width text box in the Image Size section (see Figure 16.10) and press the Tab key. The image is immediately reduced in size. Select the Optimized tab. The file size is down to a 49 KB, a mere 2 percent of the original file size while still maintaining an acceptable quality for the Web. Click Save and save the output at Painting.jpg.

FIGURE 16.10 Reducing image size in the Save For Web dialog box

You can create a Web Photo Gallery of your images using Adobe Bridge in the Output module by selecting the desired images, template, and style in the Web Gallery window.

Rendering Images to Video

The ability to work with video has been added to Photoshop CS6 (and Photoshop CS6 Extended). Previously, video editing was only available in Photoshop CS5 Extended. In addition to allowing you to open and manipulate video files such as QuickTime MOV, Photoshop now lets you render a sequence of still images to a variety of video formats, including MOV. In the following steps you will create a short video from a sequence of time lapse stills and then render it to video output.

Certification
Objective

1. Choose File➤ Browse In Bridge.

2. Navigate to the Time Lapse folder and view the 157 images showing people walking about a train station (see Figure 16.11).

3. Press Cmd+Tab on the Mac or Alt+Tab on Windows and switch back to Photoshop. Choose File ➤ Open and select Frame001.jpg in the Time Lapse folder. Select the Image Sequence check box and click Open. As long as the files are named sequentially, they will be converted into a single video layer. Click OK to accept the default frame rate of 30 frames per second.

You can download the Time Lapse folder from this book's Downloads page at www.sybex.com /go/photoshop essentials.

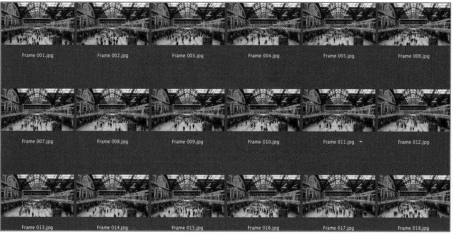

VIDEO COURTESY OF ISTOCKPHOTO, ©ADAM WATSON,
IMAGE #5657285

FIGURE 16.11 Still thumbnails in Bridge

If adding titles, text, or credits to your video, be aware that it must be constrained to a "title-safe" portion of the frame. This avoids any clipping that might result from differences in file formats.

4. Click the Play icon in the Timeline panel and watch the time lapse video play (see Figure 16.12). Press the Spacebar to stop playback.

FIGURE 16.12 Playing a video clip with controls in the Timeline panel

Ideal image file formats for video include Targa, OpenEXR, or Cineon. Ideal image file formats for Word or for PowerPoint or Keynote presentations are JPG, GIF, PNG, and BMP.

5. Choose File ➢ Export ➢ Render Video. Type **Train Station.mp4** in the Name box. Leave all the other settings at their defaults and click Render.

6. Locate the Train Station video on your hard drive and open it in the free QuickTime Player. Figure 16.13 shows the result: a video that anyone can play whether they have Photoshop or not.

Windows users download the QuickTime player from apple.com/ quicktime. Mac users already have it installed.

FIGURE 16.13 Playing the MP4 video in the QuickTime player

THE ESSENTIALS AND BEYOND

In this chapter you have learned how to print with Photoshop, managing color for best results. In addition, you learned how to save images for the Web at reasonable levels of quality, compression, color, and file size, and you have learned how to render multiple images as a video. Congratulations on completing this book! You now understand the essentials of Photoshop. Good luck and have fun with this amazing software.

ADDITIONAL EXERCISE

Select one of your favorite images that you have created in Photoshop and print it so that what you see on the screen is as close as possible to how the output appears on paper. In addition, save the file for the Web such that its file size is greatly reduced while maintaining an acceptable level of quality for use in an online portfolio.

Adobe Visual Communication Using Photoshop CS6 Objectives

The Adobe Certified Associate (ACA) certifications are industry-recognized credentials that can help you succeed in your design career—providing benefits to both you and your employer. Getting certified is a reliable validation of skills and knowledge, and it can expand your career opportunities, improve your productivity, and help you stand apart from your peers.

This Adobe Approved Courseware for the ACA can be an effective component of your exam preparation. To prepare for certification, review the most current exam preparation roadmap available at www.adobe.com/support/certification, where you will find information on where you can take a test and how to promote your status once you've passed.

To help you focus your studies on the skills you'll need for these exams, Table A.1 shows each objective and the chapter in which you can find information on that topic—and when you go to that chapter, you'll find certification icons like the one in the margin here.

Certification Objective

These Adobe exam objectives were accurate at press time; please refer to www.adobe.com/support/certification for the most current exam roadmap and objectives.

Good luck preparing for your certification!

TABLE A.1 Adobe Visual Communication Using Photoshop CS6 Objectives

Topic	Exam Objectives	Adobe Photoshop CS6 Essentials
Objective 1.0 Setting Project Requirements	1.1 Identify the purpose, audience, and audience needs for preparing image(s).	Chapter 1
	1.2 Demonstrate knowledge of standard copyright rules for images and image use.	Chapter 1
	1.3 Demonstrate knowledge of project management tasks and responsibilities.	Chapter 1
	1.4 Communicate with others (such as peers and clients) about design plans.	Chapters 1, 9
Objective 2.0 Identifying Design Elements When Preparing Images	2.1 Demonstrate knowledge of image resolution, image size, and image file format for Web, video, and print.	Chapters 1, 3, 16
	2.2 Demonstrate knowledge of design principles, elements, and image composition.	Chapters 1, 3, 6
	2.3 Demonstrate knowledge of typography.	Chapter 6
	2.4 Demonstrate knowledge of color correction using Photoshop CS6.	Chapters 7, 15
	2.5 Demonstrate knowledge of image-generating devices, their resulting image types, and how to access resulting images in Photoshop.	Chapters 1, 3
	2.6 Understand key terminology of digital images.	Chapters 3, 4, 5

(Continues)

TABLE A.1 *(Continued)*

Topic	Exam Objectives	Adobe Photoshop CS6 Essentials
Objective 3.0 Understanding Adobe Photoshop CS6	3.1 Identify elements of the Photoshop CS6 user interface and demonstrate knowledge of their functions.	Chapters 2, 4
	3.2 Demonstrate knowledge of layers and masks.	Chapters 6, 7, 8, 9, 10, 11
	3.3 Demonstrate knowledge of importing, exporting, organizing, and saving.	Chapters 3, 9
	3.4 Demonstrate knowledge of producing and reusing images.	Chapters 5, 9, 10, 11
	3.5 Demonstrate an understanding of and select the appropriate features and options required to implement a color management workflow.	Chapter 4
Objective 4.0 Manipulating Images Using Adobe Photoshop CS6	4.1 Demonstrate knowledge of working with selections.	Chapters 3, 7, 13, 14
	4.2 Use Photoshop guides and rulers.	Chapters 6, 10
	4.3 Transform images.	Chapters 3, 4, 8, 9, 10
	4.4 Adjust or correct the tonal range, color, or distortions of an image.	Chapters 4, 7, 10, 11, 12
	4.5 Demonstrate knowledge of retouching and blending images.	Chapters 4, 8, 11, 13
	4.6 Demonstrate knowledge of drawing and painting.	Chapters 5, 4
	4.7 Demonstrate knowledge of type.	Chapter 6
	4.8 Demonstrate knowledge of filters.	Chapters 9, 11, 13

(Continues)

TABLE A.1 *(Continued)*

Topic	Exam Objectives	Adobe Photoshop CS6 Essentials
Objective 5.0 Publishing Digital Images by Using Adobe Photoshop CS6	5.1 Demonstrate knowledge of preparing images for Web, print, and video	Chapters 3, 14, 15, 16

INDEX

Note to the Reader: Throughout this index **boldfaced** page numbers indicate primary discussions of a topic. *Italicized* page numbers indicate illustrations.